Contents

Dedication

For
Andrew, Madeleine and Mark;
Helen and Andrew

Acknowledgements

We would like to thank all the community groups and individual members of the ethnic minority community, as well as Housing and Social Work Departments, who have supported us in our research. The different elements of that research were the subject of a conference at Stirling in February 1990 and we would like to thank all those who participated in the conference as well as those who presented the papers which are reproduced in this volume.

The typing of the papers was undertaken by secretarial staff at the University of Stirling, comprising Sally Armstrong-Payne, Rachel Loudon, Sarah Pugh and Betty Skinner and we are indebted to them for their work. Ian Maxwell of the Scottish Council for Voluntary Organisations carried out the page layout and production of the book.

University of Stirling   Alison Bowes
                                                               Duncan Sim

Contributors

DAVID ALEXANDER is Senior Policy Officer with the Scottish Federation of Housing Associations. Prior to May 1990 he was Senior Lecturer in Housing Administration at the University of Stirling.

ALISON BOWES is Lecturer in Sociology at the University of Stirling.

MARY BRAILEY is Director of Integrate, a body which promotes housing and support services, based in Glasgow.

MONO CHAKRABARTI is Head of the Social Work Division at Jordanhill College of Education, Glasgow.

MIKE DALTON is Co-Director of the Scottish Ethnic Minoriities Research Unit, based at Glasgow College of Technology.

LYNNE HARVIE is a groupworker with One Plus, One Parent Families Strathclyde. She participated in the Stirling University - Crossroads Action Research project.

JACQUI McCLUSKEY was, until recently, Research Fellow in the Department of Sociology and Social Policy, University of Stirling.

MARTIN MacEWEN is Co-Director of the Scottish Ethnic Minorities Research Unit, based at Edinburgh College of Art/Heriot Watt University.

CLARE MURRAY is a Community Worker with Crossroads Youth and Community Centre in Govanhill, Glasgow.

DUNCAN SIM is Lecturer in Housing Administration at the University of Stirling.

JULIA WARDHAUGH is Research Fellow in the Departments of Criminology and Education at the University of Keele. She participated in the Stirling University - Crossroads Action Research Project

Introduction
Alison Bowes and Duncan Sim

Ethnic minorities and social services

...The response of social services department to the existence of multi-racial communities, has been patchy, piecemeal and lacking in strategy' (ADSS 1978:14)

Through the 1980s, there have undoubtedly been many attempts to remedy the deplorable situation noted by the Association of Directors of Social Services in their 1978 report. In social work (Young and Connelly 1981, BASW 1982, CCETSW 1982) and public housing (New Community 11(3) 1984, Henderson and Karn 1987) measures have been taken aimed at improving the sensitivity of services to ethnic minority needs and at eradicating discrimination and racism. Cheetham argues however that whilst these efforts at improvement must be acknowledged, there remain many 'continuing failures and insensitivities of services' (1986:2). Pearson's (1988) review of the series of studies carried out for the Department of Health in four UK regions (North West, Yorkshire and Humberside, West Midlands and London) reveals (p.7) that

... a majority of the 24 social services departments which were visited during these studies had no policy for responding to the needs of a multi-racial population.

Other writers argue the point more strongly: Dominelli (1989) for example gives a case study of social work practice operating with racist assumptions to the considerable detriment of the client, who was offered English lessons rather than practical help to alleviate poor housing conditions. Due to this failure in social work practice, the client's children were eventually taken into care. The social worker wrongly believed that the client's problems arose from her 'non-Englishness' rather than her poverty.

A similar picture can be documented for housing. Ward (1984) lists proven discrimination against black people in council house allocations in Hackney, Lewisham, Birmingham and Nottingham. Recent studies have revealed discrimination in Glasgow (Bowes, McCluskey and Sim 1989) and Liverpool (CRE 1989). Even where attempts to improve matters have been made, problems remain. For example, in Birmingham, Henderson and Karn (1987) report that after measures had been taken to eradicate discriminatory elements in the council housing allocations system, such as length of residence points, the system was still operating to the detriment of those in serious housing need, particularly ethnic minorities.

It is clear therefore that the issue of the relationship between ethnic minorities in Britain and the social services remains an important area for investigation and monitoring. This book examines policy and practice in regard to ethnic minorities in two major areas, housing and social and community work, using research material based in the Scottish experience. We are particularly concerned with the consumers' point of view, an area somewhat neglected in previous literature. We also reflect on our role as researchers in a field in which the recipients of research findings have expressed considerable scepticism about their usefulness, suggesting that often, research has been a substitute for action, and a way of diverting attention from real people's real problems.

The Scottish context

This is the first book to deal with these issues in a Scottish context, and a contribution to a very small but gradually expanding body of research on ethnic minorities in Scotland. We see our work not in isolation, but as a contribution to comparative literature in the field. Smith and Mercer (1987), referring to housing research, give three major advantages of adopting a comparative perspective, which are 'questioning the taken for granted' (p.20), checking the validity of interpretations of research material and differentiating 'between the general and the unique' (p.22). Following their suggestions, in order to allow ourselves and our readers to ascertain what are the distinctive features of the Scottish ethnic minority experience, and to enable productive comparison, it is necessary to outline the general context of the work. Inevitably, this involves us in differentiating the Scottish context from that of Britain as a whole, since previous literature has tended to generalise findings from England and Wales to cover the whole of the U.K. (eg Brown 1984).

In comparison with England and Wales, Scotland has a different institutional and legal structure, a different migration history and ideology about migrants (Miles 1980, Miles and Muirhead 1986) and a different set of minorities (Bowes, McCluskey and Sim 1989, 1990a).

Housing and social work services are organised on the basis of laws specifically applying to Scotland. Public housing is the responsibility of district level housing authorities, locally based housing associations and the recently established 'Scottish Homes', an organisation appointed by central government to oversee increasing privatisation of housing, notably that previously controlled by the Scottish Special Housing Association, also a central government body which built and let houses, but is now abolished. These aspects of housing provision can be counted forms of 'social services', though they differ importantly from other areas so designated (such as social work, education and health care) as they involve payment by their consumers and do not monopolise provision (cf. English 1988). The structure of housing tenure in Scotland is also distinctive, with a traditionally dominant public housing sector: in Scotland, 45 per cent of all dwellings are rented from public sector landlords (CIPFA 1988) compared with about 22 per cent for England and Wales (BSA 1988:21). Glasgow District Council is the largest local housing authority in Western Europe.

Social work services are the responsibility of Regional authorities. One commentator, noting the frequent lack of communication and co-operation between housing and social work departments which can result from their association with different levels of local government writes

> It sometimes seemed...that one of the principal functions of the social work department was to carry out rescue work among the human wreckage created by the evictions policy of the housing department. (Martin 1979:94)

Whilst responsibility for homelessness now lies with the housing authorities following legislative change, clearly there is still plenty of scope for problems in this area. Ford (1988:136) considers 'The largest single problem' facing social work departments in Scotland to be that of 'delineating boundaries', particularly relating to where their work ends and that of other agencies begins. She points out in particular that social work departments and housing departments continue to pursue their separate paths often with little regard for one another, thus failing to face the key issue of boundaries; and sometimes with conflicting results.

Social work departments in Scotland have somewhat wider powers than those in England and Wales, the relevant legislation being more generally phrased. Furthermore, social work services in Scotland include work with juvenile offenders, particularly significantly in childrens hearings. In England and Wales, social work and probation services are separate. In Scotland, one half of the population is covered by Strathclyde Region Social Work Department, the largest social work authority in Britain. Within this area also live the large majority of Scotland's ethnic minority population.

Migration and racism

Examining the history of migration to Scotland, it is useful to refer back to the Irish migration of the nineteenth century discussed in detail by Miles (1980). Until the 1840s, the migration was temporary, but in the latter half of the century, migrants came to Scotland to settle permanently, driven by the destruction of the Irish agricultural peasant economy and latterly by the potato famine, and drawn by the demand for labour in the expanding Scottish industrial sector, particularly in the West of Scotland. In some areas, migrants formed as much as 60 per cent of the workforce, and throughout, they experienced the worst housing, the lowest wages and the worst working conditions. Miles (1980) describes much anti-Irish activity, relating incidents involving several thousand people at a time and lasting several days, which required considerable force to subdue them. The agitation involved a process of stereotyping and scapegoating the Irish, 'racialising' them as a separate and inferior race and blaming them for the ills of society. It was overlaid with strong anti-Catholic sentiments, particularly clear in Scotland, Miles argues, because of institutional support in the established church, the Church of Scotland, more radically Protestant than the Church of England. As Miles suggests, this migration and the opposition to it can usefully be seen as historical precursors to the post World War II migrations to Scotland, and as establishing a particular form of anti-migrant ideology.

It is conceivable, though difficult to establish empirically, that the very strong anti-Irish sentiment in Scotland lessened the impact of racism on later migrants to the country including Jews and Italians who migrated in the late nineteenth and early twentieth centuries, and the NCWP migrants who came after World War II. Irish Catholics continued (and continue) to be stigmatised and scapegoated, and to come off worse in all social and economic competitions than Scottish Protestants, and the symbolism of Catholics versus Protestants continues to be strong. Miles and Muirhead (1986) mention that England also provided an alternative target, available to be blamed for the problems of Scotland. This historical heritage may have meant that the new black migrants of the 1940s onwards, at least for a time, were not needed as scapegoats. It may also have meant that rather little attention was paid to manifestations of racism against black people (other problems being thought more serious) until they became too blatant to ignore. Certainly, many commentators in the 1960s noted a widespread belief that Scotland had no problems in this area (e.g. Baker 1968, Hanley 1969), especially in comparison with England.

From the 1970s, such a view has been challenged. In 1972 for example, Jahoda et al reported acceptance among Asian schoolchildren in Glasgow of a racial hierarchy topped by white people, reflecting attitudes characteristic of the society around them. McEwen (1979/80, 1980) commented on what he saw as dangerous apathy on the part of local authorities who not only failed to perceive widespread interpersonal racism, but also complacently saw no need to examine their own practices for institutionally racist content. More recently, Tayside Community Relations Council (1987) has reported increasing racial tension in Tayside, again urging greater attention to be paid to the problem by those in positions of power. The essays in this book document racism in many forms in Glasgow and Edinburgh in particular.

Ideology about migrants in Scotland, as elsewhere, has to be considered at two levels, usefully termed the interpersonal and the institutional. Interpersonal racism is part of the ideology of an individual, and is constructed, argue Phizacklea and Miles (1979), as individuals make plausible interpretations of the world around them and their own experiences of it, drawing on a wider fund of ideas. Thus in nineteenth century Scotland, Irish migrant workers were apparently accepting low wages and thus keeping wages low all round: to the indigenous workforce, the notion that the Irish were a separate and inferior race 'explained' their actions and allowed them to be scapegoated. Racism therefore grew out of particular, local circumstances, and became linked to a wider, racist tradition. Needless to say, the Irish migrants were not in reality responsible for poor working conditions, and were not actually in competition with indigenous workers, being concentrated in particular types of jobs (Miles 1980).

Institutional racism is built into the structure of a society, and is relatively independent of individuals. To identify it, commentators have looked at a range of phenomena, as Cheetham (1986:9) notes,

> ...from the economic and other social systems which intentionally or uninten-
> tionally keep blacks in subordinate positions to those rules and practices of
> individuals and public bodies which unwittingly discriminate against black
> people.

We do not intend to debate the finer details of definition, but to cover in the book racism in all its forms, including those discoverable in Scottish institutional structures.

Black people in Scotland

Until the 1960s the black population of Scotland was tiny, and in the 1980s the proportion of black people in the population as a whole has remained small, at less than 1 per cent (Scottish Office 1983). This general picture conceals local concentrations of black people, principally in the urban centres of Glasgow and Edinburgh. The processes of development of black communities in the two cities can be separately described. The other centre of population, Dundee, is much smaller, and there is little information available.

Glasgow is the main centre of black settlement in Scotland, and is relatively well documented. Before the 1950s, there were very few black people in Glasgow, save some Indian and Chinese seamen. Kearsley and Srivastava (1974) mapped the distribution of the black population between 1951 and 1971, demonstrating early concentration in very poor inner city housing in the Gorbals, then, with expanding population, movement into other slightly better inner city neighbourhoods. Early migrants to Glasgow from Pakistan and India responded to labour demands in the transport industry, and later there was a move into small business, notably retailing, wholesaling and the manufacture and sale of cheap clothing. The population was boosted in the 1960s, as the male migrants were joined by dependent women and children. Chinese migrants from Hong Kong became characteristically concentrated in the catering industry in restaurants and take-away establishments. Recent figures for Glasgow's black community show 17,281 Pakistanis and Indians (of whom the vast majority are Pakistani), 1769 Chinese and Vietnamese (nearly all Chinese) and a small group of 310 Afro-Caribbean people (Bowes, McCluskey and Sim 1989). This total of 19,360 people form 2.66 per cent of the total city population. The highest concentration of ethnic minority electors is 258 per 1000 electorate in Woodlands (the old Park Ward), a very much higher figure than those for Dundee and Edinburgh (Bowes, McCluskey and Sim 1990a).

The picture for Edinburgh is complicated by wide disparities in published figures (e.g. marked disagreement between Scottish Office (1983) and SEMRU (1987)). SEMRU's figures are probably more reliable, being based on Census information, which householders are legally compelled to provide. They found a black population of 7,115 in 1981 in Lothian Region as a whole, concentrated in the City of Edinburgh and consisting of 5,173 Pakistanis, Indians, Bangladeshis and East African people with origins in the Indian subcontinent, 1,593 from the Far East (mainly Hong Kong) and 349 Caribbean. Thus the black minority in Edinburgh is also overwhelmingly Asian in origin, though the preponderance of South Asians and amongst them Pakistanis is much less marked than for Glasgow. Migration to Edinburgh involved people looking for opportunities to set up in business, often very small scale to start with (SEMRU 1987). Chinese people in Edinburgh today are concentrated in the catering trade (Chan 1983). South Asians are employed particularly in ethnic businesses, restaurants and small shops and the small

Caribbean group is probably mainly professional (SEMRU 1987). It is important to note, as SEMRU (1987) do, that whilst these minorities appear to have established economic niches, unemployment is high (20 to 30 per cent) and the prospects of young people finding work within these niches are not bright. The Edinburgh black population is the least concentrated of all, the highest concentration being 23 Asian electors per 1,000 electorate in St Giles District ward (Scottish Office 1983).

Jones and Davenport (1972) found a Pakistani community in Dundee numbering 500-600 people and the Scottish Office (1983) found a total 'Asian' population (including people of Pakistani, Indian and Chinese origins) of 1,700 people. In the early years of migration (1950s and 1960s), the Pakistanis were attracted to Dundee by the prospect of work in the jute industry (Jones and Davenport 1972, Tayside CRC 1987), though this has since declined, and it appears that the major source of employment in Dundee is now small ethnic business. The pattern of settlement for all Asians in Dundee shows concentration in poorer inner city areas, particularly in neighbourhoods near the old jute mills. Scottish Office (1983) figures suggest that the main centre of population has remained very similar since Jones and Davenport's (1972) survey. The largest number of Asian electors per thousand electorate was 48, in the Coldside district ward (Scottish Office 1983).

The consumers' point of view

In both social and community work and housing, recent research has paid rather little attention to the point of view of the ethnic minority consumer, at least partly because earlier work which attempted to do so was seriously flawed, operating with misleading assumptions and stereotypes. A major task of recent work has been to question these flawed views. A further reason for less attention being paid to the consumers point of view has been that researchers and practitioners in both fields have rightly been paying attention to issues of racism, seen as a problem for white people and therefore a matter of concern for most professionals.

In social work, Pearson (1988) explains that the research work undertaken for the Department of Health concentrated on examining what, if any, special provisions were made in the social service departments for ethnic minorities. Recommendations arising from the research findings focus on policy-making, promoting equal opportunity, funding, staffing and staff training and support. Regarding ethnic minority needs, there is the general statement about the need for equal access to services, and the following bland comment (1988:19-20)

> It is important to recognise the heterogeneity of the black and minority ethnic communities. A balance must be kept between recognising cultural differences and respecting the uniqueness of each individual and his/her needs. Particular attention should be given to communicating effectively with individuals and communities for whom English is not the first language.

Whilst in general terms we cannot disagree with this statement, it remains a minimalist approach to the challenge undoubtedly presented to social services of attempting to meet ethnic minority needs, and may indeed entail some risks. We have already referred to Dominelli's (1989) salutary account of the potential danger of concentrating on an assumed need for English lessons. Other work comes closer to reflecting real minority concerns. Ahmed et al (1986) for example present a series of examples of social work practice with black children and families, strongly challenging approaches which stereotype and stigmatise black people. Ahmed herself reviews the case of a sixteen year old pregnant Sikh woman who wanted to marry her Moslem boyfriend. The white social workers supported and encouraged her in this wish, opposed by her parents. They assumed that she came from a traditional, oppressive family, and that she needed her freedom. Ahmed explains that a black social worker pointed out that if the woman had been white, marriage at sixteen would have been seen as a 'cage' (1986:147) and the social workers would not have supported her so readily. Their views involved the automatic, racist notion that white society was superior to Sikh society for the woman involved. The case emphasises the kinds of problems that may arise from failure to examine minority concerns fully: the white social workers did not bother to consider the parents' wishes which, for them, simply resulted from oppressive traditional culture. SEMRU (1987) found their black interviewees in Lothian Region generally unaware of the Social Work service, and that they felt social workers themselves stereotyped black people and were generally ignorant of their particular needs.

Ohri et al (1982) and Dominelli (1988) support the work of Ahmed et al (1986) and SEMRU (1987) in a more general way, by arguing that social and community work have been racist, and that there is an urgent need for white professionals to challenge their racism and develop anti-racist practice. Dominelli (1988) goes as far as to argue that anti-racist social work can eliminate not only racism in social work, but also by implication class and gender inequalities. All this work has involved strong inputs from ethnic minority professionals and clients, and many of the contributors have worked closely with ethnic minority communities. But there remains little systematic material on ethnic minority views even of anti-racist social and community work or of ethnic minority requirements from the services. One of Dominelli's (1988) main recommendations is that social workers must listen to ethnic minority voices. She argues that they must (p.162)

...alter the existing power relationship between the users of services and workers...[and]...not deny consumers their right to determine the types of welfare provisions on offer.

Much recent research on housing, as we have already noted, has focussed on discriminatory practices in housing departments, concentrating, like the social and community work research, on service delivery and the problems of institutional racism. From the 1960s, there has been a long debate about how far ethnic minority patterns of housing in Britain are dictated by minority preferences, and how far by external constraints of discrimination and structured disadvantage (e.g. Rex and Moore 1967, Dahya 1974, Davies 1985, Werbner 1979, Henderson and Karn 1987, Sarre, Phillips and Skellington 1989). Phillips (1987) notes that the argument for external constraint has been the more convincing, and that the arguments stressing minority preferences operated with misleading stereotypes. Bowes McCluskey and Sim's (1990b) work supports this argument, questioning the myth that 'Asians prefer owner-occupation' by demonstrating that, in Glasgow at least, they have little realistic alternative. Findings like this have called the older, culturally based work into question.

A focus on ethnic minority housing needs and aspirations expressed by black people themselves remains eminently desirable, and there are indications that an approach to the question which does not stereotype minority cultures can produce important findings. One such indication appears in the work of Ridoutt (1984) in Lewisham, where black people were found to be concentrated in poorer housing in the Northern part of the Borough, with a greater proportion of white people in the better Southern part. Housing allocations officers interviewed by Ridoutt explained that black people preferred the Northern part because they liked to live with their own community. Accordingly, where possible, they would offer black people houses in their 'preferred' area. Ridoutt decided to ask the black people themselves where they would like to live, suspecting that the allocations officers had an incorrect stereotype of black housing aspirations. The great majority of black people interviewed expressed a preference for the Southern part of the Borough. In this case therefore, conventional 'culturally based' stereotypes were shown to be totally wrong. Similarly, Bowes, McCluskey and Sim (1989b) found that many Asians in Glasgow were keen to apply for council housing, but that they had had considerable problems getting information about it, and that the stereotypical view of Asian preference for owner-occupation was subscribed to by many local housing officials. In Lothian Region, SEMRU (1987) found that black people felt they were invariably allocated the worst council housing, and that staff were (p.21) 'ignorant of ethnic minority issues, unhelpful or misleading in the advice proffered'.

All the contributors to this book try to examine ethnic minority points of view on social services, and attempt to avoid the pitfalls of racist stereotyping. We have tried, as far as possible, to work with black people, and to reflect their needs and their concerns.

Research in action

Lawrence (1982) criticises sociological research for its focus on 'black "pathology"', arguing that black people have been treated as a social problem, and that their subordinate position in white society has been attributed to the pathology of their cultures. In particular he argues, Afro-Caribbean culture is considered somehow incomplete and deficient, therefore handicapping individuals and inhibiting their lifestyles and life chances. Asian culture, he argues, is seen as hidebound and traditional, holding back members of the Asian community in their attempts to make their way in the world. Social research, Lawrence suggests, has done black people some grave dis-services. As an alternative, he argues, the focus needs to be on the power structures which dictate black people's position in society, and particularly on racism. Insofar as black cultures are considered, Lawrence feels that new questions need to be asked: for example, with Carby (1982), he argues for consideration of black family structures as important sources of support and bases for resistance to oppression, rather than the simple adoption of the prevailing notion that the black (particularly Asian) family is a source of oppression.

White researchers in particular are challenged by Lawrence's work to consider how far their work is influenced by racist stereotypes. The white writers in this volume must recognise that these stereotypes may come into play in their work, which may therefore be detrimental to black people. In collecting the information on which these articles are based, we have all, in various ways, worked as closely as we could with local black people, and have tried, through so doing, to reflect their views and aspirations as closely as possible. They are not, however, responsible for what we say.

All our work has a very practical orientation, trying, in different ways, to approach, understand and suggest solutions to some problems with social welfare that local black people themselves have raised. The practitioners among us are engaged every day in working with black people towards solutions to such problems. The academics are one step removed, but co-operate with practitioners and black people to the same end. We aim therefore at an applied, anti-racist research.

The book and the contributors

Bowes, McCluskey and Sim look at the relationship between ethnic minorities and Glasgow District Council Housing Department. Locating their work in the wider literature on black housing in Britain, they focus on the demands made on the council by the minority population, the difficulties experienced in terms of access to housing and housing services, and the often negative experiences of ethnic minority tenants. This emphasis on the consumers' point of view helps stress how 'internal preferences' can challenge stereotypes of Asian culture often perpetuated in the academic literature. The research was carried out for the Housing Department, and the authors look at the Department's response to their findings and recommendations in which, as the Department had requested, they had endeavoured to ensure representation of ethnic minority views.

Sim then focusses on the whole question of minority access to smaller landlords, particularly housing associations. He reviews the English experience and comments on its relevance in the Scottish context, arguing that Housing Corporation policies have been insufficiently adapted to the Scottish situation. He argues that black tenure choice in Scotland is constrained by many aspects of housing association policies and practices, and that, whilst some recent initiatives are to be welcomed, there is still much scope for improvement.

Whereas Sim's focus is on the wider issues of access, Dalton has undertaken research with a number of locally based housing associations in Glasgow. His work, which was partly financed by the Commission for Racial Equality, is of national and local interest. It looks at the practices of specific associations in relation to the minority communities, and at black people's views of housing associations. Dalton clearly demonstrates that Scottish housing associations are doing little to satisfy the real housing needs of black people in Scotland, and that many of their policies and practices are discriminatory in effect.

MacEwen is a lawyer and university teacher and researcher who has written extensively on the legal aspects of housing allocations, particularly in respect of racial discrimination. He has also collaborated in research within Lothian Region (SEMRU 1987) in the housing and social service field. His contribution examines the effectiveness of the Race Relations Act 1976 in preventing discrimination in housing, looking at the level of understanding and commitment to implementing the law with reference to Edinburgh District Council's housing policy and practice. He is able to draw reasonably optimistic conclusions about policies, but cautions that, in the end, the practices must follow these through effectively.

Brailey works for Integrate, a voluntary organisation which exists to promote the provision of housing and related services for those who have difficulties gaining access to mainstream housing, such as the elderly, the handicapped and the disabled. These difficulties are often magnified for members of the ethnic minority communities and Integrate has, under Brailey's direction, carried out preliminary assessment of the problems. Her contribution widens the debate about housing access and explores the interaction of various forms of discrimination. She argues that there are large gaps in our knowledge of special housing needs among ethnic minorities, that it is difficult to identify people with such needs, that planning has taken no account of them, that they have not been monitored, and that ethnic minority take up rates for existing provision are extremely low. She suggests a number of measures which may go some way towards remedying the situation.

Chakarabarti's chapter begins the discussion of social and community work by raising a series of issues in social work training. He argues that for an anti-racist social work to develop, current training must improve. Illustrations are given, showing how anti-racist practice is needed in relation to family work, particularly adoption and fostering, community care and work with black elders. Chakrabarti insists that the major responsibility for implementing training improvements rests with social work management.

McCluskey (who also worked on the council housing survey as research fellow and is a qualified social worker) conducted research on access to the social work service in Glasgow which assesses the problems minorities face in making use of the services available. She has the unusual experience of both research and professional practice which facilitates her clear insight into difficulties of access, and the inappropriate structure of social work services. She concludes that in Glasgow there has been little progress in developing anti-racist social work, that black clients are 'dissatisfied with and alienated from' social work services, and that social workers in the field are frustrated that they receive little help in their efforts to work with black people.

Murray is a community worker with Crossroads Youth and Community Association, Glasgow, a voluntary community work agency in one of the main ethnic minority areas of the city. She focuses on community work with Asians, looking at Crossroads' own recent experience and drawing out general lessons for community development initiatives. Crossroads' work has been monitored and supported by an action research programme, and Murray also looks at how the programme has tried to ensure that research has practical applications and is answerable to those whose lives it investigates. Murray emphasises that Crossroads is still working on the development of ethnically sensitive practice and reviews a series of issues, including training staff and students, location in the community, tackling equal opportunities, approaching harassment and working with a women's group and a self help housing group. She traces both successes and problems at Crossroads in dealing with these issues.

Wardhaugh, who worked on the action-research programme, examines the potential for community action among Asian women. Most of the businesses and organisations within the Asian community are run by men, and men tend to be seen as the public faces of the community. Wardhaugh examines the development of a local Asian women's group, showing its growth and considerable strength, increasing independence from Crossroads and diverse campaigning and self-help activities. She contrasts this success with the relative weakness of an Asian housing group, which focussed on the single issue of harassment, was isolated, internally divided and faced much neighbourhood hostility. She argues that the women's group challenges the myth of Asian women's passivity and suggests they can offer inspiration to other such groups.

Harvie's project took up a theme raised by Asian women themselves, wife abuse, which she sees as a form of sexual violence. Her work involved providing research material to support community action, documenting women's experiences of violence and trying to get away from it, and developing analyses of the material. Her contribution, based on a UK wide survey of refuge provision, emphasises the lack of appropriate responses to such violence by existing agencies, and the extra problems therefore faced by Asian women experiencing violence.

In conclusion, Alexander, Bowes and Sim review some of the major issues arising from the work in the book. Many of these were discussed at a conference held at the University of stirling in February 1990. We conclude that there is much more work to be done, in both practice and research.

Notes:

Community Relations Councils are local bodies, set up by and answerable to the national UK-wide Commission for Racial Equality, whose remit is to work towards eliminating discrimination, to promote racial equality and to review the workings of the 1976 Race Relations Act

Housing associations, in Britain, are voluntary housing agencies, usually with charitable status, and controlled by management committees of lay persons. They provide housing for people in need, funded by central government through the Housing Corporation (in England) and Scottish Homes (in Scotland).

References

Ahmed S, Cheetham J. and Small J (ed.), 1986 *Social Work with Black Children and Their Families,* London: Batsford.

Association of Directors of Social Services and the Commission for Racial Equality (ADSS/CARE) 1978 *Multi-racial Britain: the Social Services Response* London: Commission for Racial Equality.

Baker P, 1968 *Attitudes to Coloured People in Glasgow,* Glasgow: University of Strathclyde Survey Research Centre.

British Association of Social Work (BASW), 1982 *Social Work in Multi-cultural Britain London:* BASW.

Bowes A M McCluskey J and Sim D F, 1989 *Ethnic Minority Housing Problems in Glasgow: Final Report* Glasgow: District Council Housing Department.

Bowes A M McCluskey J and Sim D F, 1990a 'The Changing nature of Glasgow's ethnic minority community' *Scottish Geographical Magazine* 106(2):99-107.

Bowes A M McCluskey J and Sim D F, 1990b 'Ethnic minorities and council housing in Glasgow' *New Community* 16(4):523-532.

Brown C, 1984 *Black and White Britain: The Third P.S.I. Survey* London: Heinemann and the Policy Studies Institute.

Carby H V, 1982 'White woman listen! Black feminism and the boundaries of sisterhood' in Centre for Contemporary Cultural Studies *The Empire Strikes Back: Race and Racism in 70s Britain* London: Hutchinson pp. 212-235.

Central Council for Education and Training in Social Work (CCETSW) 1984 *Teaching Social Work in a Multi-racial Society* London: CCETSW.

Chan E, 1983 *Needs of the Chinese Community in Lothian* Edinburgh: Lothian Community Relations Council.

Chartered Institute of Public Finance and Accountancy (CIPFA), 1988 *Rating Review Estimates of Income and Expenditure 1988-89 Summary Volume* Edinburgh: CIPFA Scottish Branch.

Cheetham J, 1986 'Introduction' to Ahmed S et al (eds.), *op cit* pp. 1-38.

Commission for Racial Equality, 1989 *Racial Discrimination in Liverpool City Council* London: CRE.

Dahya B, 1974 'The nature of Pakistani ethnicity in industrial cities in Britain' in Cohen A. (ed), *Urban Ethnicity* London: Tavistock pp.77-118.

Davies J G, 1985 *Asian Housing in Britain* London: Social Affairs Unit.

Dominelli L, 1988 *Anti-Racist Social Work* London: Macmillan.

Dominelli L, 1989 'White racism, poor practice' *Social Work Today* 20(18) : 12-13.

English J, 1988 'Housing' in English J (ed.), *Social Services in Scotland* Edinburgh: Scottish Academic Press (3rd edition) pp. 96-117.

Ford J, 1988 'Personal social services' in English J. (ed.), *op cit* pp. 118-140.

Hanley E, 1969a 'Scotland: avoiding English mistakes' *Race Today* 1(1) : 23-24.

Hanley E, 1969b 'Scotland: a more organised approach' *Race Today* 1(4): 120-121.

Henderson J and Karn V, 1987 *Race, Class and State Housing: Inequality and the Allocation of Public Housing in Britain* Aldershot: Gower Press.

Jahoda G Thompson S S and Bhatt S, 1972 'Ethnic identity and preferences among Asian immigrant children in Glasgow: a replicated study' *European Journal of Social Psychology* 2(1).

Jones H R and Davenport M, 1972 'The Pakistani community in Dundee. A study of its growth and demographic structure' *Scottish Geographical Magazine* 88 (2) : 75-85.

Kearsley G W and Srivastava S R, 1974 'The spatial evolution of Glasgow's Asian community' *Scottish Geographical Magazine* 90(2) : 110-124.

Lawrence E, 1982 'In the abundance of water the foot is thirsty: sociology and black "pathology"' in *CCCS op cit* pp. 95-142.

MacEwen M, 1979/80 'Local government and the promotion of good race relations: the Scottish lack of experience' in Scottish Council for Racial Equality, *First Annual Report* Edinburgh: SCRE, pp. 32-42.

MacEwen M, 1980 'Race relations in Scotland: ignorance or apathy?' *New Community* 8(3) : 266-274.

Martin F M 1979 'Personal Social Services' in English J and Martin F M *Social Services in Scotland* Edinburgh: Scottish Academic Press pp. 89-106.

Miles R, 1980 *Racism and Migrant Labour* London: Routledge and Kegan Paul.

Miles R and Muirhead L, 1986 'Racism in Scotland: a matter for further investigation' in McCrone D. (ed) *Scottish Government Yearbook* Edinburgh.

Ohri A Manning B and Curno P, 1982 *Community Work and Racism* London: Routledge and Kegan Paul

Pearson R M, 1988 *Social Services in a Multi-Racial Society* London: Social Services Inspectorate, Department of Health.

Phillips D, 1987 'Searching for a decent home: ethnic minority progress in the post-war housing market' *New Community* 14 (1-2) : 105-117.

Phizacklea A and Miles R, 1979 'Working class racist beliefs in the inner city' in Miles R and Phizacklea A (ed.), *Racism and Political Action in Britain* London: Routledge and Kegan Paul.

Rex J and Moore R, 1967 *Race, Community and Conflict* London: Oxford University Press.

Ridoutt T, 1984 'Ethnic monitoring in housing departments: a necessary beginning' *New Community* 11(3): 234-237.

Sarre P, Phillips D and Skellington R, 1980 *Ethnic Minority Housing: Explanations and Policies* Aldershot: Avebury.

Scottish Office, 1983 *Ethnic Minorities in Scotland* Edinburgh: Scottish Office Central Research Unit.

Smith S J and Mercer J, 1987 *New Perspectives on Race and Housing in Britain* Glasgow: Centre for Housing Research.

Tayside Community Relations Council 1987 *Racial Tension in Tayside* Dundee: Tayside CRC.

Scottish Ethnic Minorities Research Unit, 1987 *Ethnic Minorities Profile: a Study of Needs and Services in Lothian Region and Edinburgh District,* Edinburgh: Department of Town and Country Planning, EdinburghCollege of Art/Heriot-Watt University.

Ward R, 1984 'Race and housing: issues and policies' *New Community* 11(3) : 201-205.

Werbner P, 1979 'Avoiding the Ghetto: Pakistani migrants and settlement shifts in Manchester' *New Community* 7(3) : 376-389.

Young K and Connelly N, 1981 *Policy and Practice in the Multi-racial City* London: Policy Studies Institute.

Chapter 1

Ethnic minorities and housing in Glasgow: from research to action

Alison Bowes, Jacqui McCluskey and Duncan Sim

Introduction

The research on which this paper is based was carried out by the University of Stirling in 1988 for Glasgow City Housing Department. The City Council has published the main report (Bowes, McCluskey and Sim 1989) and papers on various aspects of the research have been separately published in a number of journals (Bowes, McCluskey and Sim 1990 a,b,c). This paper will outline the research findings and discuss the way in which those findings are being translated into action by the local authority concerned.

We begin by outlining the background to the research and then summarising the findings. The response of the City Council is then discussed and we continue with an account of the Action Plan prepared by the Housing Department. We conclude with a statement of the position as at summer 1990.

Background to the research

The research stemmed from decisions taken by Glasgow City Council in approving its Housing Plan 8 in March 1985. The plan drew attention to the fact that the city's black ethnic minority population was located largely in the owner-occupied sector, usually in inner city areas, and there was some speculation as to how much this reflected difficulties of access to local authority housing. It concluded: 'Only limited progress has been made towards increasing access to public sector housing amongst the ethnic groups and further research is needed on this issue' (Glasgow City Council 1985:65).

Further evidence of the difficulties faced by the ethnic minorities was provided by Glasgow City Planning Department's work on social deprivation in the city, and concern at the underuse of City Council grants and loans by minority groups was expressed as long ago as March 1984 by the Council's Housing sub-committee on the Private Sector. There was also concern at an apparent increase in incidents of racial harassment, the subject of reports by the Housing Department to the Sub-Committee on Race Relations.

The City Council formally agreed, in September 1986, that a major research study into the housing needs of ethnic minorities was required and committed itself firstly, to eliminate any discriminatory practice which the study identified and, secondly, to review all relevant housing policy and practice in the light of the research findings. The contract for carrying out the research was awarded in late 1987 to the University of Stirling.

A parallel study was carried out by the Scottish Ethnic Minorities Research Unit (SEMRU) at Glasgow College, into ethnic minority access to and experience of housing association housing (Dalton and Daghlian 1989). A summary of this research appears elsewhere in this volume. The two studies therefore represented an important step forward in ethnic minority research in Scotland.

Methodology

At the outset of the research, it was recognised that staff within the District Council who had specialist knowledge of ethnic minorities should be approached and several meetings were held in different departments. Other statutory bodies and government departments were also approached, including the Scottish Office, the Commission for Racial Equality and Strathclyde Community Relations Council. These meetings all provided important background information on the context of the research.

In particular, we were able to obtain lists of the various ethnic minority community, social and political organisations existing in and around Glasgow, and at an early stage in the research, we met representatives of many of these bodies. These meetings were important, partly as a means of informing the ethnic community about our study, partly as a means of obtaining a 'group' view on some of the housing issues we wished to explore and partly as a source of information which helped us immensely in compiling our questionnaire.

The questionnaire which we devised was lengthy, covering basic household details, questions about housing tenure, the use of the Council's housing service and experiences of discrimination and harassment. There were also a number of questions designed to test knowledge of the housing system and to establish attitudes towards council housing and the housing service. We originally intended to interview 400 households, just under 10 per cent of the total number of black ethnic minority households within the city. In the event, 341 interviews were achieved, a response rate of 85.2 per cent. Response rates were lowest within the Chinese community and within council housing, where large numbers of households had moved and given up tenancies at relatively short notice. We interviewed 68 public sector tenants and 273 other households, mainly owner-occupiers.

A housing profile of ethnic minorities

As might be expected, over two-thirds of black ethnic minorities in the city were found to live in tenement flats (68.4 per cent), with 9 per cent in multi-storey flats, 7.2 per cent in semi-detached housing and 6.6 per cent in detached housing. This breakdown reflects the location of minorities in inner city areas where tenements predominate. For those who rented their housing, however, multi-storey flats were more significant, housing 34.9 per cent of households.

We discovered, however, that the proportion of minorities living in detached and semi-detached housing was increasing and one of the results of our survey of the electoral register was the identification of a number of ethnic minority families living outwith the inner city, in Deaconsbank, Baillieston, Hogganfield, Kelvindale and Summerston (between 7 and 9 per cent of the population of these areas). In the main, these are areas of new private housing, many of which have been built with the support and encourage-ment of the District Council. It appears therefore that the Council's policy of harnessing private sector resources and encouraging low cost private house building has somewhat increased the range and availability of housing to ethnic minorities, many of whom are beginning to move out from the traditional areas of inner city settlement. We estimated that so far only 2.0 per cent of the total ethnic minority community lives in these areas but this is increasing.

These moves within the private sector serve to emphasise the propensity of Asian households for owning rather than renting. The tenure breakdown of minority households revealed 78.1 per cent in owner-occupation with 13.1 per cent renting privately, 5.3 per cent renting from the District Council, 3.3 per cent from housing associations and 0.2 per cent from the SSHA (now Scottish Homes). We attempted to make some assessment of the condition of the housing and although almost half felt their property was in good condition, problems were clearly evident. The most pressing were decoration (perhaps because of its visibility), dampness, central heating and window repairs. Households did not always feel able to tackle these problems, however, and although decoration could be and was dealt with, dampness was not a repair that was generally tackled, partly perhaps because of the expense of solutions.

We asked households why the repairs which were still required had not been carried out and the most frequent response (mentioned by 26.5 per cent) was cost. This was followed by 'problems with the council', claimed by 14.0 per cent: many of these problems seemingly concerned inability to obtain grant aid.

Despite the sometimes poor housing conditions which exist in areas of ethnic minority housing, we found high levels of satisfaction with both home and neighbourhood amongst our sample. The presence of good neighbours, the convenience of an inner city location and a strong sense of community were all positive attributes mentioned by respondents.

Perhaps as a result of these levels of satisfaction, we found families living in the same area for long periods of time and there was a general stability to the ethnic minority community. Almost a third of all households had lived at their present address for 10 years or more. On the other hand, one fifth of households had lived less than two years at their present address, and we asked about their housing history and previous place of residence. Of those who had moved, the vast majority had moved within Glasgow, although 5.8 per cent had moved from elsewhere in Scotland and 7.5 per cent had moved from England.

When asked why households had actually moved, 45.3 per cent stated reasons relating to the house (notably its size) and this motive for moving, in order to obtain more space, is common throughout the ethnic minority community (Rees and Ram 1987). A further 17.2 per cent gave family reasons and 8.4 per cent made a move associated with a job.

In 63.1 per cent of cases, the previous house was owned but when asked who had owned it, 19.3 per cent stated it had been a relative outside the current household. This suggests that some of the moves had been out of the extended family home, with younger couples moving in order to set up on their own. 63.0 per cent of previous houses were owned outright and 29.9 per cent were being bought with a mortgage.

For those whose previous accommodation was rented, 28.7 per cent had rented from Glasgow District Council, 1.1 per cent from another local authority, 2.3 per cent from a housing association and 63.2 per cent from a private landlord. The high proportion renting privately, compared with the estimate of 13.1 per cent at the time of our survey suggests that these households were either younger Asians who had rented privately in the short term, using the tenure simply as a stepping stone on the way to owner-occupation, or else they were households who had moved into Glasgow from elsewhere and had rented while looking around for a house to buy.

This housing profile of ethnic minorities within the city is valuable for raising a number of questions which were a central concern of the research. The first of these relates to the low numbers of ethnic minority households in council housing, despite the dominance of the local authority sector in the city as a whole. It was important to test whether this was due to difficulties of access, to discrimination within the allocation system or simply to a greater aspiration towards owner-occupation instead.

The second issue also relates to the small number of minority households in council housing and concerns the areas where such households were allocated houses. If these areas were too remote and the households were isolated from the rest of the ethnic minority community, then families were increasingly open to racial harassment. This was a problem highlighted by a number of the community groups which we had consulted.

The third issue concerns owner-occupiers. Given that the majority of ethnic minority families are in owner-occupation and given that these houses are, in the main, pre-1919 tenement flats, then it is to be expected that owners would be looking for some financial assistance to repair and improve them. Yet, despite the availability of grants from the District Council, there was clearly a low take up by the minority community, perhaps because of a lack of knowledge. We were asked specifically therefore to investigate the knowledge and use of the council housing service by all tenure sectors.

Knowledge and use of the housing service

a) Applying for council housing and the allocation system

The ethnic minority population in Glasgow, unlike many English cities, is predominantly Asian and there has long been an assumption that, all things being equal, Asian families overwhelmingly choose to become owner-occupiers. The absence of Asian families from much of the local authority stock has therefore been explained in these terms. Recent evidence, though not explicitly challenging this stereotype, does suggest growing demand for council housing. In particular, there are the possibly different aspirations of children of Asian families born in this country and also the changes in the make-up of the Asian population. Robinson (1980), for example, refers to the influx of East African Asians in the 1970s, many of whom sought local authority housing.

Within Glasgow, the failure of many Asian families to apply for council housing may reflect the inability of the local authority to allocate council houses in the areas in which Asian families wish to live. For example, there are few council houses in Glasgow's inner city, apart from certain areas such as Gorbals, Townhead and Woodside, and the housing which exists frequently requires a level of allocation points which many Asian families find difficulty in amassing. For this to be the reason for not applying for council housing however, a certain level of knowledge of the system would be needed and many community groups suggested to us that this was missing. Indeed, ignorance of the allocation system and in particular the points system, seemed quite widespread.

We attempted to measure the levels of knowledge about the allocation system by asking households if they knew how people qualified for a house. Only 42.8 per cent said they knew and could provide us with any details. When asked if they knew where to apply, 45.4 per cent said they did and of these 59.3 per cent mentioned Lomond House, the head office of the Housing Department. A further 32.5 per cent mentioned their local housing office. Misunderstandings clearly do arise, however, as 11.4 per cent named a housing association, and 7.3 per cent the DSS.

Only in 14.0 per cent of our sample had either the whole household or part of the household applied to the council for rented accommodation. Application rates were higher in the Pakistani community, lower amongst Indians and Chinese. We therefore attempted to discover why such a very large proportion had not applied. A total of 78.1 per cent said they wanted to own their own home, and this does tend to reinforce the view that many Asian families wish to be owner-occupiers. Certainly very few (only 6.6 per cent) said they would now like to apply for council housing. We formed the impression during our interviewing that demand for council housing was increasing amongst the younger members of Asian families who cannot afford to buy and no longer wish to live in the extended family home. In fact the average age of head of household applying for a council house, within our sample, was 39, younger than the overall waiting list average of 43. It would be interesting to analyse the full waiting list to see if any clearer trends are apparent, although this was beyond the remit of our study.

For those who do apply, the question then arises as to how well the allocation system copes with the needs and aspirations of minorities and it was our impression that the system was not coping well. There are, in fact, a number of ways in which Glasgow's points system is unsatisfactory and discriminates against the ethnic minorities. Firstly, the Council gives points for 'local connection', with the understandable intention of strengthening local communities. Unfortunately, this has the effect of discriminating against families who have lived the least time in the city and have been unable to build up such points; many of the families in this position will be ethnic minorities. In addition, those minority families who do qualify for local connection points will be allocated those points for certain inner city neighbourhoods, such as the West End and Pollokshields. These are precisely the areas where the council has fewest houses, and where the allocation of such points is of least value. Secondly, the Council allocates date points for time on the waiting list but this favours existing tenants. Thus an Asian owner-occupier will be allocated five points for each year on the list. But tenants, who are overwhelmingly white, are allocated five points per year for the first ten years, rising to ten points and more thereafter. This means that white families with relatively little housing need may take preference over a black family in greater need but with a shorter residence in the area.

If the Council wishes to use waiting time as a criterion for allocating council housing, then points should be given for waiting time in need, regardless of whether the applicant is a tenant or not.

It may also be the case that the failure to provide sufficiently large houses for Asian families is also discriminatory. Large houses (five apartments or more) are in short supply generally in Glasgow with only 3.2 per cent of local authority stock of this size. Frequently too this is stock which is popular under the right-to-buy. Nevertheless, this shortage has particular repercussions for Asian households and has meant that families have failed to be rehoused or have had to wait longer for their accommodation. The Association of Metropolitan Authorities believes that this non-provision of housing to particular groups because of lack of available large units of accommodation, may be indirectly discriminatory under the Race Relations Act (AMA 1988). A final area of indirect discrimination may arise concerning the rights of sons and daughters to succeed to a tenancy. Clearly there are very good reasons for this policy but it should be borne in mind that it does reinforce the racial mix in particular areas and reduces the availability of housing for allocation to other families in need.

Even where sons and daughters do not actually succeed to a tenancy, the 'council house tradition' in Glasgow means that many children put their names on the waiting list at 16, that is, as soon as they become eligible. They are thus able to build up waiting time points. Such a 'tradition' operates against the interests of ethnic minorities and we would reiterate our belief that 'waiting time in need' is the most important measure.

The research therefore raised a number of questions relating to the points system, where discrimination, usually indirect, was occurring. These are questions which are also identified in Martin MacEwen's paper elsewhere in this volume. We recommended that these issues, particularly relating to waiting time and local connection points, be examined carefully as part of a wider review of the allocations system which was then taking place.

b) Harassment and attitudes to council housing

Although both discrimination and racist harassment are known to exist in Glasgow, it is not always easy to get an objective measure of their seriousness, partly because of the enormous range of problems which ethnic minority families face and the differing ability of families to cope with the strain imposed by those problems. Some families are therefore more willing to talk about their experiences than others.

The question of satisfaction with house and neighbourhood has already been referred to. Generally the greater levels of satisfaction existed where minority families felt a sense of community support; in other areas such as the peripheral council housing estates, isolation and vulnerability to harassment led to dissatisfaction with the neighbourhood being expressed. A total of 13.3 per cent of those interviewed were dissatisfied or very dissatisfied with their area and of the various specific problems identified, harassment was mentioned by 10.5 per cent and unfriendly people and neighbours by 12.4 per cent.

When asked if they or anyone in their household had experienced violence, threats or harassment in the area, 35.7 per cent said they had. The three major problems were verbal abuse, cited by 58.1 per cent, personal attacks, cited by 29.9 per cent, attacks on the home, mentioned by 19.7 per cent. Other problems which were identified were the throwing of objects, rudeness, graffiti and attacks on children and family cars.

Of particular concern was the fact that relatively few people bothered to report these experiences. Only in the case of attacks on the home and burglaries, did more than half report it. Even in the case of physical attacks on the person, more than half failed to inform the police or other authorities. When asked why they had not reported a particular problem, the majority stated that they felt there was no point and nothing would be done, and many were critical of the police who were also felt to be guilty of racism. Even where the problem was reported, little action seemed to have been taken and it is not surprising that the proportion of the sample who were satisfied with the outcome of their experiences was generally relatively small.

There is no doubt that these experiences have soured attitudes towards the Housing Department and, indeed, towards local authority housing in general. It was important to try and assess these attitudes, as they would help perhaps to explain why relatively few people actually applied for council housing. We did this by reading out various statements in our interviews and asking if the respondents agreed or disagreed with them.

In a number of cases, interviewees felt unable either to agree or disagree but many clearly did feel positively towards council housing, with for example, almost a fifth agreeing strongly with the notion that everyone had the right to a council house and 44.4 per cent disagreeing or disagreeing strongly with the notion that council housing was only for whites. On the other hand, council housing was not seen as being particularly well maintained and most seemed unconvinced that the council took care of its tenants or that officials assessed housing need impartially. Of greater concern perhaps, from the District Council's point of view, were the very negative feelings that respondents had regarding the ethnic minority experience of council housing. More than half agreed that Asian/Chinese families in council schemes were isolated and subject to harassment while 20.9 per cent agreed strongly that officials did not treat minorities fairly. Even more worrying for allocators of housing was the fact that 43.8 per cent agreed or agreed strongly that Asian or Chinese families were always offered bad housing. Interestingly, the experiences of the Pakistani community seemed to be particularly negative, compared with the Indians and Chinese. Given that Pakistanis have a greater representation in the council sector and arguably, therefore, are better placed to comment on the District Council, then this is an especially depressing finding.

Clearly, the Council has some way to go in two respects. Firstly, there is a need to convince ethnic minorities of the impartiality of the allocation system, bearing in mind our own reservations regarding some aspects of it. Secondly, access to council housing on its own is not enough and in order to prevent problems of isolation and harassment, support systems need to be developed to sustain ethnic minority tenancies.

(c) Grants and loans for owner-occupiers

The private sector division of Glasgow City Housing Department is responsible for allocating money for repair and improvement grants. Given that the majority of ethnic minority householders are owner-occupiers, it was felt that this section of the Department would be of particular relevance.

We began by asking if respondents knew how people qualified for a grant or loan for repairs or improvements and only 25.9 per cent said they did. When asked if they knew where to go to apply, 34.0 per cent said yes and of these 71.2 per cent mentioned Glasgow District Council itself. 19.5 per cent however mentioned their bank or building society as a source.

We then asked if the families themselves had ever applied for such a loan or grant. Only 11.6 per cent had applied for a grant for repairs, of whom 74.4 per cent had been successful, 15.4 per cent unsuccessful and in 2.6 per cent of cases, a decision was awaited from the District Council. A total of 7.4 per cent of households had applied for a grant for improvements, of whom 78.3 per cent had been successful. As far as loans were concerned, only 0.9 per cent had applied for a loan to carry out repairs or improvements. When asked if households had experienced difficulties applying, 33.3 per cent said they did, of whom 72.2 per cent said they had difficulty getting information and 61.1 per cent found filling in forms a problem.

Given the fact that much of the housing in inner city areas, where ethnic minorities are concentrated, is in relatively poor condition, the extremely low take up rate for grants is disappointing. Knowledge of the grants system was particularly low within the Chinese community with only 9.5 per cent stating that they knew how households qualified. This suggests that ignorance of the system has led to many households missing opportunities to improve and repair their properties, particularly when grants were available at a level of 90 per cent, between 1982 and 1984. The contrast is particularly noticeable in Woodlands, immediately north west of the city centre; in East Woodlands, where the population is predominantly Asian, property is in a poor state and is only now being renovated by the actions of the District Council, Charing Cross Housing Association and the Woodlands Development Trust. To be fair, the problem was aggravated by Housing Corporation cost limits, which prevented some improvement work getting underway, and there are also severe mineral problems, but the absence of common repairs schemes and individual improvement work has hardly helped. In West Woodlands where there is a greater white population, there is no doubt that a concerted approach by local residents who understood the system, resulted in substantial amounts of grant being paid into the area.

This question of low take up was raised with District Council staff who shared our concern. However, since grants are less freely available than they once were, the money is being channelled more into priority repairs areas including Garnethill and East Woodlands. Because there is greater targeting on areas of poor housing conditions, it is believed that Asian families should no longer lose out. Nevertheless, targeting alone will not achieve a greater take-up of grants unless Asian households know that such targeting is taking place and are able to take advantage of the increased availability of grants in their area. There is still therefore a need to make information available to the families concerned, and careful monitoring of the situation must take place.

The need for changes in service delivery

The results of our research, parts of which are summarised in the preceding sections, led us to make a number of recommendations to the District Council. Some of these recommendations were specific, relating to aspects of the allocation system or repairs grant targetting. Others, however were more general and we focussed here on the issues of staff training, recruitment, the provision of information, and ethnic monitoring and record keeping.

As far as staff training was concerned, we felt that the numbers involved had been too small in relation to the total staff employed and that the front-line staff in particular were inadequately trained. Simple racism awareness training was not always appropriate and a more specific 'anti-racist' approach was better.

The question of recruitment was particularly problematic. Although Glasgow is clearly a multi-racial city, the image presented by the Housing Department is almost exclusively white. Within the District Council as a whole, there were only 26 white collar and 16 manual staff from the ethnic minority community, out of a total of 14,000 employees. This proportion (0.3 per cent) is much smaller than the proportion of ethnic minorities in the city as a whole (2.6 per cent). Most of the community groups we spoke to raised this as a problem and stated that they believed Asian families would feel happier if there were Asian housing workers who could help overcome difficulties of language and understanding. Many District Council staff themselves felt that there was a need to recruit more ethnic minority staff.

One important way of trying to achieve this is to examine the specifications for jobs, taking into account the fact that candidates will be working in a multi-racial environment. It is important therefore not only to avoid requirements which might be discriminatory but positively to welcome aptitudes such as knowledge of a second language like Urdu, Punjabi or Chinese. For example it would seem quite appropriate for job descriptions for certain Allocations and Estate Management posts, particularly in the Area Offices, to state that 'proficiency in Urdu or Chinese would be preferred'.

Secondly, the advertising of posts is a crucial area. If the ethnic minority community is to be given an equal opportunity in employment, then it is important that people are aware of vacancies and know that the District Council is open to applications from ethnic minority candidates. We recommended therefore that vacancies were advertised in ethnic minority newspapers and that the Council's vacancy list was circulated to local community groups. In England, Section 11 of the Local Government Act 1966 permits the Home Office to fund local authority posts which meet the needs of ethnic minorities. In many authorities such posts have been established to deal with housing management, improvement grants, homelessness and housing advice. Unfortunately Section 11 funding does not apply in Scotland but there is no reason why local authorities such as Glasgow should not appoint specialist staff whose role is exclusively to work with ethnic minorities.

The third area covered by our recommendations concerned access to information and this is bound up with the availability of translated material. Many families have difficulties with the English language and the results of our survey showed that there was a demand for translated material, or some sort of interpreting service at Area Offices.

Glasgow District Council did in fact translate material on the allocations system into Urdu, Punjabi and Chinese in 1985 in the form of A5-sized booklets. Only one Area Office we consulted was able to produce these but informed us that they were simply left on the counter and there was no indication as to how well they were used. The information in the leaflets they suggested was probably out of date and as no-one seemed to know what the leaflets actually said, it was difficult to see how useful they could be in practice. Information supply and recruitment need to be considered together for there is no doubt that the provision of translated material raises the expectation that housing inquiries can be dealt with in a language other than English. Thus 'there seems little point in handing out leaflets if staff are not equipped to deal with the relevant enquiries' (Frempong and Rawlinson 1990:10).

The final area where recommendations were made was in regard to ethnic monitoring and record keeping, where Glasgow has made extremely slow progress. A few years ago, a question on ethnic origin was added to the Housing Application form but it was and is optional; it was not based on self-assessment by the applicant, it was not integrated into the application form but was on a separate piece of paper of a different colour, and the ethnic origin categories listed were inappropriate for the Glasgow situation. Unsurprisingly, the question was generally inadequately answered and this had made monitoring of applications almost impossible.

Thus, of the 75,633 application forms filled in at the time of the Council's re-registration exercise in 1984, the ethnic origin question was not completed or coded in 52,502 cases. This is a non-response rate of 69.4 per cent and renders the brief analysis which was done completely useless. This is not the place to reiterate the arguments for monitoring. They are referred to elsewhere in this volume and are summarised in many of the publications by the Commission for Racial Equality (for example CRE 1989). Many authorities have successfully adopted the practice and we felt that Glasgow should do the same.

Completion of the report

Our research for Glasgow District Council was completed in the late autumn of 1988 and the preliminary results, together with a first draft of our report, were presented to an invited audience of Council officials, community groups and other interested bodies on 13 December. Several workshop sessions were held and individuals were able to comment on the findings and suggest amendments to the final document. Thus the ethnic minority community was closely involved at both the beginning and the end of the research.

We felt this involvement was vital, so that the community could see the direct relevance of what we were doing. We were all too conscious of the suspicion held in some quarters regarding our study. Hence:

> More often than not the problem is already known and there is no need for
> even more research. When the findings of the research are published, there is

a great fanfare of publicity which is followed by inaction, with dust collecting on the report. It is with such cynicism, unfortunately, that we view the Survey of Ethnic Minority housing problems being undertaken by the University of Stirling on behalf of Glasgow District Council. (Scottish Asian Action Committee 1988:9).

We quoted this comment in our final report to the District Council as a way of illustrating the need for speedy action on our findings. In fact, although the report was finally submitted in January 1989, there was no reaction from the Council, and no publicity, although a seminar was held in February in Lomond House, the housing headquarters, for staff and interested researchers. This was addressed by Duncan Sim from Stirling and Mike Dalton, co-author of the SEMRU report on housing associations. A similar joint presentation was made in June 1989 to the annual conference of the Scottish Federation of Housing Associations.

The lack of any apparent movement by the District Council led to a certain amount of concern. The Scottish Asian Action Committee wrote to the Housing Department in May 1989 and then published the response in their 1988/89 Annual Report. The Council was at pains to refute criticism and emphasised its commitment to action.

The Council recognises that sympathetic rhetoric is not enough, that it has to be backed up by actions. The nature of the action which the Council proposes has to be effective, workable and sensitive to the real needs of ethnic communities. Is the real priority not to ensure that we spend time getting the action right than worrying about cynics who might suspect other motives? (Allan 1989).

Allan, the Head of Development within the Housing Department, went on to state that Housing Conveners were to discuss final proposals for action that week.

Another organisation expressing concern at the lack of progress was Integrate, formerly Glasgow Special Housing Group:

Many Integrate members were involved in the preparation of the Stirling University report and have been anxious to see Glasgow District Council's response to the recommendations of the University team. The report had all but disappeared from sight in the last eight months since the District Council convened a seminar on the draft in January (Integrate 1989:1).

In fact the Council seems to have hoped that the implementation of the report could be delayed until its two new Race Equality Advisors were in post, in October. These posts had been created in early 1989 but did not stem directly from our research. The Council then took the opportunity of announcing their appointment and releasing the report to the press at the same time. The plan, however, went badly wrong and the press focussed immediately on the delay between the completion of the report and its public launch, with a clear implication that the Council had been trying to withhold it. The Glasgow *Evening Times* of October 9, 1989, led with the story, entitled 'Secrets of Race Report' and the accounts they published focussed on the more 'sensational' findings relating to harassment and racism within the Housing Department. Clearly a more balanced and thought out press release might have prevented this.

The next day the rest of the Scottish press picked up the story under headings such as 'Shock claim in city racism attack' *(Daily Record)*, 'Concern over racism link' *(Scotsman)* and 'Council anger over racist claims on housing policies' *(Glasgow Herald)*. The appointment of the Race Equality Advisors was lost amidst the racist 'scare' stories.

The problems which this posed for the District Council were well illustrated by the next issue of the *Bulletin*, the Council's monthly newspaper. Instead of a more positive feature, with references to our report and the Race Equality Advisors, the Council was forced very clearly on the defensive with a story entitled, ' "City Housing is not racist". Bailie Brown responds to press allegations'.

There is no doubt that the launch of the report was badly mishandled and it is unfortunate that community groups were left for so long in ignorance of the Council's intentions, after being so closely involved in the research. It made it doubly difficult for the Council to obtain a sympathetic response from the ethnic minority community. Nevertheless, the Council pressed ahead and in December 1989 held a Consultative Forum with community groups, at which it launched its Action Plan.

Action plan for racial equality in housing

The District Council's Action Plan was developed so as to ensure that the policies and practices being pursued provided equality of opportunities for ethnic minorities. Following the acceptance of our report by the Policy and Resources Sub-Committee on Race Relations, the Director of Housing was asked to report back within six months on the action the Department was intending to take. The Action Plan formed the basis of that report back. The plan included these points:

i) Racial harassment policy. The Department aimed to investigate the existing guidelines, revise them, and set out detailed procedures for the handling of harassment cases. There was no indication, however, as to how victims or perpetrators would be dealt with, although the existing system had been strongly criticised in our report.

ii) Communications. There seemed to be a strong commitment to the provision of translated material and to promoting the activities of the Housing Department among the ethnic minority communities. Local forums with community groups were to be developed.

iii) Personnel and training issues. The Council intended to increase the number of employees from the ethnic minority community, and ensure that staff received appropriate equal opportunity and anti-racist training.

iv) Special needs. There was to be new research on the special needs of, for example, ethnic minority elderly, and housing provision was to be better tailored towards meeting those needs.

v) Allocations. The allocation system was to be reviewed so as to ensure that all allocations were fair and did not discriminate against minority applicants. Council housing and its availability was to be promoted among the minority communities.

vi) Private sector. The availability of repair and improvement grants was to be promoted. In this area, as in others, careful monitoring would be undertaken.

The timescale for implementing the Action Plan varied depending on the various areas of concern but it was intended that, by the end of 1990, most of the areas would have been dealt with, to a greater or lesser extent. The Plan itself, interestingly, identified key staff who would take the lead in implementing particular forms of action, so the areas of responsibility were clear.

Since the launch of the Action Plan, two more events are worthy of note. Firstly, the Commission for Racial Equality has visited the District Council to see for itself the progress that is being made. The involvement of the CRE has been at the invitation of the Council and this has been in contrast to many authorities who have been less open to CRE attention. Thus, although progress has been slow so far, the CRE appears relatively satisfied. They are, however, returning in Autumn 1990 to assess the situation (Hann 1990).

The second event was the holding of a major conference on racial equality in March 1990, with speakers from the CRE, academic institutions and other local authorities. Entitled "Is Scotland Unique?", the conference sought to explode the myth that Scotland has no race problem and to help raise consciousness of discrimination and harassment issues.

Conclusion

The original research on ethnic minorities in Glasgow was commissioned by the District Council because of a belief that ethnic minorities were the victims of discrimination within the housing system, a belief which was borne out by the results of our study. The acceptance of our report by the District Council and the launching of its resultant Action Plan has shown that there is a commitment to trying to tackle that disadvantage. At the time of writing, it is difficult to assess the success of the Council's actions so far but it is clear that there is still a long way to go. Research is being turned into action, but slowly. The real issue will be whether the slow progress is acceptable to the minority community in the interests of 'getting it right', and the involvement of the community at all stages of development is therefore crucial.

B

References

Allan B 1989 Letter to Scottish Asian Action Committee reproduced in *Scottish Asian Action Committee Annual Report 1988-89* Glasgow: Scottish Asian Action Committee p.7

Association of Metropolitan Authorities 1988 *A Strategy for Racial Equality in Housing: 3 Allocations* London: AMA

Bowes A McCluskey J and Sim D 1989 *Ethnic Minority Housing Problems in Glasgow* Glasgow: Glasgow District Council

Bowes A McCluskey J and Sim D 1990 a 'The changing nature of Glasgow's ethnic minority community' *Scottish Geographical Magazine* 106(2): 99-107

Bowes A McCluskey J and Sim D 1990 b 'Ethnic minorities and council housing in Glasgow' *New Community* 16(4): 523 -532

Bowes A McCluskey J and Sim D 1990 c 'Racism and harassment of Asians in Glasgow' *Ethnic and Racial Studies* 13(1): 71-91

Commission for Racial Equality 1989 *Positive Action and Racial Equality in Housing :A Guide* London: CRE

Dalton M and Daghlian S 1989 *Race and Housing in Glasgow. The Role of Housing Associations* London: CRE

Frempong G and Rawlinson G 1990 'Research into action: Developing multi-cultural housing practice in Glasgow' *Black Housing* 6(5): 10-11

Glasgow City Council 1985 *Housing Plan 8* Glasgow: City Council

Hann C 1990 contribution to conference 'Is Scotland Unique?'Glasgow 1990

Integrate 1989 'Ethnic minority housing problems in Glasgow Update on Stirling University report' *Integrate News* 4 September: 1

Rees P H and Ram S 1987 'Projections of the residential distribution of an ethnic group: Indians in Bradford' *Environment and Planning A* 19: 1323-1358

Robinson V 1980 'Asians and council housing' *Urban Studies* 17: 323-331

Scottish Asian Action Committee 1988 *Annual Report 1987 - 1988* Glasgow: SAAC

Chapter 2
Ethnic minority access
to housing associations
Duncan Sim

Introduction

This chapter aims to give an overview of Scottish housing association policy and practice in relation to the housing needs of the black population. It has long been apparent that most associations in Glasgow have adopted a 'colour blind' approach to their work, not only in areas where few black people live but also in areas of high black settlement. Black people appear to have little involvement in the affairs of Scottish associations.

In England the National Federation of Housing Associations placed the issues of race and housing and a fair housing policy on the agenda of English associations in 1982. In Scotland, however, no similar dialogue within the movement was stimulated and few associations seemed to treat this issue with the seriousness it deserves.

More recently, however, race and housing has assumed greater relevance for all Scottish associations for a number of reasons. Firstly, the Housing Corporation in Scotland (now Scottish Homes) issued Guidance on the subject, mirroring the earlier Housing Corporation (England) Circular issued previously. Secondly, there has been a major research study of Glasgow housing associations carried out by the Scottish Ethnic Minorities Research Unit and the subject of Mike Dalton's chapter within this volume. Thirdly, there has been the funding by Scottish Homes of ethnic minority outreach workers in Glasgow, and the associated development of a training scheme for black people.

Nevertheless, it seems that, while some Scottish housing associations may be aware of the issue, few have given priority to establishing a fair housing policy. Although the black population in Scotland is significantly smaller than in England, it is contended that the principle of equal opportunity is relevant to all Scottish associations, not just those working within areas of major black settlement. Finally, the question of whether the registration of black associations is applicable in the Scottish context is considered.

Race and housing associations: England

(a) Role of the NFHA

Research into local authority practice has shown not only sustained disadvantage for black households in access to housing, but also in the types of accommodation allocated. Thus, questions of status, influenced by race and class have been shown to affect the decisions taken by Housing Departments (Henderson and Karn 1984; Phillips 1986). It is important to question whether this criticism could also be directed at housing associations. In September 1981, the National Federation of Housing Associations, at its annual conference, proposed that its Housing Management Committee produce guidance to formulate a Fair Housing Policy, which should include advice on ethnic record keeping and monitoring. This decision was influenced by civil unrest in areas where affiliated members were established. Amongst the associations who were concerned with issues of race and housing were those working in Toxteth (Liverpool), Moss Side (Manchester), and Wood Green (London). It was considered that poor housing conditions were a factor contributing to unrest within those areas.

The Commission for Racial Equality (CRE) was asked to help in the production of the policy document. The result was the circulation to all associations of the guide entitled 'Race and Housing' (NFHA 1982), a comprehensive, easily read piece of work for which the NFHA should be commended. However, it should not be forgotten that issues such as monitoring were brought to the attention of housing practitioners five years before (Hammond 1977).

The NFHA document recommended that a Fair Housing Policy be established in each association and, to aid in the process, a checklist was produced, covering advice on equal opportunity statements, how to review policy and procedures, as well as employment, consultation, implementation and development issues. Because it was felt that further encouragement and specific guidance was required, the NFHA published two further guides. These publications were entitled 'Race and Housing: still a cause for concern' (NFHA 1983) and more recently, 'Ethnic Record Keeping and Monitoring'. (NFHA 1985). The issues relating to disadvantage for black households were therefore grasped by the NFHA and clearly translated into proposals for change. It was the NFHA which took the first steps to persuade associations that they should adopt a Fair Housing Policy and, until 1985, it stood on its own without the institutional blessing of the Housing Corporation. It was only in 1985 that the Housing Corporation followed the NFHA lead. Clearly, the autonomy of associations enabled them to influence Housing Corporation policy and practice.

(b) Role of the Housing Corporation

In April 1985, the Housing Corporation in England issued a circular entitled 'Race and Housing' (Housing Corporation 1985). The following summary of the circular sets the tone for proposed action;

> All eligible groups shall have the same opportunites. Because minority groups are overrepresented amongst those in urgent housing need, special initiatives to assist minority groups are likely to be necessary.

The policies of the Housing Corporation were to be carried out, firstly by monitoring the activities of housing associations; secondly by promoting and developing with the housing association movement, good practice both in housing management and administration; and thirdly through registration and practice. The monitoring section carry out regular monitoring of associations, their main function being to establish whether the management committee have control over the affairs of an association and that the staff are carrying out their duties in a satisfactory manner. The monitors are responsible for pinpointing weaknesses and helping to resolve them.

The monitoring teams were issued with clear guidance on approaching the issue of Race and Housing (Housing Corporation 1985). The main theme running through this guidance was sensitivity in dealing with the issue. An educational approach was advised where time could be spent with staff and committees to make them aware of the nature and extent of racism. Caution was advised when opening up a debate within a housing association about shifting advantage and power from one group to another. It was clearly understood that should a less sensitive approach be taken, that the door would be closed on achieving a gradual change.

The Housing Corporation faced the task of assessing how much effort should be spent on persuasion before taking action, namely, recourse to the law or withdrawal of funding. The circular clarified the procedures to be adopted:

> We shall look for answers to the questions posed in the NFHA checklist, and the written committee reports showing action taken and planned. Where these answers appear to demonstrate practices which fall below the standards set by the NFHA, we will discuss corrective action and agree specific remedies to a specific timetable (Housing Corporation 1985).

Nowhere in the circular was there a mention of withdrawal of funding; however, this has since become the final sanction. The Chief Executive of the Housing Corporation, David Edmonds, saw the role of the Corporation as 'persuader' rather than 'dictator', and stated it was only in the last resort that action to withdraw funding would be taken. Doubts about the commitment or likelihood of this sanction being implemented have been expressed by the Federation of Black Housing Organisations (FBHO) (Clarke 1986). On reflection, it is unlikely that such punitive action would have been taken because an association under threat would probably have given a commitment to changing its policy and practice, albeit in a token fashion.

The results of monitoring 140 associations in 1987 showed that only two associations were found to be making 'unreasonably slow progress'. In one, the association agreed to make changes, while in the other case, the threat of cutting funding was made 'unless the association puts its house in order swiftly'. Twenty associations were found to be 'performing inadequately' and were given a chance to remedy the situation. According to the Housing Corporation, because the majority of remaining associations were small and operated in mainly white areas, they would not require to see equal opportunities as an issue (Edmonds 1986). Without further information, it is difficult to see whether the same conclusions would be drawn by the CRE, whose investigation into Collingwood

Housing Association in Manchester, referred to later, showed that the Association had not given the issue of race the priority that it should have been accorded. Section 35 of the Race Relations Act 1976 provides a general exception for discriminatory acts to be performed, enabling the special needs of particular racial groups to be catered for. It permits access to facilities or services to be restricted to one group. Within the housing association movement this section has been used to justify the establishment of black associations, run by black staff, and catering for the needs of black people.

The Housing Corporation's views on registering black associations was summarised in the 1985 circular:

> Registration policy does not discriminate on the grounds of race or nationality and many associations that cater for minority groups are already registered. However, since there is a larger number of associations that must be funded from current resources, the Corporation does not normally register new associations where needs which they aim to fulfil can be met by a voluntary group working within an existing organisation. It will therefore expect registered associations to cooperate with ethnic minority groups seeking to provide housing ..... when this type of cooperation does not meet identified needs, or associations are unable to or unwilling to work with ethnic minority groups, the Corporation will consider registering new groups.
> (Housing Corporation 1985)

The argument has therefore been established that black housing associations will be required where predominantly white associations do not cater for the needs of black households.

As at March 1990, there were 58 black housing organisations (both associations and co-operatives) registered with the Housing Corporation. Over half of these are based in the London and Home Counties area and many are developing 'special needs' schemes such as sheltered and extended family housing (Black Housing 6.3.1990). Housing Corporation action has achieved two things. Firstly, it has heightened the profile of race and housing as an issue within existing white associations. Secondly, black associations have been registered but only where it can be shown that white associations cannot meet an existing need. Although black associations have been registered, they are small and it is therefore of continued importance that white associations adopt a fair housing policy and the Housing Corporation monitor those associations effectively.

(c) Research into the English housing association movement

There have been few studies of race and housing association issues in England, even though work on local authorities is abundant. Perhaps the most important research is that carried out by Niner (1985), while there have been investigations by the CRE into Collingwood Housing Association (CRE 1983), and more recently into nominations to Liverpool associations (CRE 1989).

Niner (1985) does not suggest that her research into associations in England, and specifically Birmingham, gives a comprehensive picture of association activities but it does provide pointers to the important aspects of the issue related to unequal treatment. It is these points which require to be highlighted as they provide a backcloth against which to view the current policy and practice of Scottish associations. Thus, in the Birmingham study, Niner showed that the Bournville Village Trust (BVT) were shown to have received only 8 per cent of their applications from black households, while the level of applications directed to Family Housing Association (FHA) was also low. Both associations were pointed in the direction of setting objectives which would:

> increase the number of ethnic minority applicants; ensure that the number of ethnic minority applicants at least equals their representation in the local population; ensure that the ethnic minority population are fully aware of the existence of the association and what it can offer, and that they are encouraged to apply if the association can meet their needs; to examine the development programme to ensure it meets the needs of ethnic minorities.
> (Niner 1985)

It is clear each of these suggestions would be applicable to all housing associations to encourage demand from black households.

Part of the problem centred around the issue of closed waiting lists. Niner found that associations preferred to open and close lists because, firstly there was considerable administration involved in keeping the list open and, secondly, it reduced the disappointment caused to applicants who would require to wait a long time. Research carried out amongst housing associations in Birmingham showed that none operated an allocation system based on housing need such as a points system. This, coupled with the existence of closed waiting lists, creates a situation in which those in most need may not be considered. In such circumstances, the importance of nominations from local authorities for black access to housing associations cannot be over-emphasised. Local authorities may have formal or informal agreements with housing associations but can usually nominate up to 50 per cent of the tenants. In Birmingham, it was found that local authority nominations to housing associations were 'tiny'. (Niner 1985). Although speculative, it would seem that local authorities are either too disorganised or would prefer not to rock the boat in areas where nominations are weighted in favour of black applicants. The solution proposed to overcome this problem is that local authorities require to carry out ethnic record keeping and monitoring.

The issue of nominations was considered more recently, during the investigation by the Commission for Racial Equality into Liverpool City Council Housing Department. (CRE 1989) The CRE investigated nominations made by the Council to six housing associations in the city between 1984 and 1986 and found that black nominees had consistently received poorer property than white nominees, across all the measures of quality, including type of housing, type of letting, type of building, the age of the property and whether the property had central heating and a garden. The CRE therefore, concluded that the Council had directly discriminated against black applicants, in that those nominated to associations were treated less favourably than white applicants.

The conclusions which must be drawn are that, while local authorities must shoulder much of the blame for the discrimination which has occured, housing associations are not blameless. It is clear that few associations are addressing the question of equal opportunity as they should.

Race and housing associations: Scotland

(a) The Scottish Federation of Housing Associations

The NFHA Guidance (1982) had no apparent impact in Scotland. At the time of its publication the SFHA were either unaware of its existence or did not see the need to consider its validity for Scottish associations. The question of whether this guidance was valid in Scotland was raised by the Housing Corporation early in 1986, when they suggested that the SFHA consider working on a code of practice for Scotland. This suggestion was rejected because it was felt that race and housing should not be looked at in isolation but incorporated into a review of other aspects of discrimination in housing management practice which was initiated at the time. The response perhaps reflects the view, frequently expressed, that there is a perception in Scotland that there is 'no problem'. It may also be argued that it reflects a 'new right' notion that policy should relate to individuals rather than groups (Smith and Mercer 1987).

Rosenburg (1986) provided some pointers as to why associations may hold this view by highlighting the characteristics of properties which Asian people occupy in Glasgow. Firstly, such properties tend to be above the Tolerable Standard, although in poor repair; secondly the houses are larger than average and have standard amenities; thirdly the properties are generally outwith Housing Action Areas, although this is gradually changing. Glasgow Special Housing Group (GSHG), now Integrate, put a different perspective on this proposition and suggested (GSHG 1986) that:

> Tenements with a high proportion of ethnic minority residents are dealt with late in development programmes, that black people are unclear about the role of associations and in particular about special needs provision.

GSHG went on to state that in areas where there is a concentration of housing association activity:

> There is no evidence that even these associations have made any effort to ensure that new services are accessible and appropriate to ethnic minority groups.

Clearly, the SFHA lost the opportunity of tackling an issue which does affect its members. Perhaps as a result the Housing Corporation in Scotland (now Scottish Homes), through pressure exerted from colleagues in the South, felt it necessary to introduce the Scottish guidance note without any consultation with Scottish associations.

(b) The Housing Corporation in Scotland

A major strategy adopted by the Housing Corporation in Scotland, was 'area renewal', involving the renovation of Below Tolerable Standard housing by locally based housing associations. Approximately 23,000 houses have now been improved (Scottish Development Department 1989). Investment has been targetted at the inner city areas, a number of which have high concentrations of black people. It is for this reason that the consequences for black households of association policy and practice have major significance. The summary of the guidance to associations by the Corporation used the same words as the English version, and while this may be helpful as a basic source of information, there is still a need for a Scottish code of conduct to be published.

The wisdom of issuing a mirror version of English guidance must be questioned. Glasgow Special Housing Group suggested sometime before the guidance was issued that:

> A Scottish circular would have to take account of the fact that ethnic minorities are less vocal in pursuit of their rights and demands than in some parts of England. Positive action (rather than monitoring reaction to expressed demand) has to be taken by service providers here. (GSHG 1986)

The advice given was sound but was not taken on board. Although the SFHA did not react to the invitation to work on a code of practice, the Housing Corporation should have consulted a number of individuals who are interested, or active, in the race and housing field in Scotland.

As far as the registration of black associations is concerned, the criteria in Scotland reflect those adopted in England. Prompting came from GSHG not to use the registration of black associations as a fall-back position (that is only allowing a registration where an existing association does not cater for existing needs) (GSHG 1986). Guidance on Section 87 funding which allows for the financial backing for a supportive framework to be provided for black groups has not been circulated to Scottish associations. The precedent here had already been set in urban policy generally, for example when Section 11 funding was not publicised in Scotland. When an attempt was made to use Section 11 funding in Scotland it was refused on the basis of size of the black population. Alternative urban aid funding has been made available in Scotland, but there in no focus on housing. (Thwaites 1986).

It is this Section 87 funding which is most needed in Scotland to employ black workers to guide groups through the difficulties of registration and development. There is an acceptance that provision is likely to be needed by the elderly, single and women and their children who require refuge (Rosenburg 1986). Scotland does not have the equivalent of the Federation of Black Housing Organisations and black groups will require encouragement. There are as yet no black associations. Neither the Housing Corporation nor the SFHA have, until recently, firm proposals on this sort of training, although things may move on with the appointment of a black outreach worker and the introduction by SHARE, the housing association training organisation of a scheme similar to the PATH scheme in England. These are dealt with later in this paper.

(c) Research into Scottish housing associations

During 1988, a major study of the role of housing associations in satisfying the needs of ethnic minorities was carried out in Glasgow. Four associations were involved - Charing Cross, Govanhill, Southside and West of Scotland - and the study was funded partly by the CRE and partly by the Housing Corporation in Scotland. The results of the research are outlined by Mike Dalton elsewhere in this volume and are published in full by the CRE (Dalton and Daghlian 1989).

The only previous research appears to be that of Lear (1987) whose questionnaire survey of Scottish associations showed a sadly familiar pattern of under-representation of black people as tenants and on Management Committees, and a general lack of priority given by associations to equal opportunity policies.

Recent Developments

It seems clear from the limited research so far undertaken that there is a demand from black people for housing association property. What is not known is the extent to which this demand might increase if certain constraints were removed. The constraints which affect black household tenure choice are fairly clear and are seen to be similar to those operated through the policy and practice of English associations.

The main policies and practices constraining black tenure choice in Scottish associations may be summarised as follows:

i) The lack of representation of black people on the staff and committees of associations;

ii) The lack of contact with the black community or representative organisations;

iii) Constraints on development options, resulting in the shortage of housing large enough for extended Asian families;

iv) The use of waiting list exclusion policies against owner occupiers -many of whom may be black;

v) The system of an open/closed waiting list, whose opening times may not be advertised widely enough for minority groups to be aware of them;

vi) A points system which allows weighting for local connections, which may operate against black families who have moved into an area more recently than white families;

vii) The existence of allocation systems which allow a high degree of subjective decision making;

viii) The lack of any policies relating to the racial harassment of tenants;

ix) The lack of use made by District Councils of nomination of black people to associations and agencies in making referrals;

x) The non adoption of equal opportunity policies.

The issue of ethnic monitoring and record keeping deserves special mention as most associations clearly feel that, due to the small size of the black population resident in their area, there is no need to adopt such a practice. Associations should recognise the relevance of the system of monitoring 'race' amongst a set of variables, including gender, age and family size.

Although monitoring is of importance, it has already been noted that there should be more emphasis on positive action in Scotland. Positive action requires to be taken in establishing the needs of black groups and whether these could be met by black housing associations. There may well be potential for existing predominantly white associations to work in liaison with black groups. If this is not feasible then the registration of black associations will follow the established pattern in England.

There are, however, some recent developments which are significant in raising the awareness of black issues within the housing association movement and in possibly helping to improve access to housing association stock.

The first of these has been the establishment of an Ethnic Minorities Outreach Project in August 1990, derived from the Dalton and Daghlian (1989) research. The aims of the Project are twofold. Firstly, it aims to build close links between the ethnic minority communities in the Govanhill, Pollokshields, East Woodlands and Garnethill areas and the community-based housing associations operating in those areas. The project staff aim to work closely with the associations to encourage the participation of minority groups and the development of anti-discriminatory policies and practices. The second and wider aim is to encourage, across all associations in the West of Scotland, a greater understanding and sensitivity to the issues of race and housing.

Funding of £50,000, spread over two years, has been provided by Scottish Homes and the project is managed by SHARE (Strathclyde Housing Associations Resources for Education) the Strathclyde training and educational organisation. The Project Committee membership is made up of representatives of the three sponsoring housing associations (Charing Cross, Govanhill and Southside), SHARE, Scottish Homes and various minority organisations. Mono Chakrabarti of Jordanhill College of Education (whose paper on social work training appears elsewhere in this volume) has been appointed project consultant. The project leader has now been appointed and work has now started.

The second important initiative has been the development, also by SHARE, of the PATHWAY project. This is a training and education scheme, aimed at providing an opportunity to individuals to train for a job in housing. The scheme is targeted at individuals who, because of social, education or ethnic background, might find it difficult to enter housing as an occupation. The training programme lasts for a year and includes college-based education and workplace training and experience. Funding for the project is not, at the time of writing, fully secured, although it is hoped to enrol the first trainee in April 1991.

Unlike the PATH (Positive Action for Training in Housing) schemes in England, which are aimed exclusively at black people, the PATHWAY project is targeted also at the unemployed, the disabled and women wishing to return to work. It is anticipated, however, that at least half of the 12 trainees per annum will be from ethnic minority backgrounds.

Conclusion

There is no doubt that the race issue has been taken far less seriously by Scottish housing associations than by those in England and the advances that have been made have resulted from English pressure. The situation is beginning to change as independent research is carried out in Scotland and the appointment of outreach workers and development of the PATHWAY project are signs that the issue is now taken seriously. There remains a long way to go, however, if the disadvantages experienced by the black community are to be countered by the housing association movement.

References

Clarke V. 1986 *The work of the Federation of Black Housing Organisations* Paper presented at seminar 'Eliminating Racial Discrimination in Housing ': Housing Centre Trust:.

Commission for Racial Equality 1983 *Collingwood Housing Association Ltd: Report of a Formal Investigation* London: CRE.

Commission for Racial Equality 1989 *Racial discrimination in Liverpool City Council. Report of a formal investigation into the Housing Department* London: CRE.

Dalton M. and Daghlian S. 1989 *Race and Housing in Glasgow. The role of housing associations* London: CRE.

Glasgow Special Housing Group 1986 *Race and Housing Associations* correspondence to Housing Corporation Glasgow: GSHG.

Hammond R. 1977 'Ethnic records for local authority housing' *New Community* 6(1): 105-112.

Henderson J. and Karn V. 1984 'Race Class and the Allocation of Public Housing in Britain' *Urban Studies* 21(2): 115-128.

Housing Corporation 1985 *Circular 22/85: Race and Housing* London: Housing Corporation.

Lear A. 1987 *Black Access to Housing Association's Stock* Unpublished Diploma dissertation University of Glasgow.

National Federation of Housing Associations 1982 *Race and Housing: a guide for Housing Associations* London: NFHA.

National Federation of Housing Associations 1983 *Race and Housing -Still a Cause for Concern* London: NFHA.

National Federation of Housing Associations 1985 *Race and Housing: Ethnic Record Keeping and Monitoring* London: NFHA.

Niner P. 1985 *Housing Association Allocations: Achieving Racial Equality: A West Midlands Case Study* London: Runnymede Trust.

Phillips D. 1986 *What Price Equality?: A report on the allocations of GLC housing in Tower Hamlets* GLC Housing Research and Policy Report No.9 London: GLC.

Rosenburg L. 1986 *Asians and Housing - the Scottish context* Paper presented at SFHA seminar 'Race and Housing Associations' Glasgow.

Scottish Development Department 1989 *Statistical Bulletin* Edinburgh: SDD.

Smith S. and Mercer J. 1987 *New Perspectives on Race and Housing in Britain* Studies in Housing 2 Glasgow: Centre for Housing Research.

Thwaites F. 1986 *Local authority housing and ethnic minorities - a preliminary study of demand and supply in Edinburgh 1981 - 1985* Unpublished Diploma dissertation Edinburgh College of Art.

Chapter 3
Housing association access: achieving racial equality
Mike Dalton

Introduction

Persistent racial disadvantage and discrimination in housing markets has been shown to be commonplace. Allocative mechanisms, both formal and informal, cemented by racial stereotyping and set within institutional frameworks, increasingly appear to legitimise racial bias in publicly rented and owner-occupied tenures (Brown 1984, CRE 1984, Phillips 1986, Sarre et al. 1989). Recently, attention has been focused on the housing association sector, in which a situation little different from that existing in other tenures has been revealed (CRE 1983, Niner and Karn 1985, Dalton and Daghlian 1989), and during the past few years there has been some response to discrimination in access and allocations and the need for the implementation of fair housing policies in this sector (NFHA 1982, 1983). Yet reactions have been muted and the majority of associations remain complacent. Indeed in England, such has been the disaffection amongst ethnic minority communities with a white dominated movement that in several major cities black housing associations have been formed. In Scotland, a situation of benign neglect has prevailed until very recently, when research was undertaken within three Glasgow-based community associations, Charing Cross, Pollokshields (now Southside), and Govanhill, and a fourth regional association, West of Scotland, each with large ethnic minority communities living in their respective areas of housing activity (Dalton and Daghlian 1988).

This chapter begins with a review of the role of community-based housing associations in improving housing conditions in the inner city, together with the tenure and housing conditions of local ethnic minority families, and highlights the significant under-representation of minority families housed by inner city associations. Subsequently, this issue is explored by identifying the barriers faced by ethnic minority applicants which impede access to association tenancies. These include the levels of awareness amongst ethnic minority families of housing opportunities offered by the associations and the extent to which discrimination exists in their selection and allocation procedures. These concerns were raised within the framework of a much larger study in which 210 ethnic minority households, living in the inner city areas of Woodlands, Garnethill, Pollokshields and Govanhill, were interviewed in Autumn 1987. In addition, the participating associations agreed to a detailed examination of their housing and management practices to determine their impact on potential ethnic minority applicants. It was from this analysis that recommendations for positive action were made as to how these practices might be improved to facilitate access to housing association tenure and enable the associations to achieve equal opportunity through fair housing policies for all who lived in the local community (Dalton and Daghlian 1988).

Housing associations and inner city redevelopment

During the past 15 years, community-based housing associations have been a significant element in the regeneration of Glasgow's, indeed Britain's worst slum housing (Robertson 1990). This rehabilitation of nineteenth century tenement property plus, to a lesser extent, new build projects has become a cornerstone of the city's fight to overcome its inner city housing problem. In the first ten years, 1974-84, this drive to achieve acceptable modernised accommodation in inner city areas saw community-based associations improve over 10,460 properties in the city, plus 820 owner-occupied homes during the overall rehabilitation of closes, and complete a further 300 new build dwellings. These impressive statistics are the outcome of several interweaving strands of organisation, policy and action. The process was led by a top-down initiative involving Glasgow district and its massive Housing Action Area programme. In turn, central government finance was channelled largely through the Housing Corporation. This was set within a legislative framework, the Housing (Scotland) Act 1984, drafted with Glasgow's sub-standard tenemental stock as a key variable giving shape to this legislation (Armstrong 1985). In addition, a bottom-up approach was adopted, recognising the role of residents living in neighbourhoods who were to be directly affected by the rehabilitation programme. In this, the Glasgow/Scottish model of locally based housing associations was established, containing approximately 2,000 pre-improvement housing units. The locality dimension was further reinforced by local accountability, for membership, management and participation were rooted firmly in the local community. Hence, community-based housing associations became the key facilitators of the redevelopment strategy, financially accountable to the Housing Corporation and responsible for identifying and carrying out specific improvement programmes, with the active involvement and approval of local communities.

Thus, this tripartite relationship, of an innovative local authority Housing Action Area programme with a neighbourhood focus; of housing associations, responsive to and controlled by local residents, and functioning as the essential deliverer of rehabilitated tenements; together with the backing of substantial funds (Housing Corporation, 1987), has meant that high quality housing has been provided in previously deteriorating neighbourhoods. At the same time, these neighbourhoods have retained the strong ethos of community and avoided incipient gentrification of properties and closes. All this has led to a significant success story of inner city regeneration whose major beneficiaries have been families living in poor, inadequate housing and who are amongst the worst off. Yet this success has not been all-embracing, for it has largely by-passed a minority of Glasgow's inner city population concentrated in significant numbers within these problem areas, the ethnic minority communities.

Ethnic minority housing in the inner city

In residential terms, the ethnic minority communities mainly occupy those parts of the city built before 1914 to the west and south of the city in areas such as East Pollokshields, Govanhill, Woodlands and Garnethill (Dalton and Daghlian 1989) where, at the scale of street and tenement close, levels of concentration can be very high (McEvoy 1978). Although increasing numbers of ethnic minority households have begun to appear in the middle class suburbs of the city, a reflection perhaps of middle class aspirations in housing location (Scottish Office 1983), the traditional residential areas have displayed remarkable residential stability in housing South and East Asian families over the past few decades, with 12 years being the average length of stay in the local area (Kearsley and Srivastava 1974, Dalton and Daghlian 1988: 14). This residential pattern is a reflection of several factors stemming largely from the ethnic minority communities' position in the housing market, where restricted access to public sector property combined with minimal funds forced the communities to look at other tenures. In the past, many inner city tenement properties were either relatively cheap to buy or formed a substantial part of the city's dwindling private rented sector and, importantly for employment prospects, offered proximity and access to central area locations.

Today, ethnic minority tenure in the inner city's housing markets is dominated by owner occupation.

Table 1: Tenure Status of Households (per cent)

Tenure	Ethnic Minority Households in Survey Area	Ethnic Minority Households Citywide	All Households in Glasgow
Owner-occupied	83.2	70.8	24.9
Publicly rented	-	8.9	62.9
Housing assoc.	10.4*	1.1	3.7
Privately rented	6.4	17.3	7.5
Other	-	1.9	1.0
total number	(210)	(3423)	(273,582)

* a combined figure for public sector and housing associations

Source: Census 1981, City of Glasgow Special Tables, Census Scotland 1981,
Strathclyde Region, vol. 1, Table 26, Survey 1987

The majority of households live in tenement properties that have already stood for between 70-100 years and today are faced with the costly burdens of fabric maintenance. For many of these flats have been bought at the bottom end of the housing market within the price range of £5-10,000, and less than five per cent of purchases have exceeded £30,000 (Dalton and Daghlian 1988:35). The lack of tenure in the public rented sector is not unexpected, partly because of restricted access, but also, with the exception of Govanhill, public sector property is not found on any significant scale in the study areas. More surprising perhaps is that privately rented accommodation accounts for such a small proportion of current tenure status. Furthermore, Table 2 contrasts present tenure status with previous status and reveals important issues which deserve comment.

Table 2: Tenure Status, Present and Previous Home (per cent)

Tenure	Present Home	Previous Home
Owner occupier	83.2	42.4
Publicly rented	10.4	3.8
Privately rented	5.3	12.9
Living with family	-	22.2
Rented from relative	1.1	11.9
Other	-	6.8
total number	(209)	(209)

Source: Survey 1987

The direct move by newly formed households, as well as those privately renting, into owner-occupation means that both groups are foregoing access to social sector housing which dominates the overall tenure pattern of the city. This trend is the more remarkable in that one in three heads of households interviewed and eligible for work were unemployed (Dalton and Daghlian 1988:26). Such a pattern raises important questions concerning the community's perceptions of this sector and the allocation policies and institutional practices of the city's housing department and housing associations. For neither the District Council nor community-based housing associations have succeeded to any degree in acquiring ethnic minority families as tenants. Indeed, the latter's records were to show that only two per cent were from the minority communities, the majority of whom had sold their homes to associations during rehabilitation schemes and elected to become tenants (Dalton and Daghlian 1988:68).

An examination of housing circumstances highlighted the fact that owner occupation does not necessarily equate with good housing and reveals conditions which were far from problem-free.

Table 3: Housing Circumstances (per cent)

Fitted with bath/shower	98.6
Possessing inside WC	100.0
Separate kitchen	99.5
Sharing basic amenities	1.0
No central heating	84.5
Lack of garden/backcourt access	26.7
More than one person/room	57.6
Kitchen used as sittingroom/bedroom	20.9
Livingroom used as a bedroom	15.7
Kitchen as the only sitting room	4.8
(total number = 210)	*Source: Survey 1987*

Although the quality of housing conditions as measured by the range of basic amenities (Table 3) indicates that the community is well provided for, with the exception of central heating facilities and garden or backcourt access, further indicators give rise to major concerns for the living circumstances of many minority families. Room occupancy levels and the use of rooms for purposes other than their normal function show a lack of space for many families which lead to problems of over-occupation. Several instances of very severe over-occupation were revealed, with the most extreme being 14 families with more than seven members crowded into two or three rooms. When asked to indicate levels of satisfaction with their present home (Table 4) the responses produced an illuminating commentary on the quality of property bought by many minority households.

Table 4: Levels of satisfaction and dissatisfaction with present home (per cent)

Likes	Household mentions	Dislikes	Household mentions
Large size of rooms	43.8	Heating inadequate	17.1
Neighbours	37.6	House too small	16.2
Heating	30.5	Dampness of house	13.8
Number of rooms	28.6	Rooms too small	12.4
House position in close	26.6	Lack of garden	9.5
Quiet	26.2	Neighbours	8.6

Source: Survey 1987

The favourable responses identify a mixture of neighbourhood and housing characteristics, not least the generously proportioned rooms offered by some pre-1914 tenements. In contrast, those expressing dissatisfaction with their present home not only highlighted the demand for more living space, but also identified several housing faults common within the city. More than one in three households indicated the need for major repairs or improvement to their property, ranging from rotting window frames to structural matters or improvements within the communal parts of the building (Dalton and Daghlian 1988:29-30).

Whilst it is clear that housing associations have had a major role in recent years in rehabilitating older tenemental housing in inner city areas which had escaped earlier slum clearance programmes, and in many of these areas sizeable ethnic minority communities have settled during the post-war years, it is equally clear that many continue to live in poor housing conditions. Yet a major disconnection has occurred in that, by 1987 out of 2,209 tenancies in the four inner city associations, only 45 ethnic minority families were their tenants.

Of the issues which emerge for consideration, perhaps the starkest is the under-representation of ethnic minority families in housing association accommodation. This provokes questions, not simply of the minority communities' awareness and attitudes to social sector housing, but also of the access policies, practices and institutional workings of such organisations. For inadequately housed families, together with newly formed households of Scots-born Asians with a strong attachment to the inner city, may well turn to this sector for housing in increasing numbers as owner occupation moves beyond their financial reach (Dalton and Daghlian 1988:49). This presents a major challenge to associations to ensure that access and allocation procedures do not act as barriers which prevent such households from gaining housing association tenancies.

Ethnic minority households in association tenancies

The policy aims of associations may determine access to waiting lists and eventual tenancy and the three community-based associations have produced written policies which detail their aims and objectives throughout the eighties, and which were generally available and in some cases were being translated into the most commonly used minority languages. The fourth, the West of Scotland Housing Association, had published a general statement of its lettings policy in one of its newsletters. Charing Cross Housing Association stated that its aims is 'to rehouse those applicants in most housing need' whilst keeping 'a sense of local community'. Such aims were echoed by Govanhill Housing Association which added a third factor to shape its allocation policy - that of the size of housing stock available. Pollokshields Housing Association aimed simply 'to meet all forms of housing need', whilst for the West of Scotland its aim was 'to house homeless and underprivileged people'. In principle, therefore, each of the associations had an allocations policy based on need. Finally, the three community-based associations, whilst having introduced equal opportunity policies, had barely begun the record-keeping and monitoring process. The West of Scotland had neither a specific equal opportunities policy nor monitoring procedures, arguing that all applicants were deemed to be treated equally: thus the association had a 'colour blind' approach.

By 1987, the four housing associations housed only 45 ethnic minority families. (Table 5)

Table 5: Tenants and Allocations, 1987

Association	Total tenancies	Ethnic minority tenants	Allocations (1987)	Ethnic minority allocations
Charing Cross	200	12	18	4
Govanhill	1073	22	71	1
Pollokshields	166	4	4	-
West of Scotland	770	7	210	1
Totals	2209	45	303	6

Source: Housing Association records 1987

All of those tenants were in mainstream general needs housing. There are two main routes to housing association tenure, the improvement programme and the waiting list which may include District Council nominees to tenancy. Only stock which is surplus to the needs of those affected by the development programme is offered to direct applicants from the waiting list. Historically, therefore, a majority of a housing association's tenancies are the result of acquisitions of previously factored or owner-occupied properties, rather than of allocations from the waiting list. Ethnic minority tenants appeared to reflect this pattern. Taking the first pathway, nearly all ethnic minority tenants of Govanhill Housing Association had either sold their property to the Association or had been sitting tenants in property acquired for private landlords. The remainder had been housed via the waiting list either as direct applicants or District Council nominees. This trend was confirmed by a survey of ethnic minority households in the other associations.

Turning to the second pathway of the waiting list, the number of ethnic minority families housed by this route so far is very small. In large part this is due to the lack of numbers on the associations' General Needs Waiting Lists. (Table 6)

Table 6: Ethnic Minority Households on Waiting Lists

Association	Total on waiting list	No. of ethnic minority households on list	Per cent of total
Charing Cross	193	23	12
Govanhill	59	-	-
Pollockshields	226*	21	9
West of Scotland	300**	2	0.6
TOTAL	778	46	5.9

* Does not include applicants on sheltered house waiting list, all of whom are white
** Includes 'ground floor only' applicants (Dalton and Daghlian 1988:87)

Source: Housing Association records 1987

This statistical evidence shows that few ethnic minority households over the years have become either tenants of, or waiting list applicants to, the housing associations. Such under-representation may reflect a limited awareness of housing opportunities provided by the associations, it may be the result of barriers to access which black applicants find great difficulty in overcoming, and it may result from the operation of discriminatory policies and procedures within the housing associations.

Barriers to access: the awareness of housing opportunities

Despite the efforts made by the three community-based associations during the course of 1986 and 1987 to raise their profiles within their local communities, the survey carried out during the autumn of 1987 revealed a low level of awareness amongst the communities of both the existence and purpose of housing associations. Just over half of the ethnic minority sample, 57 per cent, had heard of the associations and further questioning revealed much confusion between other forms of association, such as residents' and tenants' associations, as well as Glasgow District Council housing department. Indeed, only a quarter of households interviewed knew the name of the association operating locally and the location of its office. Such knowledge had either resulted from direct contact with the association through living in a Housing Action Area or through passing the association's offices during the course of their daily lives. Very few had been made aware of the existence of the association through publicity materials. Indeed, similar low levels of awareness have been found amongst an almost exclusively white resident population in the east end of the city (Reidvale Housing Association 1987-88). If the awareness of housing associations and their activities is restricted amongst largely white communities, it is even more restricted amongst the minority communities and is compounded further by language barriers. The failure to publicise activities widely in the past was recognised by the housing associations and somewhat faltering efforts were being made to redress the situation. The process was certainly not being helped, even where material had been translated, by employing white staff. Complacency was at its most extreme when the argument was put forward by the West of Scotland, who hitherto had not considered the issue of advertising, that 'everybody knows about us'. Publicity was therefore considered unnecessary and the Association's newsletter, circulated to tenants and friends of the Association, remains the major publicity vehicle. During the course of 1987 over half the tenancies awarded by the West of Scotland were either referrals by statutory and voluntary agencies or nominations by the District Council, but over a third of new tenants were drawn from friends, neighbours or relatives of existing or former tenants. As Table 5 shows, almost all the Association's tenants are white and their 'word of mouth' advertising clearly places ethnic minority families at a great disadvantage and indeed may be unlawful and constitute indirect discrimination.

Such levels of awareness reflect the extent to which information on housing opportunities is communicated to the local community. It has been limited and poorly targeted and appears to be the first structural constraint to obtaining a tenancy.

Barriers to access: the application process

Having become aware of the existence of a significant provider of housing in inner city areas, the potential ethnic minority applicant faces the task of gaining access to the waiting lists. For the prospective housing association tenant, the first contact with a housing association is an important stage in the filtering of applications. This covers two key areas in particular, the initial contact either at the reception desk or over the telephone, subsequently followed by the completion of application forms. No data were available for analysis of the first stage, although at the time of the survey no employee of any association was from the ethnic minority communities; indeed, the majority of minority community tenants interviewed were in favour of employing ethnic minority staff, indicating that this would generate confidence, make it easier to explain problems, reflect the cultural diversity of the area and undoubtedly facilitate initial contact.

As to application forms, their length and complexity varied, each attempting to document personal and housing circumstances within the context of individual associations' allocation policies. Applicants undoubtedly have difficulty with form filling and genuine misunderstandings arose, particularly for those whose first language was not English. One example will serve to illustrate this point of ambiguity. One applicant, responding to the question of whether he was related to a committee member, understood 'related' to mean 'knowing' rather than having blood or marriage ties. He gave a wrong positive answer which could have barred him unjustly from a tenancy under the terms of the Housing Associations Act 1985, as amended by the Housing (Scotland) Act 1986. Clearly, in order to facilitate the filling-in of application forms, they should be simple to read and use, accompanied by translated documents explaining association policies and with a clear and prominent invitation to seek help and advice in completing the forms if difficulties arise.

Whether associations operate open or closed waiting lists, and all three community-based associations had or were about to implement the former, access to the waiting list is determined by eligibility evidence. Not only may eligibility criteria be a major block on access to association tenure, but certain exclusions may substantially disadvantage ethnic minority households to the point of indirect discrimination. Three criteria in particular are cause for concern. First, the ineligibility of particular tenure groups may disproportionately disadvantage ethnic minority groups. As owner-occupiers, and eight out of ten households were in owner-occupied housing, a number were experiencing poor housing conditions associated in particular with the need for repair and modernisation and often facing severe over-occupation. For associations to exclude owner-occupiers on the assumption that this tenure category reflects both relative wealth and good quality housing is not borne out by many Asian homeowners who occupy substandard properties. Their ineligibility to take up association tenancies not only disproportionately disadvantages them but may also constitute indirect discrimination under the terms of the 1976 Race Relations Act. District Council tenants are a second tenure group suffering from restrictive eligibility criteria. Here, the issue is not housing fabric or standards of accommodation but the social conditions that ethnic minority tenants suffer, particularly racist harassment (Bowes, McCluskey and Sim 1989). Housing associations can provide important opportunities for rehousing and relocating ethnic minority families suffering harassment on peripheral council schemes.

The second issue concerns house size and restricting access to the waiting list to those seeking two- and three-apartment properties, the most common housing stock held by the associations. It appears that housing stock considerations greatly influence such management strategies and this is turn is further compounded, from the associations' point of view, by a cost limits system of capital funding from the former Housing Corporation, which has deterred associations from retaining or creating large family housing units (Dalton and Daghlian 1988:114-1616). It is clearly of great importance that development programmes should take account of all unmet housing needs in the local community and for associations to challenge cost limits and argue for the retention of large units within rehabilitation and new build schemes. Simply to ignore such needs, or to adopt the fact of the historical shortfall of large housing units as a justification for not housing ethnic minority families, severely disadvantages these families in the local community. Simply to argue the stereotypical view that all ethnic minority families are large and very little accommodation of that size is available is unacceptable. Although, according to the survey results, the average size of ethnic minority households of 4.6

persons is above that of all Glasgow's households of 2.8 persons, the fact remains that ethnic minority families seek accommodation of all sizes. Almost half the households interviewed had four or less members and almost one-third (28 per cent) were households with three members or less, the very household sizes that associations can accommodate with ease.

The final issue, albeit a very minor one within the context of the survey area, is the ineligibility imposed by an under-21 years of age rule. This has been shown elsewhere to particularly disadvantage Afro-Caribbean minority households who traditionally form separate households at an earlier age (Brown 1984). Although Afro-Caribbeans form only a very small proportion of the city's ethnic minority population, the disadvantageous impact should be taken into account, during the process of policy formulation.

Barriers to access: the allocation systems

The next task is to prioritise applicants and here in the inner city associations two systems are in operation, points systems and discretionary systems. Points systems are designed to provide objective measurements of housing need, each appropriately weighted to cover a range of circumstances from housing conditions to security of tenure and racist harassment. From an analysis of the different points allocation systems arise two areas of concern. The first and most important is the role of local connection and/or residence points in the allocation process. Whilst recognising the importance of such criteria to associations, who argue for the need to maintain or keep a sense of local community, and notwithstanding the view of the Housing Corporation who regard such criteria as bad management practice, the counter argument is that such a factor may outweigh other needs criteria. To illustrate, in one association the maximum number of points available for local connection was greater than the maximum number of points available for a medical condition where the need to be rehoused is severe (Dalton and Daghlian 1988:81). The use of such points may lead to the less needy being rehoused. Such criteria may also discriminate against ethnic minorities, in particular recent arrivals, including refugees, from Africa, the Middle East, and SE Asia; whilst small in total numbers, they are proving exceptionally vulnerable to exploitation in the privately rented sector (McFarland and Walsh 1988). If local connection points are to be maintained, then perhaps a wider interpretation, beyond that of residence, is more appropriate to include working and social needs. For example, ethnic minority workers in the catering industry, working into the early hours and lacking transport, may be forced to sleep on their employer's floor unless housed near their place of employment (Home Affairs Committee, 1985). Similarly, the positive features of living in areas with other people from the same community, of easy access to specialist facilities, family and friends, all enhance the quality of life for ethnic minority families. Such factors are particularly important for those who would be otherwise isolated by a lack of English. The second concern is that of points awarded for time on the waiting list. Any award for waiting time may encourage queuing, may reward those in the know, and runs contrary to the idea of urgent housing need. Indeed, ethnic minority applicants may be further disadvantaged in that their information networks are very limited in relation to housing associations, so they are unlikely to be able to benefit from these aspects of the system.

Despite these qualifications, points systems are regarded as the most objective method of assessing need and prioritising applicants. More particularly, the system lends itself to monitoring and as such is an essential aid to good management practice. In contrast, the discretionary system of allocation allows for assessment to be made according to more generalised criteria by moving away from rigid rules to allow for flexibility and judgment. Such systems allow associations to respond speedily to all possible forms of housing need. It is in the area of matching tenant and property that the starkest contrasts between the two systems occur. Under a points-based system, vacancies are offered to applicants with the highest number of points on the list for a particular size of property. In contrast, the discretionary system, lacking objective criteria against which housing need can be measured, introduces subjective judgments in which personal prejudice and stereotyping of applicants intrude. Often these value-laden social judgments are acquired during the home visit and subsequently influence the quality of lettings involved (Dalton and Daghlian 1988:86). Other research has shown that Housing Visitors are more likely to make negative comments on ethnic minority families (CRE 1984), and that assessment could be unconsciously biased because of their ignorance of the cultural traditions of ethnic minority families (Brown 1984). Although no such evidence was found in the Glasgow study because of the lack of ethnic minority applicants, it was stated by one association - West of Scotland - that all ethnic minority families want to live in Pollokshields where the association has some 100 properties. What was not clear was whether this assessment of choice was based on fact or assumption as to where minority applicants will 'fit in' and 'want to live'. Indeed, it could be that many ethnic minority applicants were unaware that the association had properties elsewhere.

Discretionary allocations are seen as an inappropriate system particularly for areas of ethnic minority settlement. Essentially, any monitoring of the system is made very difficult. For, without ethnic monitoring, the identification of discrimination is rendered almost impossible and accountability and achievement are hard to demonstrate.

Barriers to access: local authority nominations

Two further pathways to tenancy are strewn with barriers. The first of these is local authority nomination - Glasgow District - to housing association tenancy. The District Council has an important role in widening the housing opportunities of ethnic minorities, and has 50 per cent nomination rights to the associations' surplus and newly renovated properties, rights which in practice appear to be rarely taken up. At the time of the study the District Council did not keep ethnic origin records on nominations, making it impossible to assess the Council's record in nominating ethnic minority families to housing association tenancy, nor was any attempt made to probe at local area office level as to how nominees were selected. Nevertheless, a number of concerns arose in discussion with housing associations regarding the process of nomination which might disadvantage ethnic minority households. The first concern was that nominations to associations might be based on criteria which did not reflect housing need, indeed that some nominees, picked from the top of the waiting list, have reached that position by virtue of accumulated residence and waiting time points. The second concern was the practice by associations when waiting lists have been closed to refer applicants to the District Council's local area office to request nomination. This method favours those who already know about housing associations, and is therefore likely to disadvantage ethnic minority households. The final concern was revealed by a name check of nominations to two of the participating associations, which showed that for one association 37 per cent of nominations were Asian households, contrasting sharply with the two per cent received by another (Dalton and Daghlian 1988:92). As we were unable to pursue this within the context of the research brief, our reasons for such disparities can only be very speculative. For example, could it be that in local area offices there are perceptions held as to who housing associations wanted or wanted not to accept as nominees; or does this disparity reflect the choice of area by applicants; or does it reflect a system in which most nominees have themselves requested nomination? Overall, the system is weighted in favour of white residents who already knew of the existence of the association.

Thus far, the local authority has a poor record of nominating ethnic minority families to inner city housing associations, of missed opportunities for rehousing by housing associations. Clearly, housing associations have to work more closely with the local authority to ensure that quotas for nominations are filled, making clear at the same time their commitment to equal opportunity by monitoring nominations to ensure ethnic minority households are not excluded. In turn, local authorities must inform all applicants in English and minority languages of housing opportunities offered by housing associations and explain the nomination system.

Barriers to access: referral agencies

The second pathway to tenancy is through the referral by statutory and voluntary agencies of needy applicants. The participating associations had established links with a number of agencies and management agreements have been formulated which award tenancies to particular agencies whose client group may require specialised support. Disappointingly, only one association has an arrangement with a group providing specifically for an ethnic minority clientele. If ethnic minority families are to benefit from referral, and research elsewhere has shown a limited awareness generally by ethnic minority families of social service provision in the city (McFarland and Walsh 1987), and their under-representation as clients in the voluntary sector (McLeod 1988), then information and publicity about housing association opportunities need to be widely disseminated to such groups. For, as a first point of contact with those in need of housing, referral agencies perform an important role but, given the barriers posed by lack of awareness on the part of the ethnic minority communities of the role and function of such agencies, housing associations should consult more widely with ethnic minority organisations and specifically ask for referrals, particularly when seeking to fill specialised forms of housing.

Conclusion

The situation in Scotland's largest city can differ but little from that found in other major Scottish towns and cities. The Glasgow study, set within the context of housing associations involved in rehabilitating tenement properties and to a lesser degree new build projects, establishes the extent to which fair housing policies are being pursued in areas of significant Asian residential concentration and including many families in housing need. The goal of equal opportunity in this sector of housing tenure is a recent issue, not just here in Scotland, but throughout the UK. Inevitably, policies and practices have been identified which disadvantage and discriminate against ethnic minority families within the terms of the Race Relations Act 1976. Such discriminatory practices include management strategies involving word of mouth advertising and poor publicity programmes which do little to inform local ethnic minority residents; and the operation of eligibility criteria which are restrictive, inappropriate and unjustifiably exclude ethnic minority families. Such structural constraints on access are followed by allocation systems with procedures often based on subjective social judgments making accountability difficult to demonstrate and identification of disadvantage and discrimination problematic. Even associations with objective allocations criteria are not free of such charges, highlighting a need to guard against establishing and weighting criteria to the disadvantage of ethnic minority families. A key strategy is to introduce ethnic record-keeping and monitoring, for associations cannot ensure equal access and equal provision or measure their achievements without a system of ethnic monitoring. This facilitates the identification of disadvantage and discrimination, both in access to waiting lists and in allocations, by allowing for comparison between the housing outcomes of black and white households. It also facilitates the identification of housing needs (NFHA 1989).

Housing associations have been peripheral to the housing needs and concerns of ethnic minority families. This lack of past commitment has effectively marginalised their access to this form of housing tenure. Though some associations have begun to address the issue of how to achieve equal opportunity in housing access, the important issue for associations operating in areas of significant ethnic minority settlement is whose needs will they predominantly reflect and provide for in the future. The failure to address this issue will undoubtedly result in black housing associations becoming a reality in Scotland's major cities in the near future.

References

Armstrong D (ed.) 1985 *Miles Better, Miles to Go: The Story of Glasgow's Housing Association* Glasgow: Glasgow and West of Scotland Forum of Housing Associations

Bowes A McCluskey J Sim D 1989 *Ethnic Minority Housing Problems in Glasgow. A Report to Glasgow District Council* Glasgow: District Council Housing Department

Brown C 1984 *Black and White Britain; The Third PSI Survey* London: Heinemann

Commission for Racial Equality 1983 *Collingwood Housing Association Ltd. Report of a Formal Investigation* London: Commission for Racial Equality

Commission for Racial Equality 1984 *Race and Council Housing in Hackney* London: Commission for Racial Equality

Dalton M Daghlian S 1988 *Housing Needs, Experiences and Expectations of Glasgow's Ethnic Minority Population. The Role of Housing Associations. A Report to the Housing Corporation in Scotland* Glasgow: Scottish Ethnic Minority Research Unit, Glasgow College

Dalton M Daghlian S 1989 *Race and Housing in Glasgow* London: Commission for Racial Equality

House of Commons Home Affairs Committee Session 1984-85 London: HMSO

Scottish Office 1983 *Ethnic Minorities in Scotland* Edinburgh: Scottish Office, Housing and Urban Research Unit

Housing Corporation in Scotland 1987 *Investment Programme 1987/88 Note 2* Edinburgh: Housing Corporation

Kearsley G Srivastava S 1974 'The spatial evolution of Glasgow's Asian community' *Scottish Geographical Magazine* 90 (2):110-124

McEvoy D 1979 'The segregation of Asian immigrants in Glasgow. A note.' *Scottish Geographical Magazine* 94 (3): 111-113

McFarland E Dalton M Walsh D 1987 *Personal welfare services and ethnic minorities. A study of East Pollokshields* Scottish Ethnic Minorities Research Unit Paper No. 4, Glasgow: Glasgow College

McFarland E Walsh D 1988 *Refugees in Strathclyde* Scottish Ethnic Minorities Research Unit Research Paper No. 6, Glasgow: Glasgow College

MacLeod L 1988 *Irrespective of Race, Colour or Creed? Minority Ethnic Groups and the Voluntary Sector in Scotland* Edinburgh: Scottish Council for Voluntary Organisations

National Federation of Housing Associations 1982 *Race and Housing: A Guide for Housing Associations* London: NFHA

National Federation of Housing Associations 1983 *Race and Housing ... Still a Cause for Concern* London: NFHA

National Federation of Housing Associations 1989 *Race and Housing: Employment and Training Guide* London: NFHA

Niner P Karn V 1985 *Housing Association Allocations: Achieving Racial Equality* London: Runnymede Trust

Phillips D 1986 *What Price Equality? A Report on the Allocation of GLC Housing in Tower Hamlets* GLC Housing Research and Policy Report No. 9 London: GLC

Reidvale Housing Association 1988 *Housing Survey 1987-88* Glasgow, Mimeograph

Robertson D 1990 'The regeneration of Glasgow: the contribution of community-based housing associations towards Glasgow's tenement improvement programme 1964-1986' *Scottish Geographical Magazine* 105 (2): 67-75

Sarre P Phillips D Skellington R 1989 *Ethnic Minority Housing. Explanations and Policies* Aldershot: Gower

Chapter 4
Housing allocations and the law:
ethnic minorities in Edinburgh
Martin MacEwen

Introduction

Morality cannot be legislated but behaviour can be regulated. Judicial decrees may not change the heart but they can restrain the heartless (King 1963).

Whether the law embodies the highest common morality or the lowest common tolerance, it seeks to transmogrify social expectations into a code of practical behaviour. Whatever else we seek from law, we demand two dominant responses, that it generally be observed and that recidivists are effectively discouraged. We expect no less from the Race Relations Act 1976 in its attempt to police unlawful discrimination in housing. Or do we? This chapter, by reference to housing allocation, questions:

i) whether the legislation relating to unlawful discrimination in housing allocation is understood;

ii) whether, if understood, there is any commitment to secure its observance; and

iii) whether, by reference to the experience of one housing authority, we can draw any conclusions on the relevance and impact of the legislation.

Racial discrimination in housing

The first civil rights legislation in Britain was the Race Relations Act, 1965. This Act, however, was restricted to prohibiting discrimination in places of public resort such as restaurants, pubs, and theatres. It was, therefore, limited in scope and did not attempt to outlaw discrimination on the grounds of race in employment, education, or in housing. The Street Committee produced a report in October 1967 entitled Anti-discrimination Legislation: its terms of reference were to examine anti-discrimination legislation in other countries, to assess its effectiveness and to consider what types of legislation Parliament might consider most suitable, should it decide that the Race Relations Act, 1965, required amendment or extension (Street 1967). In effect, the Street Report focused on legislation in the USA and parts of Canada and made reference to the experiences there regarding discrimination in accommodation. This included both commercial accommodation and municipal housing (Chapter 13 pp.78-89). The recommendations of the Street

Report in respect of housing were summarised as follows:

The law should cover shops and factories. It should cover municipal and other public housing. Certain additional legislative and administrative controls of the allocation of housing and the treatment of persons displaced by local authority schemes of slum clearance and town planning are desirable. We do not believe that the freedom of local authorities to select clearance areas or to implement provisions about overcrowding can be interfered with by law. The law should extend to privately rented accommodation including houses let in multiple occupation. At least one exception could be admitted: where bathrooms, toilets or living facilities have to be shared by resident landlord and tenant. Sales of houses by builders and private developers should logically be covered by the law, but we cannot make a unanimous recommendation that sales by individual owner-occupiers should be regulated. Estate Agents and Banks, Building Societies and other lending agencies should be regulated, and certain miscellaneous discriminatory practices such as refusal to negotiate or to permit inspection should be made unlawful. Block-busting should be unlawful and violators made accountable to their victims. Covenants in conveyancing or leases imposing discriminatory restrictions, would be declared void and it would be unlawful to rely on such a void covenant. (Street 1967).

The recommendations of the report were substantially implemented in the Race Relations Act 1968, the first civil rights legislation to prohibit unlawful discrimination in relation to public and private housing. The 1968 Act made it unlawful to discriminate on racial grounds in the provision of goods, services or facilities to the public or a section of the public. In addition to this general prohibition provided by Section 2, Section 5 of the 1968 Act made it unlawful for any person having power to dispose or being otherwise concerned with the disposal of housing accommodation, business premises, or other land to discriminate:

i) against any person seeking to acquire any such accommodation, premises or other land by refusing or deliberately omitting to dispose of it to him or to dispose of it to him on the like terms and the like circumstances as in the case of the other persons;

ii) against any person occupying any such accommodation, premises or other land by deliberately treating him differently from other occupiers in the like circumstances; or

iii) against any person in need of any such accommodation, premises or other and by deliberately treating that other person differently from others in respect of any list of persons in need of it.

Unlawful discrimination focused on acts or omissions based on racial grounds, i.e. the colour, race or national or ethnic origin of the victim. In housing the only substantial exemptions from the Act's provisions related to 'small premises', i.e. premises where accommodation was shared with the landlord, and individual house sales where the seller did not use an agent such as an estate agent or solicitor in the actual sale and where the premises were not advertised.

Shortcomings in the 1968 Race Relations Act and housing policy generally were highlighted by the report on housing of the Select Committee on Race Relations and Immigration presented to Parliament in July 1971 (Select Committee 1971). The Government's belated response to this report was published in September 1975 (Home Office 1975a). Although this White Paper gave detailed responses to the 46 recommendations (see Annex pages 11 to 23) its approach was best summarised by its own conclusion (para. 29) which stated

> the Government looks to local authorities and other organisations concerned to continue, in the light of this White Paper, to give their considered attention to the housing of coloured people as part of a sustained campaign to improve social conditions and community relations.

Thus the whole tenor of the recommendations, while endorsing many of the concerns and sentiments expressed by the Select Committee, was to off-load responsibility to the Housing authorities, principally the local authorities responsible for public housing, rather than to provide a coherent central Government framework to co-ordinate, direct, guide and monitor local authority activities. For example, Government equivocated on dispersal policies and, while endorsing the sentiments behind record keeping and monitoring, left the format and initiative to local housing authorities. It refused to adopt any central measures providing guidance as to how local authorities were to implement the various recommendations contained in the Select Committee's Report, including that relating to monitoring. Essentially, then, Central Government avoided its own responsibility by transferring it to the local discretion of housing authorities: the good were encouraged, the indifferent were tolerated and the bad were left to their own devices.

At the same time that Government had responded to the Select Committee's Report on Housing it issued its White Paper 'Racial Discrimination' (Home Office, 1975b). Government recognised (para. 23, p.5) that legislation was the essential prerequisite for an effective policy to combat the problems of racial discrimination and resultant housing disadvantage experienced by the various ethnic minority groups and to promote equality of opportunity and treatment.

> It is a necessary precondition for dealing with explicit discriminatory actions or cumulated disadvantages. Where unfair discrimination is involved, the necessity of a legal remedy is now generally accepted. To fail to provide a remedy against an injustice strikes at the rule of law. To abandon a whole group of people in society without legal redress against unfair discrimination is to leave them with no option but to find their own redress. It is no longer necessary to recite the immense damage, material as well as moral, which ensues when a minority loses faith in the capacity of social institutions to be impartial and fair.

The White Paper continued (para. 25, p.6).

Legislation, however, is not, and can never be, a sufficient condition for effective progress towards equality of opportunity. A wide range of administrative and voluntary measures are needed to give practical effect to the objectives of the law. But the legislative framework must be right. It must be comprehensive in its scope and its enforcement provisions must not only be capable of providing redress for the victim of individual injustice but also of detecting and eliminating unfair discriminatory practices. The Government's first priority in the field of race relations must be to provide such a legislative framework. What is more, it is uniquely a responsibility which only the Government can discharge. At the same time Government fully recognises that this is only part of the subject; but the policies and attitudes of Central and Local Government are of critical importance in themselves and in their potential influence on the country as a whole.

On the effectiveness of the 1968 Act the White Paper observed (para. 31, p.8).

It is not possible to provide a quantifiable measure of the practical impact of the 1968 Act. Generally, the law has had an important declaratory effect and has given support to those who do not wish to discriminate but who would otherwise feel compelled to do so by social pressure. It has also made crude, overt forms of racial discrimination much less common. Discriminatory advertisements and notices have virtually disappeared from both the press and from public advertisement boards. Discriminatory conditions have largely disappeared from the rules governing insurance and other financial matters, and they are being removed from tenancy agreements. It is less common for an employer to refuse to accept any coloured workers and there has been some movement of coloured workers into more desirable jobs....and yet at the end of the decade both statutory bodies [the Race Relations Board and the Community Relations Commission] have forcibly drawn attention to the inability of the legislation to deal with widespread patterns of discrimination, especially in employment and housing, a lack of confidence amongst minority groups in the effectiveness of the law, and the lack of credibility in the efficacy of the work of the Race Relations Board and the Community Relations Commission themselves.

The continuing unequal status of Britain's racial minorities and the extent of the disadvantage from which they suffer provided ample evidence of the inadequacy of the existing policy. Government acknowledged that it was insufficient for the law to deal with only overt discrimination. It should also prohibit practices which were fair in a formal sense but discriminatory in their operation and effect. Clearly, too, the sanctions against perpetrators were perceived as inadequate: in 1974 the sums awarded in compensation varied between £2 and £150 and averaged £23.50.

The new regime heralded by the White Paper was effected by the Race Relations Act

1976. The most important innovation was the introduction of the concept of indirect discrimination. Thus it was not only unlawful to discriminate, in the circumstances specified on the grounds of colour, race, nationality, ethnic or national origins directly, but it became unlawful to impose a condition or requirement, the effect of which was a proportionally greater adverse impact on one racial group in comparison with others. An exception to such a condition or requirement being unlawful in the specified areas was when it was otherwise justifiable on non-racial grounds, i.e. on the grounds of a reasonable job specification or a reasonable test of eligibility in respect of allocation on a housing authority's waiting list.

In respect of housing and related services, the 1976 Act, by Section 20, virtually replicated the provisions relating to unlawful discrimination in the provision of goods, facilities and services while Sections 21 to 24 expanded the area of unlawful discrimination in the disposal of premises, in the granting of consent for assignment or sub-letting and in the treatment of individuals in relation to lists of accommodation.

The exception relating to small dwellings was virtually repeated in Section 22 while clubs and associations (including housing associations) were specifically targeted by Section 25, where there were 25 or more members. Section 26 of the Act enabled housing associations to be formed for the purpose of providing a particular benefit for a racial group so long as this was not defined by reference to colour: this enabled the formation and promotion of Afro-Caribbean and Asian housing associations.

Section 71 of the 1976 Act placed a new duty on local authorities to review their policies with a view to eliminating unlawful practices and promoting equality of opportunity. Clearly the former was otiose: it is the nature of law to expect compliance. The latter was seen as a cosmetic exhortation without resourcing or sanction (MacEwen 1985). The new provisions relating to indirect discrimination were borrowed from the US and the judgement in the US Supreme Court in Griggs v. Duke Power Company (1971) 401 US424. Other innovations included the amalgamation of the Race Relations Board and the Community Relations Commission into a new body, The Commission for Racial Equality, the availability of direct access to employment tribunals by complainants in respect of employment cases and otherwise to the County Courts and Sheriff Courts in Scotland, and extended powers of the new Commission in respect of employment cases and otherwise to the County Courts and Sheriff Courts in Scotland, and extended powers of the new Commission in respect of investigations. The legal provisions are discussed more fully in White et al (CRE 1990) while the implications for housing are detailed in MacEwen (1990a,).

Despite the deficiences of the 1976 Act, in the CRE's opinion, expressed in the review of the Act in 1985, its structure and general thrust was right. 'Eight years experience of working with it and the consultative process that preceded this submission has convinced us of that' (CRE, 1985). Accordingly, in a formal sense, the 1976 Act provided a powerful and coherent weapon to challenge discriminatory practices generally and to make an impact on racial disadvantage experienced by ethnic minority groups in respect of both public and private housing. That it has not had the impact desired is generally acknowledged (Bindman 1980, Lustgarten 1987, McCrudden 1987, MacEwen 1990a).

C

The PEP surveys of racial disadvantage in the 1960s and 1970s and the PSI survey of 1982 (Brown 1984), provide fairly convincing evidence of racial disadvantage continuing at the extensive scale in both the public and private sectors. Certainly overt discrimination, particularly that exemplified in advertisements prior to the 1968 Act, has diminished and there is probably greater public acceptance of the desirability of legislation to stem discriminatory practices. But clearly such changes in themselves have not had a major impact on the housing circumstances, in relative terms, of the various ethnic minority communities in Britain.

Before we examine why this should be so in respect of public housing, it is necessary to examine, albeit briefly, the framework of current legislative provision relating to public housing allocations, an area where major improvement might have been anticipated with the introduction of the 1976 Act.

The law relating to public housing allocations in Scotland

Although certain statutory provisions such as the Land Compensation Acts of 1973, the Tenants Rights Etc (Scotland) Act of 1980 and the Housing (Homeless Persons) Act of 1977 imposed some restrictions on local authorities in the exercise of their discretion relating to waiting lists and allocations, in aggregate these provisions made few inroads, whether procedural or substantive, into the broad array of allocations systems and policies adopted by local authorities. No machinery for selection was prescribed, and there is no opportunity for scrutiny, challenge or review. Central Government persists in the view that broad discretion is 'good' enabling decisions sensitive to local needs, despite a simultaneous recognition that improvements were necessary and desirable (e.g. Scottish Development Department 1980).

The current law in respect of allocations in Scotland is found, for the most part, in the Housing (Scotland) Act 1987, as amended. These provisions focus on openness. Thus housing authorities, including New Town Development Corporations, Scottish Homes and Housing Associations, are obliged to publish any rules in existence governing admissions to the waiting list, allocations, transfers and exchanges and to make them available in full for a charge and in summary form without charge. A right is also given to applicants to have access to information which they have provided to the housing authority: the Local Authorities (Access to Information) Act 1985, which deals with public access to local authority documents and meetings, enables applicants, amongst others, to inspect and obtain copies of relevant minutes, reports and documents considered by committees etc., so far as these documents etc., are neither confidential nor exempt. Such documents clearly may relate to allocation policies and procedures, even where not incorporated in the published rules, as amended from time to time. Following the publications of the rules under the Access to Personal Files Act 1987, an applicant should have access to all information relating to his application, whether or not provided by him. As a result any applicant, or potential applicant, for local authority or housing association accommodation is now in a better position to judge not only the equity of the general system of allocations adopted but also the fairness of the treatment which has been afforded him or her. In making allocations to housing, housing authorities are required to give a 'reasonable preference' to those occupying insanitary or overcrowded houses, those living under unsatisfactory housing conditions or those having large families. Moreover, by Sections 19 and 20 of the Housing (Scotland) Act 1987, local authorities, in admission to the waiting list, must disregard, generally, the question of age, income, ownership, marital status and rent arrears not attributable to the applicant. In addition, local authorities should ignore whether or not the applicant is resident in the area provided he or she is employed in the area, wishes to seek employment in the area, is over 60 and wishes to be with a younger relative, or where special social or medical reasons are provided, justifying an applicant's requirement to be rehoused in the area. Similarly, once admitted to the waiting list, the above considerations must not be taken into account in respect of the allocation of housing itself and the housing authority may not impose any requirement that the application should have remained in force for a minimum period, that a divorce or judicial separation be obtained or that the applicant no longer be living with some other person.

Essentially these measures are reactive rather than proactive. Those aspects of local authority practice which are considered restrictive - such as age and income barriers in Scotland - are outlawed but there is no requirement to deploy a points or group allocations system as consistently advocated. Moreover, given that the allocations system increasingly operates as a way of metering out a scarce resource amongst an over large number of potential beneficiaries, it will remain open to two major criticisms. These are, firstly, that it is a welfare net designed to catch and accommodate the worst off and most underprivileged people, secondly that it takes inadequate account of various forms of housing needs (Hughes, 1987).

In addition, the processes involved in residualising council housing may encourage management practices which accentuate social division by categorising "bad" tenants and placing them on the worst estates, and by channelling those in greatest housing need into less popular areas by dint of waiting time to points gaining significant allocation preferences.

The courts have been reluctant to interfere in the discretion afforded local authorities in their admissions and allocations systems (Shelley v. LCC (1949) AC56). It may be possible, where a housing authority has refused to consider those things which it was legally obliged to do for the courts to provide a remedy (R v. Canterbury City Council, ex p. Gillespie (1986)) 19HLR7. At best such judicial review is a broad gauge safety net against legal abuse: no statutory appeal is provided in respect of admissions and allocation policies and there is no requirement on any housing authority to institute any process of administrative review. The legal framework relating to admissions and allocations may . be summarised as follows:

i) Wide areas of discretion remain in the hands of the housing authorities;

ii) Where demand exceeds supply, such discretion is exercised to determine the match between the most suitable applicants and the best housing stock;

iii) There is an absence of effective administrative and judicial review of the exercise of such discretion;

iv) Applicants are not required to be fully advised of how their own needs and requirements are assessed nor of how the housing authority exercises its discretion in practice;

v) Those classified as 'undeserving' are likely to obtain the least desirable housing but are unlikely to be in a position to challenge the determinations made.

Such conclusions relating to the legal framework do not imply that all or even the majority of housing authorities exercise their discretion in an arbitrary or insensitive fashion,. But where bad decisions are made, and no authority can safeguard itself against such occurrence, the authority is under no obligation to have any system of review. In this situation, all tenants, irrespective of ethnic origin, are placed in a weak bargaining position: any discrimination which may occur, whether on the grounds of sex, race or disability, is likely to go unchecked and both the applicant and the housing authority may well be unaware of its occurrence.

Race legislation and public housing allocations

Direct discrimination in allocations is likely to occur in one of eight principal ways:

i) Steering black applicants to specific areas because of staff perception that all black households want to live in the same area, or because of dispersal policy;

ii) Offering poorer quality accommodation to black applicants irrespective of circumstances;

iii) Providing different or selective information and advice to black applicants;

iv) Applying different assessment criteria to black applicants, thus affecting points allocations and/or waiting list priority;

v) In seeking to conform with management advice or policy objectives, to let properties quickly, selecting offers on racial grounds on the assumption that, for example, blacks would more readily accept offers in areas of relatively high black concentrations than whites;

vi) In response to pressures from external groups such as the police and tenants associations or from internal groups or individuals, such as housing letting subcommittees, refusing to offer blacks accommodation in specific areas, or limiting or restricting such offers;

vii) Through housing visitors or otherwise, applying different standards relating to housekeeping to black applicants/tenants, affecting the assessment of 'good' or 'bad' applicants/tenants;

viii) Operating a discriminatory lettings policy, in which certain decisions may influence lettings to the disadvantage of black applicants.

In addition to overt discrimination in housing allocations, indirect discrimination may also take place, most frequently in one of the following ways:

i) Applying a points system which gives significant advantage to longevity on the waiting list, the effect of which is disproportionately to disadvantage ethnic minority applicants;

ii) Applying a points system or allocations system, which disadvantages large households with the same effect;

iii) Through communication difficulties, failing to advise a racial group on how to optimise their choice of better housing, through first or subsequent refusal;

iv) Allocating the least desirable housing/estates to the homeless or any other group where there is a disproportionate representation of ethnic minority applicants;

v) Applying any other requirement or condition in determining allocations, the effect of which is to the relative disadvantage of ethnic minority applicants, for example relating to employment, to separated families or to 'sons and daughters' of existing residents.

vi) Operating differential access from different housing channels, for example for decants, for the homeless, from housing action areas or relating to the locality of existing residence, the effect of which is to disadvantage ethnic minority applicants;

vii) Operating a referrals or nominations system in respect of housing association lets to like effect (CRE 1989b).

Determining whether unlawful discrimination has occurred requires extensive analysis, such as that undertaken by the CRE in their formal investigations into Hackney (CRE 1984a), into Liverpool (CRE 1984b and 1989a), and into Tower Hamlets (CRE 1988). An extensive array of other studies (see MacEwen 1990a) from Bristol to Bedford, from Lewisham to Birmingham and from Glasgow to Edinburgh have either identified unlawful discriminatory practice or uncovered evidence which points strongly in that direction. The report Queuing for Housing (SCPR 1988) demonstrated that the majority of local authorities surveyed in England employed criteria in allocations, such as a requirement to be resident or employed locally or not to be an owner-occupier which are likely to discriminate against ethnic minorities: the legality of such criteria will, of course, depend on the 'justifiability' test.

Ethnic minorities and council housing allocations in Edinburgh

A local authority survey (AMA 1985), which confined itself to England and Wales, demonstrated that the vast majority of housing authorities did not keep records. Those that did, did not analyse the statistical base sufficiently to determine whether or not practices had the effect of discrimination against ethnic minorities. Such a pattern of neglect was confirmed in respect of Edinburgh District Council by an initial survey in the mid-1980s (Thwaites 1986). That survey was followed up with further surveys by Taylor (1987) and Hancock and MacEwen (1989).

Cumulatively these surveys provided evidence that ethnic minority applications and allocations approximated to their proportion of the whole population in Edinburgh and the proportion of applications respectively (approximately 2 per cent). Because there were no reliable data on relative housing need of the whole community and by ethnic group, whether such formal equality was objectively fair was unknown.

The studies by Thwaites (1986) and Taylor (1987) indicated that there was under-representation of ethnic minority applicants who were actually allocated tenancies, but the study by Hancock and MacEwen (1989) which focused on more recent applicants did not support such a conclusion. It would appear therefore that ethnic minority applicants now have a like expectation of securing housing as other applicants (18 per cent). The earlier studies showed a maldistribution of property types (including high-rise) in respect of ethnic minorities. The later study by Hancock and MacEwen (1989) suggested, conversely but again in respect of more recent applicants, that the property types allocated were proportional by ethnic group.

All three studies indicated that ethnic minority applicants were allocated to high. medium and low demand estates in a similar proportion to other applicants.

However, all three studies also indicated that ethnic minority applicants were allocated in a significantly greater number than other applicants (50 per cent as opposed to 10 per cent: 1989 study), to Wester Hailes. This is a large estate on the west of Edinburgh, peripheral in its location and unpopular with tenants. It has a number of high rise blocks within it and is regarded as 'difficult-to-let'. Area preference, house type and size requirements, urgency of housing need and points allocated failed to explain this discrepancy either individually or cumulatively.

The study by Hancock and MacEwen (1989) indicated that there was some evidence of racial stereotyping by housing staff, principally a presumption that ethnic minority applicants would prefer a tenancy in Wester Hailes for reasons of community support. On this basis, and in the absence of any other tenable explanation, Hancock and MacEwen concluded that unlawful direct racial discrimination had occurred in the allocation of some ethnic minority applicants to Wester Hailes.

The latter study also indicated ethnic minority applicants averaged a significantly greater number of needs points than other applicants. So far as the points system gave greater weight to waiting time points and so far as this was not justifiable on non-racial grounds, the practice was seen to constitute unlawful indirect discrimination in terms of Section 1(1)(b) of the Race Relations Act 1976.

The experience of ethnic minorities in respect of applications and allocations to the outlying areas was not examined by any of the three studies referred to but it was apparent that the restrictive rules applied in those areas were likely to affect ethnic minority applicants disproportionately. Consequently, unless the policies were otherwise justifiable, they were seen to constitute unlawful indirect discrimination in terms of the 1976 Act. Despite the fact that the Edinburgh District Council Housing Department had issued directions previously that staff should not require applicants or tenants to produce passports, the study by Hancock and MacEwen showed that ethnic minority applicants were requested to produce passports purportedly to verify information required. As no white applicants in the control sample were so required to produce passports it was concluded that direct unlawful discrimination had occurred. None of the studies indicated that there was any discernible difference in the information or advice offered to applicants but it was apparent that ethnic minority applicants, in respect of the study by Hancock and MacEwen, were less well informed than others regarding the implications of the allocations system in respect of refusal of the first offer.

Ethnic minority tenants were, generally, more satisfied than other tenants with both the service provided by the housing department and the offers of accommodation made. This finding extended to tenants in Wester Hailes. One possible explanation was the greater improvement in housing conditions afforded by council housing to ethnic minority applicants in comparison with others.

Despite a dominant view of satisfaction about Wester Hailes in the study by Hancock and MacEwen and that it was a relatively safe place to live, ethnic minority tenants in Wester Hailes (82 per cent) were significantly more likely to suffer racial attacks or abuse within the neighbourhood than ethnic minority tenants living elsewhere (50 per cent). In 1986 Lothian Regional Council and Edinburgh District Council sponsored a survey and report undertaken by the Scottish Ethnic Minorities Research Unit which was submitted and published in November 1987 (SEMRU 1987). That report included a summary of the services provided by the housing department and their impact on ethnic minority needs. The report also made a series of recommendations in order to improve the housing service, one of which critically related to the requirement to undertake ethnic minority monitoring in respect of applications and allocations for council tenancies. Neither at the time the Hancock/MacEwen report was published (October 1989) nor at the time of writing this chapter (January 1990) has that recommendation, endorsed as a first recommendation in the Hancock/MacEwen report, been effectively implemented.

Clearly, the larger the bureaucracy and the greater the dependence on democratic decision making, the longer it takes to consult on recommendations made and to implement policy change to reflect the inputs emanating from that process. Despite that, it is hard to escape from a conclusion that had the District Council housing department or indeed the political administration in control, considered this central recommendation a priority, it would have been implemented much earlier. Currently a voluntary question on ethnic origin is provided for new council house applicants but this does not reflect the needs of a comprehensive record keeping and monitoring system embodied in the CRE draft Code of Practice (CRE 1989b). Moreover that draft recommends that equality targets should be set in order to achieve fair shares of the properties and services available. Edinburgh District Council have yet to consider this.

Local authority attitudes to race relations have been characterised as those of 'thrusters, learners, waverers, and resisters'. At one time Edinburgh District Council questioned the need for any special provision for ethnic minorities, put the onus on Lothian Community Relations Council (LCRC) to establish needs, refused to provide staff training on equal opportunities and, generally, failed to adopt any policy to promote good race relations (as required by Section 71 of the Race Relations Act 1976). Today Edinburgh District Council has a Race Relations Sub-Committee of its Policy and Resources Committee, it employs a full-time race relations officer (one of the first in Scotland), has financed jointly with Lothian Region, the study of ethnic minority needs and local authority service provision (SEMRU 1987) and has issued a series of policy documents to promote equality of opportunity. It has increased its financial support to Lothian Community Relations Council (LCRC), has contributed to the establishment of a Lothian Translation and Interpreting Trust and is committed, at least notionally, to the introduction of ethnic monitoring in respect of employment and a selection of service provision. Consequently it would be unfair to suggest that Edinburgh District Council housing department has resisted change. What is fair to question, however, is why such change that has taken place can be characterised as 'too little too late', and why it has been as a response to largely external initiatives including the SEMRU reports and pressure exerted, from time to time, by Lothian Community Relations Council. Given the findings of the report by Hancock and MacEwen it might have been argued that the provisions of the Race Relations Act 1976 would have led to earlier complaints of unlawful discrimination by individuals or, alternatively, to a formal investigation by the CRE followed by a Non-discrimination Notice. Why this has not occurred begs questions as to the efficacy of the 1976 Act and it is this to which we now turn.

Knowledge and discrimination

In a fairly cursory examination of reports relating to discrimination in local authority housing allocations, a number of common features can be identified (MacEwen 1986). Firstly, despite the significant differences in the nature, composition and concentrations of the ethnic minority groups affected, in the allocation systems deployed and in the geographical location of the local authorities examined, unlawful discrimination, in one form or another, appeared a constant. Certainly it could be argued that the CRE formal investigations (Hackney 1984, Walsall MRC 1985) and CRC inquiries (Nottingham, Simpson 1981) were focussed on local authorities where discrimination was suspected. Similarly, inquiries into Birmingham (Flett 1979), Lewisham (Ouseley 1981) and

Bedford (Skellington 1980) may have been initiated by a suspicion that ethnic minority applicants were being treated unfairly. Nonetheless, and a point also reflected in the more recent CRE investigations into Tower Hamlets (CRE 1988) and Liverpool (CRE 1989a), the view that unlawful discrimination was occurring was not one shared by the housing authority concerned until after the inquiries were complete and the relevant report published. The examination by MacEwen (1987) also established that policies with a discriminatory effect were place and time specific. In other words, it was too crude a process to identify a specific policy as discriminatory in one location and expect it to have the same impact some years later on in the same place or, conversely, contemporaneously in a different location.

Moreover, while policies, practices and procedures have been demonstrated to have an adverse impact, it is artificial to separate these from the administrative systems and structures which sustain them (Ouseley 1981) or to suggest that racial stereotyping is not intricately interwoven with those of class and gender (Henderson and Karn 1987).

Because of such complexity it is virtually impossible to isolate an individual act or omission or a specific policy and to conclude that it is 'responsible' for a specific discriminatory outcome. Consequently, identifying racial discrimination in housing allocations is more likely to depend on the rigorous statistical analysis of comparative outcomes by ethnic group over a period of time. More often than not, such a process does not positively identify racial discrimination but merely eliminates all other plausible explanations for adverse treatment. This leads to the following conclusions:

i) The individual applicant is unlikely to have the knowledge of or access to information which would enable him or her to present a prima facie case to the housing authority (or to the courts) alleging unlawful discrimination;

ii) The housing authority itself, including the councillors and senior officials, may be unaware of the differential impact of policies and practices on particular ethnic groups, a probability where there is no record keeping and monitoring;

iii) Individual discriminatory acts or omissions may be submerged in the otherwise acceptable array of discretionary value judgements on which the process of allocations usually depends;

iv) In the absence of complaints of unlawful discrimination, the housing authority may see the introduction of record keeping as an unnecessary burden and may even oppose it because it may demonstrate discriminatory outcomes (Cowen 1983).

Inquiry led strategies

The above conclusions question the efficacy of inquiry led strategies particularly those dependent on individual complaints. An examination of individual housing complaints received by the CRE over the eleven year period from the inception of the 1976 Act demonstrated that they average only 7 per cent of all complaints received. Clearly this is the tip of the iceberg. Testing of discrimination in the housing market was conducted by the BBC in its series of programmes entitled Black and White (BBC, 14.4.88) which, in comparing the treatment received by a black applicant and a white applicant showed that, in the Bristol area, less favourable treatment might be expected in 30 per cent of applications for bed and breakfast and 18 per cent of applications for rented accommodation on the basis of colour, purely at the stage of initial inquiry. Accordingly, and in keeping with the previous PSI surveys, there is a continuing high expectation of discrimination in housing. Given that housing, along with employment and education, is one of the most important areas of an individual's living experience, it is apparent that the low figures referred to are not indicative of an absence of discrimination but are much more likely to reflect either a reluctance to complain or, as exemplified above, the absence of relevant knowledge by a potential complainer which would justify the pursuit of a complaint.

In respect of formal investigations between 1977 and 1988 some 44 reports were issued by the CRE, 11 of which related to housing. There have been no successful individual complaints nor any formal investigations originating or conducted in Scotland relating to housing.

While the CRE has adopted deliberate strategies to correlate investigations with promotional activities and, in the housing sphere, can record some success, there can be little doubt that neither individual complaints nor investigations, in themselves, constitute an effective strategy for implementing the Race Relations Act 1976 (MacEwen 1990a).

Why so few complaints?

This question is only partially answered by the issue of knowledge about the legislation and knowledge of how a particular application has fared, in comparison with others generally and others from the same racial group. Clearly such knowledge is relevant, not only to initiating a complaint, but also to its pursuit in the Courts. Although a pursuer may seek the assistance of the CRE, may ask relevant questions preliminary to the hearing, and may expect the Court to make inferences on racial discrimination where no other plausible reason for disadvantage is presented or favoured, the onus remains with the pursuer to prove his/her case, albeit on the balance of probability. The specific difficulties of doing so, however, are multifarious. The fact has been acknowledged by the Courts and demonstrated by research (Dhavan 1988). But such problems are not unique: in the US, from which the concept of indirect discrimination was borrowed, similar difficulties are encountered by pursuers. Despite the significant differences in the extent and provision of public housing in the USA, the law there has had a greater strategic impact (MacEwen 1990b). Although the differences in the context of racial discrimination and the legal systems may be critical determinants of different outcomes, even a superficial comparison makes it difficult to avoid a conclusion that the remedies available in the US encourage redress for legitimate grievances while redress is inhibited in the UK. There are seven discrete reasons for this.

Firstly, the amount of damages available and imposed by the Courts acts as an important salutary lesson and disincentive against such discrimination. By the same token it encourages record keeping, analysis and review. Thus although the risks of being caught may be no greater in the US than the UK (and arguably less, MacEwen 1990b), the consequences in purely financial terms may be considerable even for an individual act.

Secondly, unlike the opportunities in Scotland and England and Wales, the US Courts entertain Class Actions. Thus a group of individuals adversely affected by a particular policy may decide to club together to obtain redress. This not only cuts individual legal costs if the action is unsuccessful but also results in class damages. In monetary terms this may do, and has, resulted in multi-million dollar awards.

Thirdly, and in contrast to the limits imposed by the Local Government Act 1988, to tender for public (federal and state) contacts, contractors must demonstrate positive equal opportunity action. While this may have limited direct significance for housing it generates a climate of opinion in both the public and private domain, which recognises the value of such action in hard economic terms.

Fourthly, but of limited significance in housing cases (MacEwen 1990b), access by the pursuer to public enforcement agencies at the State and Federal level together with access to public action law firms provides a more coherent network of support agencies than those available to pursuers in the UK (Runnymede Trust 1980).

Fifthly, the Courts, albeit without notable consistency, are obliged to treat both Constitutional and Federal provision as paramount and to interpret such provision in a liberal manner to redress the mischief it was designed to alleviate. Such constitutional underpinning is absent in the UK: any counter and subsequent legislative provision, including rules and regulations by Statutory Instrument, takes precedent over the provision of the Race Relations Act 1986.

Sixthly, while the defence of 'justifiable' indirect discrimination is available in the US, it has not been equated with commercial convenience, as it has in the UK (MacEwen 1990b). The test is much closer to necessity. Moreover, while UK Courts have belatedly accepted statistical data, the position in the US has been to require it. In contrast the UK Courts have refused to require the production of statistical evidence when not readily available from the respondents: see Carrington v. Helix Lighting Ltd (1989) EAT.

Lastly, in the US, the defence of ulterior motive is not available to obviate damages in indirect discrimination cases as it is in the UK. Thus any housing authority in the UK, which has imposed some conditions which, for example, discriminate against non-residents in the area, may be found guilty of unlawful indirect discrimination but will have no damages to pay should they demonstrate a lack of intention to disadvantage the minority applicants for housing.

Consequential damages

A number of authors have provided critiques of both the CRE (McCrudden 1987) and the EOC (Gregory 1987) as regulatory agencies suggesting both internal factors (such as lack of staff and limited strategic planning) and external causes (including those alluded to above) which inhibit their effectiveness in respect of law enforcement. Cumulatively, these factors provide not only a barrier to formal complaint initiations and resolution but also an imperfect backdrop - a topography of informal complaint resolution - to the climate in which organisations, agencies and individuals conduct their affairs and their resultant receptivity to change, to challenge and to complaints. The research into housing allocations in Edinburgh demonstrated that some housing officials were, despite race training, ill informed as to the meaning of indirect discrimination, apathetic regarding the implementation of an effective equal opportunities policy, resistant to positive action and expressed doubt concerning evidence of racial disadvantages in housing. Most significantly, a number of officials, who had the greatest public interface, were defensive in considering the possibility of unlawful discrimination occurring in their own organisation.

While such attitudes are understandable, reflecting more broadly held social views, collectively they comprise a coherent countervailing force against the effective progressive implementation of policies promoted by senior officials and adopted by Edinburgh District Council. In doing so, they crystallise a division between theory and practice. While the reasons for such a defensive stand may be complex, one prominent consideration is the supposition that indirect racial discrimination is necessarily limited to acts and omissions stemming from overt racial considerations, reflective of crude individual expressions of racism. Consequently, when a particular agency is accused of indirect discrimination, there is a knee-jerk response to defend the high moral ground held by the service provider. In such circumstances, the complainant is denied the opportunity for rational and objective dialogue concerning his or her situation - an opportunity which may lead to informal and satisfactory resolution of the housing complaint - and, instead, is faced with the very dubious alternative of seeking legal redress. Even if successful, such a process is psychologically enervating: the results - likely to occur months if not years after initiating the process - will not resolve the immediate housing need and are unlikely to resolve it in the longer term.

Court cases generally have been likened to a Casino, not merely in respect of the arbitrary prospect of success but, more particularly, in the context of housing, in respect of the odds favouring both the repeat player, whose experience includes a knowledge of the odds, and the player with greater resources to ride the short-term losses. Clearly the housing authority, by such analogy, are better equipped to defend legal proceedings, than the majority of applicants is to pursue them.

Conclusions

Joseph (1985) in his book, Lawyers Can Seriously Damage Your Health, describes an appalling array of incompetence by the legal profession in the pursuit of negligence claims in tort. Claims relating to racial discrimination are claims in tort (in Scotland 'delict'). Fundamentally, he argues, the legal system in England and Wales, has evolved under the cloak of Justice to provide for the interests of the profession at the expense, both literal and metaphorical, of their clients. Racial discrimination in the legal profession, from bridge to boiler-room is evident (Goulbourne 1988). The Scottish legal profession, through the 1980's, has been equally negligent towards the cause of racial justice (MacEwen 1990a). While there are signs of improvement, it is too early to conclude that the culture of indifference in the legal profession, both north and south of the border, is capable of the critical introspective appraisal necessary to impact on day to day practice. Even if it is, the process will be painfully slow. In this light, while there is an ineluctable conclusion that the law relating to racial discrimination in housing has proved ineffectual, such failure is attributable less to the intrinsic shortcomings of the legislation and the enforcement agency, the CRE, and more to pervasive ignorance of the concept of indirect discrimination and the social context which tolerates, in its apathy, the consequential racial disadvantage which is evident. The capability of judicial decrees to restrain discrimination cannot be viewed as a Kantian abstraction of pure law but must be judged by results. Such a conclusion does not refute the pertinence of law in the pursuit of justice but it clearly questions its efficacy when isolated from concomitant central and local government strategies to secure both comprehension and enforcement.

So much was obvious to Government when it observed (Home Office 1975b, para. 25):

Legislation ... is not, and never can be, a sufficient condition for effective progress towards equality of opportunity. A wide range of administrative and voluntary measures are needed to give practical effect to the objectives of the law.

While that opinion, expressed by a Labour Government in 1975, may have been echoed by the Thatcher Government of 1990, Whitehall admits that race relations has been put on the 'backburner' (MacEwen 1990a). It is not indifferent to all matters concerning race: it clearly wishes to control racial disturbances and has promoted a number of initiatives to quell inner city unrest and to stem racial harassment (Jacobs 1986). But the record shows that it has not been concerned with 'racial' justice, despite statements to the contrary. If it were it would, for example, have secured the changes to the race legislation advocated by the CRE (CRE 1985); it would have directed local authorities to implement ethnic monitoring; it would have piloted strategic monitoring of housing authority allocations; it would have directed the CRE to undertake formal investigations, as it is empowered to do; it would have required local authorities to adopt and implement equal opportunity policies; it would have issued up to date guidance on the requirements of the Race Relations Act 1976; and it would have required contract compliance premises similar to those required under the Fair Employment (Northern Ireland) Act 1989; it might even have included a concern for racial disadvantage in its reforms of the legal profession.

Accordingly, it is fair to conclude, in addressing the three questions posed in the introduction, that the implications of indirect discrimination are seldom thought through at the local government level and that Central Government has failed to provide an effective administrative network of support to secure the observance of the legislation. With reference to the third question, (Can we draw any conclusions for the Edinburgh experience?), a glimmer of qualified optimism can be seen. Firstly, although some fifteen years after the introduction of comprehensive legislation, there might be an expectation that racial discrimination in public housing would not, by now, be pervasive, the recent CRE investigations suggest the naivety of that generalised expectation. Accordingly, the absence of pervasive discrimination in housing allocations in Edinburgh may be viewed as reassuring. Nevertheless, the evidence of attitudes in the housing staff which resulted in racial discrimination, most unequivocally in respect of the request for passports, demonstrates that the culture in which institutional practices emerge has not yet been radically changed. Consequently, the 'new deal' of incipient policies on monitoring and racial harassment, for example, have been and may continue to be retarded from effective implementation. The arguments have drifted from the espousal of sympathetic policies, to which Edinburgh can provide evidence, to the prioritisation of good practice and its systematic monitoring. As noted above, the AMA Survey of local authorities (AMA 1985), demonstrated that those that kept ethnic records failed to integrate them effectively into the process of policy review and management by objectives. Ultimately Edinburgh will be judged, not by what it says, but by what it does.

References

Association of Metropolitan Authorities 1985 *Housing and Race: Policy and Practice in Local Authorities* London: AMA Publications

Bindman G 1980 'The Law, Equal Opportunity and Affirmative Action' in *New Community* 8(3): 248-60

Brown C 1984 *Black and White Britain: the 3rd PSI Survey* London: Heinemann

Commission for Racial Equality 1984a *Report of Formal Investigation into Hackney LBC* London: CRE Publications

Commission for Racial Equality 1984b *Research Report into Liverpool City Council* London: CRE Publications

Commission for Racial Equality 1985 *Review of the Race Relations Act 1976: Proposals for Change* London: CRE Publications

Commission for Racial Equality 1988 Report of Formal Investigation into Tower Hamlets LBC London: CRE Publications

Commission for Racial Equality 1989a *Report of Formal Investigation into Liverpool City Council* London: CRE Publications

Commission for Racial Equality 1989b *Code of Practice ... in the field of rented housing, a Consultative Draft* London: CRE Publications

Cowen H 1983 *Homelessness Among Black Youths: Policies and Planning* Gloucestershire Papers in Local and Rural Planning 18 Gloucester: Department of Town and Country Planning Gloucestershire College of Arts and Technology

Dhavan R 1988 *Why So Few Cases: a survey of the Race Relations Act 1976'* unpublished report to CRE London: CRE

Flett H 1979 *Black Council Tenants in Birmingham* Working Paper 21 SSRC Research Unit on Ethnic Relations University of Bristol

Goulbourne S 1988 'Minority entry to the legal profession' *Policy Papers in Ethnic Relations No 2* Coventry: Centre for Research in Ethnic Relations Warwick University

Gregory J 1987 *Sex, Race and Law* London: Sage Publications

Hancock D and MacEwen M 1989 *Ethnic Minorities and Public Housing in Edinburgh* London/Edinburgh: joint CRE/SEMRU Publication

Henderson J and Karn V 1987 *Race, Class and State Housing* Aldershot: Gower Publications

Home Office 1975a *The Government's Reply: to the report Race and Housing from the Select Committee on Race Relations and Immigration* Cmnd 6232 London: HMSO

Home Office 1975b *Racial Discrimination Government White Paper* Cmnd 6234 London: HMSO

HMSO 1975 *Race Relations and Housing* Observations on the report on Race and Housing by the Select Committee on Race Relations and Housing London: HMSO

Jacobs B D 1986 *Black Politics and The Urban Crisis in Britain* Cambridge: Cambridge University Press

Joseph M 1985 *Lawyers Can Seriously Damage Your Health* London: Michael Joseph

King Martin Luther 1963 *Strong to Love*

Lustgarten L 1987 in Solomos and Jenkins (eds) *Racism and Equal Opportunity Policies in the 1980s* Cambridge: Cambridge University Press

McCrudden C 1987 'The Commission for Racial Equality' in *Regulation and Public Law*

MacEwen M 1985 'Local Authority Duty to Promote Racial Equality' in *SCOLAG* No 105 June Dundee: Scottish Legal Action Group

MacEwen M 1987 *Housing Allocations, Race and Law* Research Paper No 14 Heriot-Watt University/Edinburgh College of Art Edinburgh: SEMRU Publications

MacEwen M 1990a *Housing, Race and Law* London: Routledge

MacEwen M 1990b 'US Anti-Discrimination Law in Housing' in *Housing Studies* June 1990

Ouseley H 1981 *The System* London: Runnymede Trust/South London Equal Rights Consultancy Runnymede Trust 1980

Scottish Development Department 1980 *Allocation and Transfer of Council Housing* Report of Sub-Committee of the Scottish Housing Advisory Committee Edinburgh: HMSO

Scottish Ethnic Minorities Research Unit 1987 *Ethnic Minorities Profile: A Study of Needs and Services in Lothian Region and Edinburgh District* Edinburgh: SEMRU Publications

Select Committee on Race Relations and Immigration 1971 *Race and Housing* Session 1970-71 London: HMSO

Simpson A 1981 *Stacking the Decks: a Study of Race, Inequality and Council Housing in Nottingham* Nottingham: Nottingham Community Relations Council

Skellington R 1980 *Council House Allocations in a Multi-Racial Town* Milton Keynes: Open University Publications

Social and Community Planning and Research 1988 *Queuing for Housing: a Study of Council House Waiting Lists* London: Department of Environment

Street H Bindman G and Howe G 1967 *Anti-Discrimination Legislation: The Street Report* London: Political and Economic Planning

Taylor L 1987 *Local Authority Housing and Ethnic Minorities in Edinburgh* unpublished dissertation for Diploma in Housing, Heriot-Watt University/ Edinburgh College of Art

Thwaites F 1986 *Local Authority Housing and Ethnic Minorities: a preliminary study of demand and supply in Edinburgh 1981-85* unpublished dissertation for Diploma in Housing, Heriot-Watt University/Edinburgh College of Art

White R McKenna I MacEwen M and Miller K 1990 *Race Discrimination Reports* London: CRE

Chapter 5
Ethnic minorities and
special needs housing provision
Mary Brailey

Introduction

Individuals within the ethnic minority communities who have some form of special housing need, for instance arising from physical disability, face a double disadvantage in securing access to suitable services. They experience the usual problems of racial discrimination, lack of knowledge about services and agencies, and inappropriate housing and other services. These problems are compounded by an additional and separate set of problems experienced by anyone with special housing needs: shortfall in service provision; lack of choice; rationed access; lack of knowledge about what services are available; and further prejudice and discrimination.

The interaction between the two sets of experience creates its own difficulties. For instance, a black person with a disability will often be isolated even among their own ethnic community. This in turn can lead to depression and other mental health problems, which are also known to be engendered by experience of racism (Ward 1987). Isolation also lessens still more their chance of being put in touch with service providers via word of mouth channels within the community. The housing needs of both ethnic minorities and special needs groups are low down on everyone's agenda. Rectifying this is made harder by the fact that special needs provision requires multi-agency collaboration in assembling integrated packages of care and housing, so there are more agendas which need to be influenced.

Evidence suggests that there is a very low take-up of special needs housing provision by ethnic minorities. A number of factors could account for this, such as:

i) Ignorance of available services or of routes of access to them;

ii) Exclusion from established referral networks;

iii) Inappropriateness of existing provision to the social, cultural, dietary and religious needs of different groups;

iv) Exposure of isolated ethnic minority residents to the risk of racist behaviour in communal or shared residential accommodation; and

v) Lack of ethnic monitoring by service providers, leaving considerable scope for discrimination at the point of application or selection.

This chapter examines these factors in relation to different types of special needs housing provision, with a view to informing strategies for improving the situation. First of all, the chapter outlines the nature, and what is known of the scale, of special needs housing requirements, both in general and specifically in relation to ethnic minorities. It then turns to look at the nature of existing housing services for special needs, which agencies provide those services, and how some of the services relate to the needs of ethnic minorities. Finally a number of conclusions and recommendations are made.

Much of the experience and research on which this chapter is based relates to Glasgow and the rest of Strathclyde.

Special housing needs

The term 'special needs' refers to people who need specially designed or adapted housing - such as people with physical disabilities - and those who need support or care services as a necessary component of their housing, if they are to lead independent and fulfilling lives in the community. The housing and support needs of different groups, and ways of meeting their needs have been detailed elsewhere (Brailey Daghlian and Taylor 1989). In brief, there are people needing support or care among the following groups: people with HIV or AIDS or other chronic illnesses; vulnerable young people including those leaving local authority care; women who have been subject to physical or sexual violence; ex-offenders; elderly people. A very high proportion of people with special needs also have to face poverty, homelessness, and social isolation or prejudice. But not everyone within these groups has special needs, and some might only need support for a temporary period .

The scale of special housing needs

The scale of special housing needs is notoriously hard to measure, at the levels of both strategic planning and local and individual needs assessments; and estimates vary. For instance, planning indicators for places required in the community for people with mental handicaps vary from 0.6 places per one thousand population to 1.8 places per one thousand population. However, on any estimates, it is generally acknowledged that there are serious shortfalls in the provision of suitable housing and support for special needs, and that these shortfalls are exacerbated by geographical disparities and by the unsuitable institutional nature of much existing provision. A long-standing government commitment to a shift away from hospital care to care in the community has been given renewed impetus recently with the publication of the Griffiths Report (Griffiths 1988), followed by the White Paper 'Caring for People' (HMSO 1989) and the NHS and Community Care Act (1990). There are similar policy shifts towards community-based alternatives to prison for offenders, and to residential homes for young people in care. However, it is widely expected that the funding changes heralded by the Act will not enable the potential for an expansion in services and might in fact restrict it. This is because a currently open-ended funding system, DSS board and lodging allowances, will be replaced by a cash limited budget, which is not even ring-fenced from other social services expenditure. Specific information about special housing needs among the ethnic minority communities is even harder to establish. Valuable research opportunities are lost to tie up the incidence of disability, homelessness, and other needs with ethnic origin. Some limited light should be shed on this issue by the Survey of Ethnic Minorities in Scotland which is being carried out for the Scottish Office, and which should be published in 1991. The survey includes questions on disability (for those under pensionable age) and on carers' and their dependents' use of services.

There is a clear need for the nature and scale of special housing needs among the ethnic minority communities to be researched, especially by way of feasibility studies for the development of specific services and projects. In the meantime, in view of the lack of systematic data, it is necessary to rely on local studies and the experience of agencies providing services or advice to individuals. Such evidence, while not enabling definitive conclusions to be drawn about the statistical scale of the problems, does provide useful indications from which changes can be introduced by service providers without needing to await the outcome of research.

Special needs among ethnic minorities

Whether and how the special needs of ethnic minorities differ from those of others is a vexed question. However, it is important that concern to avoid racial stereotyping and racist assumptions does not blind us to genuine implications of cultural diversity. Within the ethnic minority communities, views about special needs, about the services required, and about how those services should be provided, differ widely just as they do among any community. Needs and preferences vary between different age groups, between the sexes, between Chinese, Asian, and Afro-Caribbean groups, and indeed between individuals. Those individuals within the ethnic minority communities who wish to preserve the values and traditions of their own culture will have different views on service provision to those people who prefer to assimilate elements of Scottish culture, and both approaches need to be provided for.

In order to start exploring relevant issues around this question, Kieran Cranny carried out a small Glasgow-based study for Glasgow Special Housing Group (now Integrate) in 1988 (Cranny, 1988). He found that research already carried out in Scotland had provided very little information on the special housing needs of black people, and that forthcoming studies were unlikely to yield further information on this subject. With very few exceptions, the local service providers - Glasgow District Council, Strathclyde Regional Council, most housing associations, Scottish Homes and Greater Glasgow Health Board - do not generally keep ethnic records of clients, applicants or tenants. There is therefore little scope for identifying the numbers of specific requirements of special needs among ethnic minorities, nor for seeking consumer views about existing services.

Cranny's study involved 24 interviews with people working in agencies concerned with race and housing issues. Half of these interviews were in agencies working solely or mainly with ethnic minorities. Special needs was obviously a 'new' issue for most of those interviewed: there was a tendency to stray on to broader mainstream housing issues which, while partly attributable to the wish to avoid labelling ethnic minorities in general as 'special needs', is also indicative of a lack of familiarity with special needs issues.

The wide variety of views uncovered by the study provides helpful pointers as to how service planning and delivery should take specific account of ethnic minority needs. For instance, as has also been argued elsewhere, it was suggested that ageing occurs earlier and that eligibility for services such as sheltered housing should take account of this (Age Concern 1984). Very few ethnic minority elderly speak English and many also lack literacy skills. At the same time, inter-generational tensions create strains. This is in addition to the usual circumstances which give rise to housing needs among elderly people, overcrowding, family disputes, and ill health. Some ethnic minority families wish to have their elders living with them, but on the other hand growing numbers of ethnic minority elders live alone. Research among Asian families in Rochdale suggests that the lack of sufficient large houses, including some adapted for people with disabilities, has had the effect of undermining the extended family system (Athar 1990). In fact the assumption that the extended family system caters for all the needs of elderly people has always been something of a myth, as pointed out by ASRA, the housing association set up in Leicester to provide housing and support for Asian elders who are 'isolated, destitute, homeless, lonely and lacking family support' (FBHO 1988). The interviews highlighted young single women as a particular group needing special housing provision. Agencies are aware of a growing number of young women leaving the parental home as a response to what they perceive as an overly restrictive and isolated existence at home. A need was expressed for specialist supported accommodation to provide a safe home where help and advice are available, from which the young women could either return home or have support to set up home independently. Several projects along these lines have been established by black organisations in England.

Women who have separated or divorced, particularly as a result of domestic violence, were also often mentioned. It was felt that separated women with young children were perhaps the most isolated group within the ethnic minority communities. While needing the same access to safe refuge and support as other women escaping domestic violence, such women within ethnic minorities face particular problems resulting from stigma amongst their own community, as well as lack of knowledge about legal rights and community resources. The needs and experiences of this particular group are discussed in more detail elsewhere in this book, and also in reports of research and conferences (e.g. Mama 1989 and FBHO 1989b).

Agencies interviewed had very little knowledge of individuals with physical disabilities, mental handicap, or mental health problems, and it was clear that such individuals or families were not seeking advice or services from these agencies. Nor are such households involved in existing self-help or campaigning groups such as the Glasgow Forum on Disability. Strathclyde Regional Council and voluntary agencies are involved in setting up self-help support groups for ethnic minority families with physically handicapped schoolchildren. There is a clear demand for respite care where parents could leave their children with carers who recognise their cultural needs.

Further light was shed on the housing experience of families with disabled children by work carried out by Mr A Khan, Strathclyde Community Relations Council's temporary resource worker, during 1988. By liaising with Strathclyde Regional Council special schools, Mr Khan established contact with 49 families with disabled children. He found a very high level of ignorance of housing, social work services, welfare rights, and leisure facilities. Many families were living in upstairs apartments which they owned themselves, and would have difficulties selling because of disrepair. Offers of alternative housing from the housing department had been made in peripheral estates which were considered unattractive because of the risk of isolation and harassment. The Community Relations Council suggests that the distress of caring for a disabled child, particularly without access to support or to welfare benefits, is likely to cause mental health problems among these families.

The general picture emerging from these studies is that of a largely hidden set of special housing needs, with parents and other carers shouldering the burden of care without support. There is a low awareness of existing services, and where services are known about, it is felt they do not take adequate account of cultural and linguistic diversity, and that the planners and providers of services pay no consideration to ethnic minority needs.

Special needs housing provision

A wide variety of housing initiatives has been developed in response to special needs. This has been in the context of government policy in favour of 'care in the community', marking a shift away from a traditional institutional setting, such as large psychiatric hospitals. Initiatives include adapting or designing housing for wheelchair users and other people with disabilities; a variety of supported accommodation ranging from fully staffed hostels, through sheltered housing, to individual flats with visiting support workers; alarm systems for summoning help in case of emergency; 'staying put' and 'care and repair' projects to help elderly people who wish to stay in their own homes; respite care to give the carers of people with special needs a temporary break. In addition, some housing agencies have allocation policies and procedures which enable special needs to be met quickly and appropriately within the ordinary housing stock, with support services drawn in from mainstream social work health or voluntary services.

Service providers

This range of special needs housing provision has been developed and is run by wide range of agencies. Statutory agencies have been the main providers of residential accommodation for elderly people and for people with mental handicaps. However, voluntary organisations and housing associations have also provided for these groups, as well as being the main or sole providers for other client groups such as ex-offenders, people with drug or alcohol related problems, people with mental health problems, and women suffering domestic violence.

At March 1989, 60 per cent of Scotland's sheltered housing places for elderly people (excluding the private sector) was provided by local authorities and new towns; 7 per cent by Scottish Homes and 34 per cent by a variety of housing associations (Scottish Development Department 1990). Within Strathclyde, there are 19 district councils, 25 housing associations and Scottish Homes, all providing sheltered housing for elderly people, and over 70 agencies providing supported accommodation for other groups (Strathclyde Regional Council 1989a and 1989b). Most housing providers have some houses adapted for people with disabilities, but individual needs and preferences are so varied that there is general difficulty in matching people with disabilities with suitable adapted housing in the right place.

In some ways, this diversity of service providers allows flexibility to respond to local need, and scope for developing close ties and referral arrangements with local ethnic minority organisations. However, there is little evidence that such arrangements are being established in practice. In other ways, the diversity of providers creates additional problems. It is harder to find out about small voluntary agencies and housing associations, and what they do. There are no central registers nationally or locally for pooling information about applicants or about vacancies, so separate applications have to be made to a wide range of housing providers in order to maximise the chances of securing suitable accommodation. Given the lack of knowledge about housing providers among ethnic minorities this is a particular problem.

The Housing (Scotland) Act 1988 is intended to increase the role of housing associations and private landlords, with a corresponding reduction in the size of local authority housing stock. This will mean that a growing proportion of the housing stock will be owned and managed by community based resident controlled landlords, and great care will need to be taken to ensure the operation of equal opportunities by these organisations. Similarly, the NHS and Community Care Act is intended to encourage private and voluntary provision at the expense of the statutory sector. The Social Work Department will have a different role, assessing the needs of individuals and shopping around for the appropriate package of services from the 'independent' sector. This will increase the diversity of service providers, but at the same time it narrows access channels to any provision which might require Social Work's financial contribution, because it involves care costs which cannot be met by housing benefit and income support. The allocation of such places will in future depend on an assessment carried out or approved by the Social Work Department. This may reduce the scope for direct referral channels between providers and ethnic minority advice agencies. The government's White Paper which preceded the Act makes only a very glib reference to the specific needs of ethnic minorities (HMSO 1989), and a number of concerns about how the new provisions will operate in relation to black communities are raised in a recent article by Dutta (1990).

If housing associations and voluntary organisations are to take on more service provision, then much has to be done to improve their current performance in responding to ethnic minority needs. Analysis of house lettings made by Scottish housing associations in a six month period in 1987 showed that only three out of 1045 lettings were made to people from ethnic minorities (Scottish Federation of Housing Associations 1987). A survey of voluntary agencies in Scotland, carried out by the Scottish Council for Voluntary Organisations in 1987/88, concluded that their level of awareness of race issues is generally very low; that they have very little contact with or knowledge of ethnic minority groups; that they are not providing a service through their mainstream activities for black people including those with physical disability or mental health problems, elderly people or single parents; and that specialist services for ethnic minorities are under-resourced, hard pressed, and few and far between (MacLeod 1988).

Voluntary agencies and housing associations are not subject to the same duties as local authorities to promote equality of opportunity, under section 71 of the Race Relations Act 1976. However, the Housing (Scotland) Act 1988 (Section 56) extended this duty to Scottish Homes. It is to be hoped that Scottish Homes will implement this duty in the course of monitoring the activities of housing associations; by providing guidance and support to help associations operate equal opportunities; and by promoting initiatives to meet the particular needs of ethnic minorities. In the same way, statutory agencies could also be doing more to promote equal opportunities in the voluntary organisations to which they provide grant aid or other support, or from whom they contract services.

In England a considerable number of special needs housing projects have been established by black led organisations, mainly or solely for individuals from ethnic minorities. The Federation of Black Housing Organisations' 1989 directory of housing organisations controlled by black people shows organisations catering for the following groups: 36 for young people, (excluding those specifically for young women), nine for refugees, 17 for elderly, three for offenders, 10 for women, (including those specifically for young women), five for victims of domestic violence, three for mentally ill, 18 'miscellaneous or mixed' and 35 'general'.

The only examples of such initiatives so far in Scotland are Gryffe Womens Aid and SHAKTI, both running refuges for ethnic minority women escaping domestic violence; and SAHARA, a newly constituted group planning to set up temporary accommodation for young women from ethnic minorities who have left home. The SCVO report argues that direct service delivery by Scottish ethnic minority bodies is underdeveloped, while Strathclyde Regional Council has argued that service developments should be a joint venture undertaken in partnership with groups and organisations in the Asian and Chinese community (MacLeod 1988, Strathclyde Regional Council 1987: 50). The desirability and practicability of separate provision by and for ethnic minorities is a subject of considerable debate to which we return later in this chapter. However, experience to date shows clearly that the black housing movement in England has succeeded in creating significant numbers of places for ethnic minorities with a range of special needs, which the white housing movement in Scotland has failed to do.

The chapter now looks at some particular examples of special needs housing provision in relation to the needs of ethnic minorities.

Sheltered housing for elderly people

The most common and well known form of special needs housing is sheltered housing for elderly people. Within Scotland there are an estimated 44,000 sheltered housing places, and there is also a growing private sector. The standard model of grouped self-contained houses with a common room and an on-site warden is now being adapted and supplemented to take account of the particular needs of frailer old people and those with dementia. There is also a move towards less identifiable complexes in ordinary looking flats and bungalows. Ethnic minority take up of sheltered schemes is known to be extremely low. Anne Lear's study of housing associations in 1987 found only two ethnic minority residents in housing association sheltered projects for elderly people (Lear 1987). Research into ethnic minority housing problems in Glasgow found that there were very few ethnic minority applicants for Glasgow District Council's sheltered housing, although there were a growing number of Chinese elderly in one particular sheltered housing project (Bowes McCluskey and Sim 1989). They argue for the recruitment of wardens with an Asian language, and the recognition of racism among white tenants, which is even more difficult to cope with in sheltered housing, with its communal facilities.

More recent research into the role of housing associations in Glasgow found that 52 per cent of the interview sample had heard of sheltered housing compared to 93 per cent of the control group (Dalton and Daghlian 1989). Once the nature of sheltered housing had been explained, 83 per cent thought it would be useful to have sheltered housing for elderly people which catered positively for their cultural needs, and 29 per cent thought that there should be separate projects for different cultural groups. In particular, two-thirds of the Chinese sample wanted separate provision. This is a particularly pertinent issue among elderly people, many of whom are unable to read, unable to speak English, and have not developed many links outside their own cultural group. Fifty-nine households had elderly relatives living in Glasgow, of whom 14 lived alone. This shows that the conventional view of elderly people living together with their families in an extended family household is not always true. It is not clear how far this reflects preferences, or whether it is a result of the shortage of large houses, or the inability of younger families to meet the expense of accommodating their parents.

Supported accommodation for other client groups

Supported accommodation ranges from individual flats with visiting support workers to residential care with full time staff present 24 hours a day. Some projects are run on a fairly communal basis, and some even have shared bedrooms. Some projects have a temporary function, such as Stopover which provides emergency accommodation for young homeless people, drugs rehabilitation centres, or training flats to acclimatise people leaving long stay hospitals to living in the community. Other projects provide housing and support for as long as it is needed, in some cases on a permanent basis.

A survey of supported accommodation in Strathclyde for groups other than elderly people revealed a total of 2392 places, provided by a wide range of agencies (Strathclyde Regional Council 1989c). A small survey recently carried out by Maurianna Smith for Integrate collected information about 28 of these projects run by voluntary organisations for a range of client groups in Glasgow (Smith 1990).

Only nine of the 28 projects said they kept records which enabled them to identify and count up the number of people from ethnic minorities who applied for places, or those who obtained places. The majority of projects do not keep waiting lists. When asked how many people from ethnic minorities had applied over the past two years, 14 projects said none, four said they did not know or did not reply, and the remaining ten specified a number. The highest number was ten, in an agency with an estimated vacancy rate of 200 places per year. This agency has close ties with an international project which acts as a source of referrals. Only five of the projects received referrals from ethnic minority organisations and the range of such referral sources was tiny, particularly when compared to the number of ethnic minority organisations involved in advising individuals. This indicates a lack of awareness among ethnic minority organisations about the availability of supported accommodation. But there is also evidence that few people with special needs are using such organisations as a source of advice. Despite a willingness to collaborate in the study, these agencies found extreme difficulty in identifying individuals who might be prepared to talk to us about their special needs housing requirements.

Thirteen of the projects in the survey offered views about some reasons listed in the questionnaire for low ethnic minority take-up of supported accommodation services. The most commonly cited reason was lack of awareness among ethnic minorities of special needs housing providers: other common responses were communication barriers and insufficient demand. There is a widespread feeling, strongly expressed at a recent Chinese conference in Glasgow, that low take-up should not be attributed to lack of need but that instead service providers must address themselves to the twin problems of low awareness and inappropriateness of services. Of the seven individuals with special needs interviewed by Maurianna Smith, only two were satisfied with the services provided. The others were not receiving any statutory services and were relying on family or community support alone. Four of them expressed a need for respite care, and two for befriending services.

Only six of the 28 projects had an equal opportunities policy, although a further eight said they were thinking about it. It was encouraging that almost every project responded positively to the question 'would your agency be interested in following up ways in which special provision might be made [to respond to the needs of ethnic minorities]?' Eleven actually felt that the needs of ethnic minorities were in some respects 'different'. The willingness to change mirrors the findings of the research by SCVO in relation to some white voluntary agencies, and calls for an active training and information strategy to assist the implementation of equal opportunities. SCVO have made a start on this with their recent production of a training pack on racial equality (SCVO 1990).

It would be interesting to conduct a similar study among projects run by the Social Work Department itself. We do know that ethnic records are not yet kept and that therefore no monitoring is possible in relation to people with special needs approaching the department for access to residential services.

Other recent research into race and housing in Glasgow has also touched on special needs issues. Research into the role of housing associations found that 13 per cent of their sample of 210 had someone with chronic illness or disability in their home, and half of these thought their current home was not suitable. Eighty-three per cent of respondents thought that sheltered housing would be useful for mentally or physically handicapped adults, and 87 per cent thought that such provision should be culturally mixed, but catering positively for the range of cultural needs (Dalton and Daghlian 1989).

The Stirling University research into ethnic minority housing problems in Glasgow found that while 20 per cent had heard of old peoples homes, only between 13 per cent and 16 per cent had heard of other forms of special needs housing such as single people's hostels, Women's Aid refuges, or housing for physically disabled people. We do not know how many of these respondents had a correct understanding of the nature of the provision, nor how many knew how to apply for a place (Bowes McCluskey and Sim 1989).

Selection procedures

Selection procedures for allocating sheltered housing and supported accommodation places are fairly subjective and flexible, particularly in shared projects where judgements have to be made about how well people will get along together. It is easy to see how ethnic minorities can be excluded by such processes, partly through well-intentioned decisions that an individual black person would feel isolated and may well be victimised by fellow residents. Such situations present genuine dilemmas, which have to be resolved in ways which do not sacrifice the interests of ethnic minorities. Practical advice on this is offered by CHAR (Dutta and Taylor 1989). Rigorous monitoring is called for, plus urgent attention to realistic strategies for ensuring equality of access, deterrence of harassment, and support for minority residents. However, it has been recognised that the difficulties in achieving this are one reason for setting up specialist services in some cases (Strathclyde Regional Council 1987: 94).

Housing services to the individual's own home

Various kinds of special needs housing services are designed to give people the support they need to carry on living in their home without having to move to sheltered housing or some other specialised housing. These services raise several issues in relation to ethnic minorities, which require further investigation.

Dispersed alarms - also known as community or housing alarms - are alarm systems which can be installed in individual houses. Pull-cords or other devices enable the tenant to contact a central control point from which help can be sent. Alarm systems are run by some of the housing associations catering for elderly people, and by several social work authorities in conjunction with local housing departments. In addition Glasgow District Council has set up its own scheme with plans for a total of 30,000 alarms. Alarm systems raise particular problems, for instance language difficulties between tenants needing help and those responding to alarm calls. Additionally there is the question of how particular tenants of properties are selected for inclusion in an alarm scheme: for instance Glasgow District Council's pioneering scheme for 30,000 alarms will focus initially on council housing, which will exclude almost all ethnic minority elderly people living alone. However, GDC has undertaken to prepare promotional material for ethnic minorities on the benefits of community alarms as part of its Action Plan for Racial Equality in Housing (Glasgow District Council Housing Department 1989).

An interesting project was started in 1987 in an area of Southampton where 80 per cent of the population are Asian and an increasing number are elderly. The project employs an Asian worker who speaks several Asian languages as well as English. The worker has also become involved in community development work on issues such as an ethnic meals-on-wheels service (McTavish 1989).

Research would also be welcome into the areas selected for 'staying put' and 'care and repair' schemes which are intended to help elderly owner-occupiers adapt and repair their homes by providing technical and financial advice, helping to find contractors and apply for grants. Such schemes would be particularly valuable to ethnic minorities, of whom disproportionately high numbers live in private sector housing. We do not know whether such areas include any with significant ethnic minority communities, or whether any particular provision is made to ensure take-up by ethnic minorities in these areas. Certainly it is to be expected that take-up of grants and loans by elderly or disabled people in private sector housing would be just as poor if not poorer than among the rest of the ethnic minority population (Bowes McCluskey and Sim 1989).

Similarly it is likely that people with disabilities within ethnic minorities do not make use of the mechanisms for obtaining aids and adaptations to their own homes. These arrangements are poorly understood among the disabled population at large and usually are triggered through existing contact with occupational therapists or other relevant parts of the Social Work Department.

Specialist provision

We have seen that white organisations have performed poorly to date in providing housing and support for people's special needs. In England and Wales, we have seen that discontent with this situation among ethnic minority groups lead to the formation of black led organisations, specifically aiming to make direct provision where the white organisations have failed. This was facilitated by two complementary Housing Corporation strategies: the hostels initiative which has provided the main financial framework for special needs housing; and a specially ear-marked budget for establishing new black housing associations. Since 1976, 58 black housing organisations have been registered with the Housing Corporation, and the majority of these cater for special needs groups (Black Housing April 1990). The framework for the development of black led housing organisations is not so favourable in Scotland. Scottish Homes, and its predecessor the Housing Corporation in Scotland, has never favoured the setting up of separate black housing associations, and neither has the Scottish Federation of Housing Associations. The various pieces of research referred to in this chapter suggest a general consensus among ethnic minorities that it is preferable to develop provision which does not segregate people on the grounds of either race or special needs. The most notable exceptions to this are women leaving the parental or marital home, and elderly people, particularly among the Chinese community: for these groups it is argued there should be a choice between specialist projects or equal access to mixed provision which takes account of cultural needs. However, it is possible that growing impatience with the failure of existing white organisations to respond to ethnic minority needs, and to involve ethnic minorities in the management and running of services, will lead to growing support for setting up black led organisations. It may be that in Glasgow current initiatives, largely arising from the housing associations research, will accelerate the responsiveness of housing associations to ethnic minority needs. In addition, Scottish Homes has funded a PATHWAY scheme, run by SHARE (Strathclyde Housing Associations Resources for Education), which seeks to help unemployed individuals from ethnic minorities and other disadvantaged groups obtain training and access to the housing employment market. At the same time, there does seem to be scope for existing ethnic minority organisations to develop direct services, particularly in the context of an expanding voluntary sector under the new community care arrangements. These developments could happen in parallel with improvements within white organisations.

Conclusion

Some issues which have been highlighted in this chapter are as follows. Firstly, the scale and nature of special needs among ethnic minorities are largely unknown. Secondly, it is very hard to identify individuals with special needs among ethnic minorities. Thirdly, the planning of special needs provision takes no account of ethnic minority needs and wishes. Fourthly, there is no monitoring of ethnic minority demand for special needs provision, and finally, there is low ethnic minority take-up of existing provision for a variety of reasons.

Objectives which would be pursued in order to improve this situation are as follows:

i) increase ethnic minority involvement in committees and organisations which plan and run services for special needs, and consider the potential for black led organisations;

ii) identify the needs and wishes of black people with special needs and their carers, and then plan new initiatives and modify existing provision accordingly. Both Stirling University's research and Glasgow District Council's current Action Plan for Racial Equality in Housing support the need for this (Bowes McCluskey and Sim 1989, Glasgow District Council 1989);

iii) integrate special needs and ethnic minorities within mainstream provision, but allowing for individuals to choose otherwise;

iv) publicise services and ways to apply, particularly given increased range of agencies under new housing and community care arrangements;

v) create the right access routes, including referral arrangements with ethnic minority organisations;

vi) create links between special needs and ethnic minority organisations, with a view to increasing their profile on each other's 'agenda';

vii) specify eligibility criteria for special needs housing projects, and monitor applications, acceptances and rejections; and finally,

viii) pay special attention to the management of shared projects and to residence agreements and staff contracts and training, to minimise discrimination, harassment and racist behaviour within special needs accommodation.

References

Age Concern 1984 *Housing for Ethnic Elders* London: Age Concern/Help the Aged Housing Trust

Athar M 1990 *Survey of the Asian Community's Housing Need. The Evidence* Asian Special Housing Initiative Agency

Bowes A McCluskey J and Sim D 1989 *Ethnic Minority Housing Problems in Glasgow* Glasgow: District Council Housing Department

Brailey M Daghlian S and Taylor M 1989 *Meeting Special Needs in the Community* Glasgow: INTEGRATE

Cranny K 1988 *The Lack of Provision for People with Special Housing Needs within the Black Community in Glasgow* Glasgow: Glasgow Special Housing Group

Dalton M and Daghlian S 1989 *Race and Housing in Glasgow. The Role of Housing Associations* London: Commission for Racial Equality

Dutta R and Taylor G 1989 *Housing Equality: An Action Guide* London: CHAR

Dutta R 1990 'Community Care and the Black Communities' *Black Housing* April: 4

Federation of Black Housing Organisations 1988 'Project Profile ASRA' *Black Housing* April

Federation of Black Housing Organisations 1989a *National Directory of Black Housing Organisations* London: FBHO

Federation of Black Housing Organisations 1989b 'Chinese Women and Domestic Violence' *Black Housing*

Glasgow District Council Housing Department 1989 *An Action Plan for Racial Equality in Housing* Glasgow: District Council, pp 17 ff

Griffiths R 1988 *Community Care: Agenda for Action* London: HMSO

HMSO 1989 *Caring for People: Community Care in the Next Decade and Beyond* London: HMSO

Lear A 1987 *Black Access to Housing Association Stock* unpublished diploma project University of Glasgow

MacLeod L 1988 *Irrespective of Race Colour or Creed? Voluntary Organisations and Minority Ethnic Groups in Scotland* Edinburgh: Scottish Council for Voluntary Organisations

McTavish J 1989 'Case Study 5: Hyde Housing Association' in Fisk M (ed) *Alarm Systems and Elderly People* Glasgow: Planning Exchange

Mama A 1989 *The Hidden Struggle: Statutory and Voluntary Sector Responses to Violence Against Black Women in the Homes* London: Race and Housing Research Unit c/o The Runnymede Trust

Scottish Council for Voluntary Organisations 1990 *Working for Racial Equality* Training Workpack Edinburgh: SCVO

Scottish Development Department *Statistical Bulletin January 1990: Housing Trends in Scotland Quarter ended 30th June 1989* Table 11

Scottish Federation of Housing Associations Feb 1988 *Who do we House: Survey of Tenants of Housing Associations in Scotland* Edinburgh: SFHA

Smith M 1990 *Ethnic Minorities and Supported Accommodation in Glasgow* Glasgow: INTEGRATE

Strathclyde Regional Council 1987 *Forward in Understanding* Glasgow: SRC

Strathclyde Regional Council 1989a *Sheltered Housing Schemes March 1988* Glasgow: Chief Executive's Department SRC

Strathclyde Regional Council 1989b *Strathclyde Region Database of Supported Housing and Hostel/Residential Care Establishments* Glasgow: Chief Executive's Department SRC

Strathclyde Regional Council 1989c *Special Needs Provision in Strathclyde* Report by the Chief Executive Glasgow: SRC

Ward L 1987 *A Descriptive Bibliography of Articles and Books on Black and Ethnic Community Mental Health in Britain* London: MIND South East

Chapter 6
Anti-racist perspectives in social work
Mono Chakrabarti

Introduction

Burke (1984) described racism as a system of ideas and ways of doing things which has enabled white British people to regard themselves as superior to black British people, not only in body but in mind. Out of this frame of mind institutions have evolved which have had the effect of transmitting attitudes and beliefs of racial superiority and practices of racial oppression from one generation to another. With regard to institutionalised attitudes and beliefs, racism poses the main challenge in Britain today, and in particular to social work in a multi-racial community, surpassing in importance unemployment and poverty among the black population because it is the cause of these social evils.

Social work is thus faced with a dilemma. On the one hand, the profession and its organisation are part and parcel of the process of institutionalised racism, with which the black person is at odds. Yet, on the other hand, the profession is fundamentally concerned to help the black person to adjust to this racist society, and to ensure as far as possible, that society does provide for his or her welfare. This dilemma has been succinctly expressed in a slightly different context by Younghusband (1970), who argues that, of all the professions, social workers are particularly closely engaged with individual and societal problems and are involved with the practical realisation of 'the great democratic ideal of liberty, equality and justice in all its complexities'.

Social work is practised and taught in different settings in formal and informal organisations, both large and small, and with diverse organisational goals, but the effect of racism on the black client is the same irrespective of the setting. The black perspective should therefore permeate the base of social work knowledge to the point of practice with the black client through to the organisation responsible for providing social work services. But for it to do so will require a different frame of mind and approach which will require an acceptance of the fact that black people are not immigrants, but settlers, that their histories are not just histories of the countries from which they have come, but the history that they have made under the most difficult and adverse conditions in this country itself. Then it will be possible to arrive at diagnoses of their problems more objectively and scientifically.

This chapter documents the general lack of response to the existence of a multi-racial society by social work departments in Britain. Examples of the type of issues that social workers must face are given in a discussion of interpretations of and policies and practices directed at black families particularly black children. I argue that training social workers to the standard required by CCETSW (1989) paper 30 is essential if an anti-racist social work is to develop; and note that current practices do little to achieve this. Certain crucial curriculum issues are highlighted, and I conclude that students require knowledge about the facts of racial disadvantage and multi-cultural Britain, skill to detect and evaluate scapegoating and an acceptance of the basic qualities of all human beings. The neglected issues of community care and back elders are raised to illustrate how these particular training items are essential. I note that social work management must bear a major responsibility for implementing anti-racist practice and, indeed for complying with current law.

Racism and social work

In its Annual Report, the Commission for Racial Equality (CRE) (1980) noted the failure of most social work departments to consider the implications of providing services in a multi-cultural and multi-racial society. In particular, it drew attention to an earlier (1978) report of the joint working party of the CRE and the Association of Directors of Social Services (ADSS). This had recommended the systematic review of social work departments' policies in order to examine the relevance of their services for a multi-racial clientele. The CRE noted that this had not met with a positive response and that few departments knew how far they were meeting the needs of black people or what these needs were.

Certainly, there appear to be grounds for suggesting that social work organisations and social work teaching departments of the higher eduction system have been slow to consider the need to change their practice in the context of a multi-racial society. There are two main reasons for this lack of response. The first is that the traditional social worker's approach may not be entirely appropriate for people of non-Western origin. The Central Council for Education and training in Social Work (CCETSW) paper, Values in Social Work (1976) has confirmed this point, by suggesting that the values operating in social work tend predominantly to reflect Western, European, Capitalist, Christian or humanist values, as realised in British institutions. In this perspective, special emphasis is given to a client's individualism, to his or her own right to self determination. In accord with this basic tenet of social work theory, the social worker uses the casework method to perform a facilitating role, enabling the client to reach his or her own decision about how a problem can be best resolved and then to act accordingly.

A second reason why social work has failed to adapt to multi-racial communities is that, on the whole, insufficient effort is made to identify unexpressed or poorly articulated need. In the case of black communities, for whom English language difficulties and unfamiliarity with social work create additional problems, social workers are required to make extra efforts to uncover social problems and social needs. Moreover, as Ahmed et al (1986) have suggested, there is a contradiction in social work practice between the individual pathology approach to white indigenous clients and, in the cases of Asian and

West Indian clients, the view that problems emanate from features within the black people's social and cultural background. By adopting the latter perspective, it can be argued, social workers see the problem as being beyond their influence or control and, in consequence, regard it as not requiring their intervention.

Establishing precisely which problems fall within the realms of social work creates difficulties, not only among social workers themselves, but also between social work and other welfare agencies. More recently, however, concern about differences of perceptions has focused not so much on inter-agency relations, but on the relationship between social workers themselves and their black clients. The possible perception by clients of social workers as agents of social control, may lead to difficulties, especially if the social workers are seen as purveyors of a dominant British culture and tradition. This difficulty has led Roskill (1979) to suggest that social work with black people should focus on the relativity of value systems and the extent to which these are culturally determined. It raises very difficult questions as to whose value systems should prevail - those of the social workers or those of clients.

Social work with black people also operates through two channels which influence client-worker relationships. Dominelli (1989) identifies these as exclusion and inclusion channels. The exclusion mode operates through a mechanism of limited access to service provisions from black people. For instance, it is now well documented that black people do not get their fair share of home helps, meals-on-wheels or places in residential or sheltered homes. The inclusion channel, or over-representation of black clients in the residential sector of social services, reinforces the already held view that black people are 'troublesome'. By taking a 'colour-blind' approach, social workers may deny black people's very special experience of themselves. The traditional view that everybody should be treated in the same way inevitably leads to inequality and injustice.

As has already been pointed out, black people suffer disproportionately from poor housing, low incomes and high unemployment, and have a a higher proportion of single-parent families. They are, therefore, proportionately more likely to be consumers of social services. Social services and social work departments have a duty under the Race Relations Act 1976 to try to eliminate racial discrimination. This means they should be implementing equal opportunities of employment for their own workers, as well as revising their policies, procedures and practices in relation to their delivery of services, to ensure that they are serving the needs of the black community, including black children and young people (Chakrabarti 1990).

In the past, social work departments either adopted the 'colour-blind' approach - maintaining that they treated all people equally - or argued that they were fulfilling their obligations, for example, by appointing a few black social workers or white social workers who had become specialists in the needs of ethnic minorities. Pressure from the black community itself has caused some departments to understand the inadequacy of these approaches and to begin to look systematically at race issues in social work. Pressure has also been growing for departments to do more to ensure that black people make full use of all their services, for example, by translating information leaflets, providing interpreters and publicising services through local black organisations. Scandinavian countries,

D

and in particular Sweden, guarantee all legal residents the right to learn their own language, culture and heritage since 1984, through the Social Services Act (Chakrabarti 1988). It has been argued that a variety of culture and heritage can only enhance and enrich Swedish society and a pluralistic perspective is the only relevant path to take to make a society civilised.

Tragically, even now in Scotland it is not possible to take formal school leaving examinations in any of the Asiatic languages, even though the English Boards have incorporated these languages for nearly 20 years. There still remains a view in Scotland that these Asiatic languages are not worth studying and this has given credibility to a false social situation.

Another factor that the providers of social work services very seldom take into account is the demography of the black population in this country. As with all other public service provision, a lack of understanding of the nature and distribution of black people will inevitably lead to wrong or inappropriate policy formulation, which in turn will produce more dissatisfaction and injustice. For example, in the UK nearly 45 per cent of black people are under 15 years old, compared with less than 25 per cent of the UK population as a whole. At the other end of the age structure, only a small proportion of black people - about 10 per cent - are over retirement age - the overall national figure being about 19 per cent. However, this particular situation will start changing dramatically towards the end of this century, and it appears that very few public institutions are anywhere near taking this demographic factor into serious consideration within the context of relevant policy formulation.

The majority of black people in the UK reside in inner city areas, in poor quality houses with inferior amenities. Alienation and a propensity to small-scale delinquency are the likely companions of such living conditions, and the high level of policing in inner city areas increases the probability that offenders will be caught. For economic reasons a very high proportion of black women are in some sort of employment. To take care of children in their circumstances becomes a real issue, which is likely to require intervention by social services and other agencies. This is especially so since the majority of these children many not be considered as a priority in local authority provision for under-fives, as they are not very often defined as most in need.

Black family and child care policies

A disproportionate number of black children are in the care of local authorities. It is estimated that 60 per cent of the children in care in inner cities in Britain are black (Brown 1984). Black children are more likely to be in care without the consent of their parents and to stay in care for longer periods than white children. Once again, separate figures are not available for Scotland because the issue of being black in contemporary Scottish society is not generally regarded as relevant in the gathering of information and statistics by the Scottish Office (statistical material is due to be published in 1991: its usefulness remains to be seen). It is not surprising therefore that social work has only recently begun to address the race dimension of child care policy, but in doing so, it seems to have taken on board the anthropological and sociological explanations of three decades ago.

It was not until 1967 that Fitzherbert made the first contribution to multicultural social work. Using an anthropological perspective similar to those of the late fifties, she set out to assist children's officers 'to help people of very many different cultural backgrounds at a very different stage of assimilation into the English way of life', and thereby produced 'a comparatively short, straight-forward account of West Indian family life ... linked to the particular kinds of problems confronting them ... and social services' (Fitzherbert 1967:7-8).

Within the assimilation tradition, she mapped out a typology of family life among West Indians and applied it to all descendants of the Caribbean. To her, there were built-in cultural patterns within the West Indian family and the process of immigration and migration triggered off social consequences which the families could not have been prepared to meet. The disruption in the movement from one society to another precipitated the reception into care of back children. She identified five antecedent factors, and these were a tradition of unstable families; a large number of single mothers; Victorian child-rearing practices; a break-up of extended families through migration; and finally the housing and economic problems of first generation immigrants. Out of this kind of false analysis of black families and their social situation arose methods of social work intervention, such as the belief that social work agencies should provide a powerful casework service to black families and children. The advantage of care for these black teenagers was believed to be that they would become socialised and would assimilate the norms, attitudes and skills of white society, which would equip them to function 'more appropriately' than their parents.

Albert Memmi (1965), in a brilliant publication suggested another way of looking at the predicament of black families. He argued that as in capitalist society, where the bourgeoisie promotes a particular image of the proletariat, so in imperialism, the imperial powers promote an image of the people they dominate. In both cases, the images justify the presence of the oppressors and cover up their otherwise shocking behaviour.

The stereotypical view of the black family completely disregards the differential and healthy patterns of life and reinforces colonial prescribed views, which then become the conventional wisdom of the social work profession. These beliefs are firstly, that the family is characterised by instability; secondly that marital ties, legalised or not, are either weak links in the fabric of the family or too strong to break out. Either way, it is too dysfunctional. Thirdly, it is believed that this instability results in children coming into care; and that mothers are willing to allow this to happen. Fourthly, there is an assumed eagerness for British education and culture; and fifthly, parents are considered 'really odd'.

It is against this background of colonialisation and the colonialised, as seen through the eyes of Memmi (1965), that the framework brought to the analysis of the black and South Asian family should be seen. Because the family is always used as the unit of analysis to indicate the social health or ill-health of the individual, the family or society, any false conceptualisation necessarily results in serious consequences for the under-standing of the dynamics of the family. In multi-racial social work, it is axiomatic that the social history of the family becomes the starting point of social work intervention. In the absence of a coherent body of knowledge grounded in a trans-cultural understanding, negative stereotypes are likely to be reinforced over time. The subsequent effect is the construction and implementation of social policies anchored in the assumption that the black family is disorganised and unable to provide a social environment with the psychological and social resources necessary for the healthy rearing of black children. In fact, the family patterns, lifestyle, child-rearing practices, and attitudes of black families have developed out of a unique experience of differential power, and cultural, racial and historical configuration. The pattern which emerged was therefore born out of exigencies predicated on survival skills, developed against a host of hostile forces, the most prominent being racial disadvantage.

Similarly, the situation of fostering and adoption of black children is increasingly becoming more problematic. This is partly due to the inflexibility of social work departments, whose strict requirements concerning accommodation and amenities prevent many black parents from qualifying as adoptive or foster parents. Some black people feel that placing a black child with white parents can, and does, cause identity problems for the child, in that white foster parents can never fully understand a black child's experience of racism. Similar problems are experienced when black children are placed in local authority residential institutions where the staff are likely to be predominantly white.

What kinds of families should be provided for black children is a continuing subject of debate. One of the questions is whether black children should only be placed with black families, or whether local authorities should encourage trans-cultural placements. The research evidence regarding the latter approach is far from conclusive. The idea of trans-cultural placements is based on the assumption that human needs are broadly speaking the same and that, in genuine human relationships, colour differences are irrelevant. Those who oppose this line of argument challenge the view that it is possible for white parents to help black children to cope with discrimination and prejudice, and contend that it is impossible for a black child to develop a relevant sense of identity in a white home.

The National Association of Black Social Workers in America puts forward the latter view very positively (Cheetham 1982:78-79).

> Black children must not lose their cultural identity by being reared in a white home. Advocates of trans-cultural adoptions have tried to negate the importance of ethnic and cultural identity and have stressed 'human identity'.
> While it is true that all people have basic common human needs, it is also true that, in a race conscious society like the USA, black people are constantly judged by the colour of their skin and racial background and all the negative stereotypes that have been attributed to that colour and background, and not by their 'human identity'. It is imperative that black children learn that there are cultural differences between black and white, and that black culture provides a viable positive way of life .... Black people are now developing an honest perception of this society; the myths of our assimilation and inferiority stand bare under glaring light.

It is reasonable to conclude from this debate that a sense of positive racial identity is important; that it is desirable to seek to recruit foster parents from every ethnic group; that black children in care have special needs which must be met sensitively; and that white parents engaged in trans-cultural fostering and adoption require specific forms of guidance, help and support (Cheetham 1982).

Black community groups have maintained that the high number of black children in care is the result of racism (intentional or unintentional) on the part of social workers, who fail to understand and respond to differences in the way in which black families function. Social workers, it is said, often underestimate or misunderstand the ability of black families to raise their own children. Evidence that this may be the case comes from a survey carried out in South London in 1981-82 (Small 1982). This survey found that social workers and black parents usually had very different views on why a black child had been taken into care. It also concluded that black families received a poorer service than white families, once they became known to the Social Services Department. More than a third of black families waited over four years before being allocated to a social worker, compared to a quarter of white families; black families experienced higher levels of turnover of social workers and 50 per cent of black clients had received no services to help the families cope and prevent admission to care, compared with 29 per cent of white families.

There appears to be an accepted wisdom that black prospective parents are unwilling to come forward or apply to be carers. But what is not commonly understood in the social work profession is that, unless a carefully prepared strategy is adopted for the recruitment of potential black parents, then there will not be any positive response. The traditional approach in the recruitment of foster parents is simply to put an advertisement in newspapers. This strategy has failed repeatedly when dealing with groups of deprived people. As has been demonstrated in a project jointly run by Lambeth Social Services Department and Independent Adoption Services, it is possible to encourage and recruit black people as carers (Arnold and James 1989). Careful thought is needed regarding the selection and preparation process of prospective black parents, the rules and regulations of the agency, and the nature of the advertising campaign. this point has been highlighted by a number of publications throughout the 1980s.

Triseliotis (1980) suggested that social workers are ill-prepared to take on board the issues of the manifold disadvantages suffered by black families and their implications for fostering and adoption policies. Ahmed (1980) has demonstrated by sustained research that black families do not need an unimaginative and ultimately alienating approach from casework agencies, which apply old fashioned and often inappropriate criteria in assessing potential adopters. She went on to say (1980:305)

> ... specialism may be necessary for social workers involved in fostering work with racial minorities (or maybe) opportunities for social workers to develop contact with members of the minority communities other than client groups.

Social work education and training and black people

The race dimension in social work education is fragmentary and incomplete, often superficial and inconsequential, and varies from region to region. According to Naik (1990) there appear to be three approaches to the race dimension of social work education and training. The first approach is the technicist model. It emphasises equality of opportunity for all students and is concerned at the achievement of black students. Curriculum change is seen as improving basic skills but within a compensatory approach.

Second, there is the moral perspective approach to curriculum building in social work. This perspective aims to reduce prejudice and discrimination and to replace it with a positive attitude. The emphasis here is on materials and the use of literature to initiative student discussion and sensitise them to the race dimension.

The last approach is what he calls the socio-political perspective, which is by no means universal or even present on social work courses. It implies a shift in value consensus in society to the belief that a plural society of relatively separate but equal groups will emerge. Those committed to the idea may wish to permeate the whole curriculum with a multi-cultural emphasis and may offer their students skills with which to assist their clients. As a long-term goal, those who support this approach emphasise the identity, needs and aspirations of the minority groups.

Of late, most educationalists have begun to realise that a multi-cultural approach, as well as anti-racist perspectives, are to be taken on board when considering social work education and training. Because multi-cultural social work on its own cannot open up the social work educational system, unless it challenges the present procedure's dominance, it remains ineffective without an anti-racist thrust. Similarly, anti-racist social work education remains ineffective unless it is given a well-conceived curricular content. If it adopts overwhelmingly political objectives, it risks forfeiting the autonomy of the teaching institution.

Both groups are also beginning to realise that, by engaging in ideological rhetoric, they are failing to get down to the tasks of understanding the complexity of the social work education system, examining the experimental and research evidence, and devising effective ways of evolving a non-racial social work education system. Because multi-cultural education is essentially 'social democratic', it fails to attend to structural inequalities in society, and masks the dynamics of race, economics and political power, and how and why minority groups are disadvantaged in relation to dominant groups in society. What is needed, it could be argued, is the teaching of various subjects in social work within a clearly stated anti-racist framework.

Views of black communities in Britain range across the whole spectrum of opinion on race issues. Some black people argue that Britain cannot and should not accept the black communities and urge their repatriation. Others contend that such a step is undesirable and would like to see the black communities fully integrated into British society. However, they differ, like the rest of the country, as to what integration actually means, and what is involved. To some black people, integration implies assimilation, understood with its strict sense of obliterating the cultural identity of the respective black communities and requiring them to adopt British values and practice. Others take integration to involve the creation of a plural society in which the black communities are free to retain their cultural individuality, consistent with the demands of law and order.

This emphasis on cultural diversity raises the question of what forms of diversity should be tolerated and even encouraged, and those where uniformity should be insisted on. Almost every manifestation of cultural diversity, from diet, dress and language to marriage tradition and the socialisation of children, is potentially relevant to these issues. These views, in turn, shape the main features of social work educational policies.

The first model is one of integration and assimilation, influenced by a belief that the black community should be integrated into the Western way of life. Integration is regarded as positively beneficial to the black community as they could be assimilated within the service structure.

The second model is one of cultural diversity, in which social work practice and education would be enhanced by knowledge of the culture of black communities. This model leads to the development of cultural models designed to inform social work professionals about the 'family patterns' of their black clients. But it has unwittingly reinforced the prejudice of practitioners and narrowed their perspectives with cultural stereotypes. It is, in fact, a cultural deficit model based on the process of problem orientation with the 'problem' invariably placed within the culture of the black community.

Recently, awareness of the need to focus on social work policies and practices, and to link them with multi-ethnic practice without the damaging effects of cultural stereotyping, has developed. Attention has also been given to providing services to black communities without discriminating effects. Yet, the influence of the integration and assimilation model still persists in social service structures and operations, with the result that this ideology still determines this approach. As a result of this debate, it has been argued that a relevant model for social work education and training is neither 'assimilation' nor' cultural diversity', but that of a pluralistic society based on 'race equality'.

Pluralism means, in the context of social work education and training, the acceptance of black people as full members of British society, equally entitled to the liberties and privileges enjoyed by the rest of the community. Such a concept requires three prerequisites. Firstly, black people should enjoy full equality in legal, social, economic and political matters; secondly, their distinctive cultural identity should be respected and provision should be made to meet basic demands; thirdly, nothing should be done to denigrate black people's humanity or to undermine their self-respect, or to make them feel that they are less than full human beings, living at the community's sufferance.

Given the conceptual model, what is the role of educator in social work? Is he or she to prepare students as agents of control and conformity to social standards? If so, whose standards? Is the task to bring about social change? Should social workers manipulate the norms? What should be the value-system, practised as taught by the social worker within a pluralistic society?

At a general level, it could be argued that the main theoretical subjects of psychology, sociology, social policy and social work methods lack relevance to a pluralistic society because the trans-cultural dimension and the socio-economic and political dimensions are missing. It could be further argued that teaching and practice in social work are geared to the concept of a uni-racial rather than a multi-racial society. The uni-racial society concept suggests that Britain is a white society upon which certain marginal groups have been appended, with the consequence that there is a predominant value system based on 'whiteness', in which other cultural characteristics can be tolerated or accommodated as long as they do not threaten white values, norms and mores.

At the other end of the spectrum, the pluralist view of society recognises the existence of opposing interests and that a different distribution of power and resources can be protected and enhanced. The structured origin of such group conflicts manifests itself in social roles which are endowed with expectations of domination or subjection. It appears that social work has embraced the theory of integration as its ideology, based on the concept of a uni-racial model of society. The black community regards British society as made up of different racial groups. The black community thus interprets events within the framework of a conflict and coercion theory and the social work educationalist and the practitioners interpret the same events within a consensus theory. This divergence implies that the two (the practitioners and their subject) adhere to different sets of premises. This two-party model implies different ways of viewing and relating to social work. A practical manifestation of social work's perspective, therefore, is the exclusion of conflict strategy from the professionals' knowledge base and techniques. Practitioners who engage in or actively encourage the use of conflict are denounced as performing illegitimate professional roles.

The present 'system' (Ouseley et al 1980) comprising managers, tutors of social work courses and administrators who run these institutions is not only powerful, but its attitudes, actions and practices ultimately distort the student composition of the course structure and its underlying ideology. English language is also used as a powerful means to obscure primary issues (Ohri 1982). This is particularly so in relation to racism. For example, white racism is not highlighted as a primary issue; instead the emphasis is placed on the phenomenon of racism and stress is laid on the victims of racism as a phenomenon for study rather than emphasising the structural dynamics of a fundamentally racist society. The result is that racism is reduced to racial disadvantage and the question raised is how to address that inherent disadvantage as opposed to how to change the system using the strategy of anti-racism.

Curriculum issues and black people

Objectives of social work teaching can be defined in terms of the behavioral and content aspects. What are the ways of thinking, feeling, and acting that the student needs to learn to become an effective social worker in a multi-racial society? What knowledge content will the student be expected to understand? The content and behavioral aspects are so closely related that they must be defined almost as one process in developing the curriculum. In the behavioral model, the process starts by the selection of objects, goes on to the identification of learning experiences to achieve those objectives, and terminates with an evaluation of how successful the learning experiences have been. For evaluation to be positive and effective, the objectives must be behavioural, that is, precisely stated, observable and assessable. Learning experiences are interpreted as a purely instrumental function, and it is assumed that those which will lead to the achievement of stated objectives can be ascertained. The difficulty for social work educationalists is the translation into teaching terms of race related issues and their impact on social work practice.

Social work teaching requires a balance between how blacks view their place in British society and cope with its imperatives, in experimental rather than empirical mode on the one hand, and the research related material on the other. It must also be acknowledged that research related to black experiences, uses methodological and conceptual tools which are not rooted in, and informed by, a living contact with their subject matter. Until research can offer coherent and vigorous theoretical accounts of black experiences in Britain, which are theorised by blacks, the experiences of the black communities and black students on social work courses will have to be used in a positive teaching form, rather than be dismissed as lacking in empirical evidence. There are additional myths surrounding anti-racist practice which have acted as barriers to anti-racist and ethnically sensitive practice, for example - that such work is either 'too difficult' or 'too risky' or 'highly specialised' or too 'different'. Such myths and stereotypes only serve to undermine the confidence and competence of students, making them feel de-skilled and putting them off engaging in trans-cultural and sensitive practice. Black people are generally welcoming towards white social workers and are prepared to make allowances for possible ignorance about customs and beliefs, provided social workers are prepared to listen, try to understand, and learn. Black people are neither unapproachable nor too fragile to be patronised, avoided, or to be over-circumspect with in approach. Again, it is only through direct work experience and personal contact that the myths can be dispelled. No doubt ignorance about services and roles, and sometimes suspicion, are bound to be found among black people as a result of many negative experiences and oppression. Many of the skills used by social work students in their practice placement with their white clients have commonalities in work with black people and with other ethnic groups. Skills such as relating, listening, communicating, observing and starting where the client or group is, are common in work with most people and situations during a beginning phase. What is usually skilful work is the accurate assessment of need that takes account of different traditions, ways of behaving, and of value systems and, in the case of the black population, recognises at the same time the impact of racism and the values that sustain it. Without equating difference with pathology, interaction can be based on informed opinion that neither disregards differences, nor ascribes everything to these.

The underpinning, however, for an anti-racist curriculum could be based on the following areas (CRE, 1982):

(i) Cognitive (knowledge): All social work students should know the basic facts of race and racial difference; the customs, values and beliefs of the main cultures

represented in Britain; and the history of patterns of immigration and government policy towards it.

(ii) Cognitive (skills): Students should be able to detect stereotyping and scapegoating in what they see, hear and read; and evaluate their own cultures objectively.

(iii) Affective (attitudes, values and emotional sets): Students should accept and value the uniqueness of each individual human being; the underlying humanity we all share, the principles of equal rights and justice and the achievements of other cultures and nations.

Community care and black elders

Post-war consensus on community care existed largely at the level of political rhetoric and provides a good example of the symbolic use of language in public policy: 'Words that succeed and policies that fail' (Edelman, 1977). Underlying this precarious consensus was, on the one hand, ambiguity and uncertainty of purpose and, on the other hand, a power struggle between competing institutional and community interests.

In theory, the term 'community care' implies that help is provided by ordinary members of local communities, like friends, neighbours, or volunteers. According to Abrams (1977:6), it is the 'provision of help, support and protection to others by lay members of societies acting in everyday domestic and occupational settings'. The development of community care policy, however, puts stress on care 'in' rather than 'by' the community. In practice, therefore, community care became help and support given to individuals, such as children, people with physical and mental disabilities and older people, by professional and quasi-professional staff in non-institutional settings.

All major reforms or suggested reforms are guided by specific considerations over a timescale, humanitarian, ideological and financial. To understand the basis for the timing and content of the Community Care Bill, and subsequently the Act, one needs to examine three important issues. First, the demographic changes cannot be ignored: the elderly population will more than double by the year 2025. Second, the report Making a Reality of Community Care (Audit Commission 1986) stated that the primary focus for many community care policies was institutionalisation and was less concerned with meeting clients' needs effectively. Third, in line with its other policies, whether in the manufacturing or welfare sectors, over the last ten years the government has sought large private sector involvement in the care of the elderly.

The analysis offered above may lead to the conclusion that the alarm caused by this increased private sector role is not an issue for black elders. After all, it could be argued, what have they gained from the public domain? What is there to be gained? Is the issue about achieving a better share in the private sector, (referred to as the independent sector in the Act) or a change in the mainstream services in the public sector? The central emphases of the Act rest on the assessment of individual needs, the determination of care packages, consumer choice and self determination, and competition to ensure the provision of better services.

In the context of social service provision for black elders, the question of assessing individual needs and devising care packages assumes centrally that these recognised that black elders have entered the market for social care, and that the assessment, identification and provision of services can be carried out. Stereotyping, gatekeeping, organisational and direct racism effectively work to keep black elders out of the 'market'. In the analysis of market dynamics, the inter-play between demand and supply assumes that black elders are willing, able and can effectively express their demands for care provision, while the suppliers - that is the providers - can supply accessible, appropriate and adequate services to them. This is essential for the determination of care packages; assessing what is required, in what form, and who can supply it at a particular price. Will this be cost-benefit analysis work, at the purchasing, budgeting, forecasting or planning stage? Will they develop new services and re-distribute resources to increase the low or even zero base services from where black elders start? Regarding consumer choice and self-determination, again one assumes that this will not only be articulated by individual black elders, but that the case managers have the required skills and knowledge to translate choice into services.

Certainly, CCETSW's new Social Work Award, the Diploma in Social Work (CCETSW 1989) incorporates, for the first time, regulations on anti-racism as requirements for this qualification. It is also anticipated that anti-racism regulations will appear on the other two levels, that is Social Care and post-qualifying studies. It can only be hoped that social work education will provide newly qualified staff with some grounding in anti-racism and the capacity to work with black elders, but what is to be done with existing personnel?

Finally, there is the issue of competition. To engage in competition in the marketing of services, not only is information of the 'market' required, but also substantial skills to tender, contract, budget, plan and utilise resources. Hence, structurally, black voluntary organisations are the weak players in any competitive tender to provide for services to black elders at a competitive price to the social work departments.

The White Paper (HMSO 1989) only afforded 57 words, compared to 75 in the Griffiths Report (1988) to people from ethnic minorities. Meanwhile for black elders, the community care promises not only more of the same but perhaps a restrictive, chaotic and ever shrinking welfare society - unless care managers are equipped and committed to black elders' needs; and black voluntary organisations are resourced to move from a weak to a competitive position in providing services to black elders.

Strategic management issues and social work provision for black people

In July 1978, a working party of the Association of Directors of Social Services in England and the Commission for Racial Equality produced a report, Multi-Racial Britain: The Social Services Response (ADSS/CRE 1978). The report made specific recommendations for the implementation of equal opportunity policies by all social services departments. One of its conclusions was that the response by social services departments to the existence of multi-racial communities was 'patchy, piecemeal and lacking in strategy'. Since the publication of this report, other research has been carried out into the delivery of services of black communities. In 1982, the British Association of Social Workers published guidelines for working in a multi-cultural society, in which it stressed the inadequacy of social services departments' practice of adopting a 'colour blind' approach to the provision of services.

In view of the lack of up-to-date information on service provision in social services departments, the Commission for Racial Equality (CRE) decided in 1988 to conduct a further detailed survey of local authority social work departments to identify progress made on the development and implementation of equal opportunity polices in the provision and delivery of services. This survey (CRE 1989) has identified that nearly two thirds of the 116 social work departments surveyed in England, Scotland and Wales do not have written equal opportunity polices to cover the delivery and provision of services to black communities. Of these, only 24 (34 per cent) submitted written policy documents. This is a matter for great concern, as most of the departments covered in this survey have a substantial black population. It was found that those departments which had equal opportunity policies in employment were more likely to have considered equal opportunity measures in the provision of services. A key issue raised by the survey is the need for a formal written policy, rather than simply a general intention to treat all service users fairly. It is argued that it is not good enough simply to have good intentions; what is needed is a specific written equal opportunity policy, the implementation of which can be systematically monitored and regularly revised.

In these circumstances, there is clearly a great deal of work to be done if local authority social work departments are to fulfill their obligations under the Race Relations Act 1976 and provide services free from racial discrimination. Equally important in a multi-racial society is that authorities carry a responsibility to provide services that are appropriate to all black groups of people.

The Act of 1976 contains many provisions that are directly relevant to social work managers in formulating their strategic thinking and planning in the delivery of service provision. The most important section of the Act in respect of service provision is Section 20, which makes it unlawful for anyone concerned with the provision of goods, facilities or services to the public, or a section of the public, to discriminate on racial grounds by refusing or deliberately omitting to provide them, or as regards their quality or the manner in which or the terms on which they are provided. This discrimination referred to may be direct, that is less favourable treatment, or indirect that is, applying a requirement or condition which has a disproportionately adverse effect on a particular racial group, and which cannot be justified.

Section 71 of the Act places a duty on every local authority to make appropriate arrangements with a view to ensuring that its various functions are carried out with the due regard to the need to eliminate unlawful racial discrimination and to promote equality of opportunity and good relations between persons of different racial groups.

Sections 37 and 38 of the Race Relations Act positive measures for the encouragement of employees who are members of a particular racial group to take up training or employment, where that racial group is under-represented. However, discrimination at the point of selection is not permissable under these sections of the Act. Similarly, Section 5(2)(d) of the Act allows the appointment of a member of a particular racial group where the holder of the job concerned provides persons of that racial group with personal services promoting their welfare, and those services can most effectively be provided by a person of that racial group.

Section 35 of the Race Relations Act makes lawful any act done in affording persons of a particular racial group access to facilities or services to meet the special needs of that person or that group in regard to their education, training or welfare, or any other ancillary benefits.

Under all the above sections of the Act, it is possible for social work management to take a strategic position in developing appropriate services for black communities, as well as ensuring that black people do get a share of employment opportunities in social work departments. For example, given the political will it is feasible to take advantage of Section 5(2)(d) in recruiting black employers to provide a sensitive and appropriate range of services to black consumers. A number of social work departments have taken this positive move, but a significant number of social work managers may not be aware of the potential of this particular section of the Act.

The Social Work (Scotland) Act 1968 also provides an opportunity to managers to take a strategic stance in terms of the promotion of welfare. Section 12 of the Act says that 'it shall be the duty of every local authority to promote social welfare ....' The word 'promote', it could be argued, requires an active involvement in encouraging others to determine needs. It involves proper and genuine consultation based on the principle of equality. The managers could, and perhaps should, consider entering into partnership with black communities in identifying the areas of concern. On the basis of information received, it should then be possible to develop policies which will be relevant and appropriate to needs of black communities.

It is a well established fact, as demonstrated by a number of studies, that often black people either do not know the range of welfare services that are available to them, and hence the very low take-up rate of social work provision (McFarland, Dalton and Walsh 1987), or that black people have little confidence in public agencies and their ability to provide a sensitive and unbiased service (Bowes, McCluskey and Sim 1989). In these circumstances, it is imperative that managers consider how best to intervene in order to be a responsible public service provider. In the short term, it has been suggested that an appropriate resolution could be for policy makers in social work departments to provide relevant and urgent support to the existing local black organisations who have already established confidence amongst black communities. It may mean offering financial support in developing community-based projects targeting black people. It could also take the form of seconding properly qualified and knowledgeable members of staff to working alongside, and with, black organisations. This course of action will enhance the credibility of a statutory agency and, as a by-product, will also create a resource within a department.

Another important area which requires strategic management thinking is how to use in-house training in a most effective way for the eradication of racial discrimination from social work practice. In the main, three developments can be charted on the current progress of training on combating racism. These are:

(i) Modified Race Awareness Training (RAT): In this there is a change in terminology to incorporate some of the 'buzz' words of anti-racism, with a 'softer' delivery of training. However, this approach retains the centrality of the individual, i.e. the examination of racism at a personal level with 'white people as the problem'.

(ii) Anti-Racist Training (ART) with RAT skills: This appears to offer serious analysis of racism based on power relations. It is expanded to include an institutional dimension. Action is stressed and strategies to combat institutional racism are promoted. The approach and skills of RAT are still retained through raising the consciousness of individuals whose personal attributes and behaviour are the prime focus.

(iii) Radical Anti-Racist Programme: This approach focuses on power relations; it locates the politics of racism in the context of the socio-economic and political life of people in society. It recognises inter-relationships with material forces, which also create class and gender relations and incorporates them in its understanding of exploitation and oppression.

'Race' awareness is deemed particularly attractive, plausible and relevant to social work because its traditions and values lie very much in 'seeing people as individuals'. The major problem with any type of anti-racist training is that it has been viewed and accepted as the panacea for eradicating racism from the system.

Conclusion

Despite three very important Acts of Parliament (1965, 1968 and 1976) passed to outlaw discrimination on the grounds of race, ethnic or national origin, any increase in tolerance amongst diverse majority and minority groups has been difficult to establish. The overall impression from various studies tends not to be optimistic, casting serious doubt on Roy Jenkins' view, expressed in 1966 when he was Home Secretary, that it should be possible to achieve 'equal opportunity accompanied by cultural diversity in an atmosphere of mutual tolerance'.

In the end, the effectiveness of social work can only be judged by its ability to produce 'good practice'. Racism in social work not only projects poor professionalism as far as black people are concerned; it also augments deficient service delivery to white people.

Note: In this chapter the term 'black' is used to refer to people of Asian, Afro-Caribbean, or other New Commonwealth origin or descent.

References

Abrams P 1977 'Community Care: Some Research Problems and Priorities' *Policy and Politics* 6

Ahmed A 1980 'Selling Fostering to the Black Community', *Community Care* 305

Ahmed S, Cheetham J and Small J 1986 *Social Work with Black Children and their Families,* London: Batsford

Arnold, E and James M 1989 'Finding Black Families for Black Children in Care: A Case Study' *New Community,* 15 (3) : 417-425

Association of Directors of Social Services and Commission for Racial Equality 1978 *Multi-Racial Britain: The Social Services Response* London: ADSS/CRE

Audit Commission 1986 *Making a Reality of Community Care* London: HMSO

Bowes A, McCluskey J and Sim D 1989 *Ethnic Minority Housing Problems in Glasgow.* Glasgow: Glasgow District Council.

Brown C 1984 *Black and White Britain: The Third Policy Studies Institute Survey* London: Heinemann

Burke A 1984 'Racism and Psychological Medicine', *International Journal of Social Psychiatry* 30(1)

Central Council for Education and Training in Social Work 1976 *Values in Social Work* CCETSW

Central Council for Education and Training in Social Work 1989 *Requirements and Regulations for the Diploma in Social Work* London: CCETSW Paper 30

Chakrabarti M 1988 'Social Welfare Provision in Sweden' in Ford R and Chakrabarti M (eds) *Welfare Abroad* Edinburgh: Academic Press

Chakrabarti M 1990 *Working with Children and Young People: Racial Prejudice* Unit K254, Milton Keynes: Open University

Cheetham J 1982 *Social Work and Ethnicity* London: Allen and Unwin

Commission for Racial Equality *1980 Annual Report* London:CRE

Commission for Racial Equality 1982 *Further Education in a Multi-cultural Society* London: CRE

Commission for Racial Equality 1989 *Racial Equality in Social Services Departments* London: CRE

Dominelli L 1989 'An Uncaring Profession? An Examination of Racism in Social Work' New Community 15(3):391-403

Edelman M 1977 *Political Language* London: Academic Press

Farrah M 1986 *Black Elders in Leicester* Leicester: Leicester Social Services Department

Fitzherbert K 1967 *West Indian Children in London* Occupational Papers on Social Administration No 19, London: Bell and Sons Ltd

Griffiths R 1988 *Community Care: Agenda for Action* London: HMSO

HMSO 1989 *Caring for People* Cm 844

McFarland E, Dalton M and Walsh D 1987 *Personal Welfare Services and Ethnic Minorities - A Study of East Pollokshields.* Glasgow: Glasgow College of Technology

Memmi A 1965 *Colonizer and the Colonised* London: Onogan Press

Naik D 1990 *'An Examination of Social Work Education within an Anti-Racist Framework'* Unpublished Paper - Lancaster Conference

Ohri H 1982 *Community Work and Racism* London: Routledge and Kegan Paul

Ouseley H et al 1980 *The System* London: The Runnymede Trust

Roskill C 1979 'A Different Social Work' *Social Work Today*, 10(2)

Small J 1982 'Black Children in Care' in *Good Practice Guide for Working with Black Families and Black Children in Care* London: Lambeth Social Services Department

Triseliotis J 1980 *New Developments in Fostering and Adoption* London: Routledge and Kegan Paul

Younghusband E 1970 'Social Work and Social Values' *Social Work Today* 1(6)

Chapter 7
Ethnic minorities and the
social work service in Glasgow
Jacqui McCluskey

The social work response

The historical legacy of racism has dominated and influenced the life experiences of black people in Britain. This racism does not only occur at an individual, personal level, but is also entrenched within the major institutions of our society. Social work, indeed, is not immune from its influence and practice.

Social work has been reluctant to tackle the inequalities and disadvantages faced by ethnic minorities and hesitant to accept the reality of the multi-racial society we now live in. The Association of Directors of Social Services Report (ADSS, 1978) was the first major document to criticise social work's response to ethnic minorities. They found that,

> Few departments have specifically and explicitly worked through the
> implications to social services of a multi-racial clientele
> (ADSS, 1978:15).

Unfortunately, according to research, only limited progress has been made since the report was published in 1978 (Young and Connelly 1981, Ely and Denney 1987, Dominelli 1989). Much of the progress has taken place in England, with very little in Scotland. The slowness of response in Scotland can be accounted for by additional factors, outwith the ones that apply country wide. It may be explained partly by the entrenched view that Scotland has 'good race relations' and that there is 'no racism here'. These statements are taken at face value by many agencies who prefer to believe them, rather than admit there are problems which they are not dealing with. Ethnic minorities' experience of racism and discrimination are, in the main, still being denied and dismissed under the veil of tolerance and acceptance of the Scots. The needs of ethnic minorities have, until recently, not been perceived as a priority. The expectation has been that existing services will meet their needs. There is a lot of time-wasting involved in the numbers debate, where many agencies and individuals argue that there are too few ethnic minorities in Scotland to bother about. Consequently it is expected that they will have to 'fit in' with the existing provision. Concerns are now being raised about the fact that a large and increasing section of the population's needs are not being met or else are being met inappropriately by social work services.

On a wider basis, part of the reason for this reluctance is to be found in the prevailing philosophy of the Welfare State and the professional orientation and context of social work. More important, perhaps, is the operation of institutionalised racism within Social Work Departments and the racism of individual social workers.

To treat ethnic minority groups as different strikes at the heart of the philosophy of the Welfare State. Ideas of different or separate provision for these groups contradict the universalistic principles that lie at the heart of contemporary liberalism, that all should be equal before the law and have equal rights to public facilities. It is argued that social work practice should be good enough to encompass all the range of cases and that, within social work, sufficient attention to cultural differences is guaranteed, because of the importance it attaches to the individual. In effect, the adoption of such universalistic principles has served to deny the cultural rights of distinct ethnic groups, resulting often in a de facto refusal to make any provision at all.

A major barrier to the development of policies and practices that allow effective provision of services to ethnic minorities is the operation of racism. According to the Race Equality Unit (1988:13),

> Racism permeates social services structures and all aspects of service delivery with harmful and damaging effects. Racism results in denying black people their welfare and rights and leaves white people with a distorted view of reality.

The application of general rules, derived in pursuit of fairness and equality can raise questions about indirect discrimination. For example, a rule that children of single parents should have first priority for day nursery places could discriminate against Asians, amongst whom there are few single parent families, unless it could be proved that such a criterion could be justified on non-racial grounds. Racism and prejudice can be manifest in judgements about different minority traditions. Social workers have considerable power in their reaction to different cultures which they may perceive as quaint, regrettable, eccentric or admirable. Until recently, there existed an assumption that recognition of differences would perpetuate them and that this was undesirable. There was also fear about arousing white hostility. As a consequence, social work did nothing to tackle often glaring inequalities and disadvantages, as this was seen as the safer course. Cheetham comments,

> Social work practice, if it is to combat racism, must therefore reflect the multi-racial society which pays for it and take positive account of its diversity. (Ahmed et al 1986:9)

Social work's response to ethnic diversity then 'has been characterised more by assertions of muddled principles than by experiment and practical action'. (Cheetham 1982a:4). Social work agencies assumed they could always adapt to changing needs but, as regards their involvement with ethnic minorities, this has not been the case. For too long apathy and inertia, to the point of racism, has been social work's reaction to distinct ethnic groups.

The study

While working with Asian families in the voluntary sector as a volunteer, and a social work student, I often heard these families airing their dissatisfaction and distrust with regard to social work and social workers. I was interested in pursuing further ethnic minorities' experience and perceptions of social work and its services. To date, too little has been done to establish an understanding of the specific needs of ethnic minority clients, as they are defined.

For this particular study I decided to concentrate on one area office situated in an area with a high ethnic minority population, which had been heavily criticised. As well as speaking to ethnic minority customers of this office, I also wanted to speak to social workers to discover their perceptions of the services social work provides to ethnic minorities.

According to Husband (1980) and Young and Connelly (1981), the major initiatives, innovations and expertise in social work with ethnic minorities are occurring at practitioner level, where the significance of our society being multi-racial has been grasped. Husband believes (1980:4)

> It is these individuals who in their work have begun to question the relevance of traditional social work provision, and of their personal professional skills, for an entirely new client population. It is they who are developing practice expertise through faltering innovation, through personal reflection, and through incipient networks for sharing and comparing this expertise.

By means of a structured interview, using a questionnaire, I interviewed eleven ethnic minority clients and twelve social workers, from May to August 1987. Due to the time scale and nature of the study, my research had to be limited and small-scale. However, I hoped to begin to show where problems exist, to highlight the main issues and to stimulate further discussion, debate and research on this area.

Before I look at the results of my study, I feel it is worthwhile to set them in the context of the local area and the overall response to Strathclyde Region Social Work Department.

The ethnic minority population

The area where my study was carried out is one with a large concentration of ethnic minorities. According to the 1987 Electoral Register, out of a total electorate of 9,567 in the area (defined by electoral ward) 1,026 belong to an ethnic minority. This breaks down into an electorate of 3 Afro-Caribbean, 97 Chinese and 926 Asians.

According to the findings of a local survey (Watson 1984), the Asian population is fairly well settled in the area with a continuing influx from elsewhere, especially England. With regard to religion, 82 per cent were Muslims, 12 per cent Sikhs and 5 per cent Hindu. 78 per cent of Watson's sample were under 40, with young families. The largest occupational group were shopkeepers, with many working in family businesses outwith the local area. The overall unemployment rate for the area was 23 per cent for males, compared with 15 per cent for Asians. One third of the homes visited contained at least one person not proficient in English. These were nearly all older people whom it was claimed by the families had sufficient to get by and were too old to learn.

The local area and its provision

The area where my study was completed is one of the forty five Areas for Priority Treatment throughout the Region. It is an inner city tenemental area of mixed local authority, privately rented and owner-occupied housing.

An Area Profile and Assessment Report (Strathclyde Regional Council 1982) identified that, according to caseloads and reports prepared, the workload generated in the area is much heavier than the average for Glasgow as a whole. The Report also examined existing provision and identified existing need. The needs of the relatively high proportion of under fives were served by nursery schools providing 190 places, one playgroup and two mother and toddler groups. In 1981, there was only one registered childminder in the area, partly due to restrictions imposed on childminding in tenements. The Report highlighted the need for more day care facilities, childminders, a Day Nursery and proper playing areas. As regards youth, there existed an intermediate treatment group work project, and youth workers and voluntary youth leaders. There were no youth employment projects, latch key projects or purpose built youth centre. The main issues identified in the Report regarding youth were those relating to education; lack of community and recreation facilities; unemployment; the need to carry out a joint assessment of the needs of young people, including the joint use of available facilities for social, educational and recreational purposes; and measures to reduce solvent and alcohol abuse.

Services for the elderly included two lunch clubs, a day centre, a street warden scheme, a number of meals-on-wheels services, and the 56 Home Helps working in the area. Concern was expressed at the increasing number of infirm elderly who could not be looked after by existing 'Good Neighbours' schemes. A need for sheltered housing and the need to develop further services by joint planning between Regional Council, Health Board and DSS were noted. The Report also highlighted that support was required for carers in families with chronically sick, disabled or elderly dependents.

With regard to the ethnic minority population in the area, the Report made some revealing comments. It began by identifying that the main issues related to the need to develop better links with, and services to, the local 'immigrant' community. The Report went on to claim that the mainly Asian community had tended to set up and operate its own system for dealing with family and 'community problems': but how did the Region know this? This claim was not based on a systematic survey of the needs of ethnic minorities but on assumptions based on stereotypical and racist beliefs. For example, the expectation of 'conflict' between the second generation and their parents, and also the problems of strict patriarchal authority were overstressed, to the neglect of other more serious problems. The lack of service use by ethnic minorities was highlighted and the fact that their contact with the Social Work Department seemed to be through crisis, for example, children unattended, wife battering and children coming before a Children's Hearing. While this type of intervention was held as necessary, the problem was as regards the one-sided view of the agency and the reinforcement of distrust. There was no questioning of why this distrust and reluctance to approach the Department existed.

There was no examination of the Department's own role or its insensitivity in meeting the needs of the ethnic minorities.

The Report blamed the minority ethnic groups poor socialising with the general population and lack of take up of services as the reason for their (Strathclyde Regional Council's) lack of knowledge of these communities. Very little effort had been made by the Social Work Department to redress their ignorance and to seek to adapt and change services for the ethnic minority population.

The discussion in the Report tended to emphasise that effort and change needed to be made by the ethnic minorities themselves; for example, with regard to elderly provision, it stated that appropriate provision should be provided for those who 'find difficulty in adapting'. Thus the expectation was that, other than the elderly, the ethnic minorities would adapt themselves to fit in with existing provision.

While some practical suggestions were provided, such as advertising services in various languages as a matter of policy, major change was seen as coming about through the training and teaching of the cultural background of ethnic minorities to social workers, and the recruitment of ethnic minorities onto social work courses. There was no discussion of the changes required in policy and services, or of the operation of racism throughout the Department. Within this climate, there was little opportunity for the needs of ethnic minorities to be identified and met by appropriate, effective and sensitive services.

The social work response in Strathclyde

The first major response from Strathclyde Region in considering social work with ethnic minorites, was Forward In Understanding, a report drawn up by its Social Welfare Services Sub-Group and published in 1986. This report made an attempt at highlighting the shortcomings and failings of the Social Work Department in relation to work with ethnic minorities. In particular, it examined the issues of training, employment, access, monitoring and services. The report has subsequently been criticised in many quarters for not going far enough, and it was widely seen as a cosmetic exercise. The Scottish Asian Action Committee (SAAC 1987) provided written critical comments on the Report.

The overwhelming conclusion of the Social Welfare Services SubGroup was that services were not widely known and, where they were known, people were deterred from approaching them. The factors identified in the Report as inhibiting the use of services were lack of knowledge of what was available, communication problems, and the inaccessibility and inappropriateness of certain services. The recommendations to inform the users of available services and to make services more accessible and relevant to the needs of ethnic minorities, were presented, according to the SAAC, as though they were new inventions. They believed the Region's intention was the creation of an image that the hierarchy of the Social Service Authority are doing their best to help the Blacks, but that it is the Blacks who are not responding' (SAAC 1987:3).

They further added that the uptake of services had been low due to the lack of attempts made by the Department to provide any suitable services for ethnic minorities.

Other issues addressed by the Report were the need to employ ethnic minority staff and to involve the community in the provision of services. While the Department claimed that a 'colourblind' approach had been adopted, the SAAC believed that, in reality, a racist approach was in operation.

One does not need to set up a Working Party to debate the reasons why black people do not use the services organised by the white establishment, i.e. seek help from whites. The answer is obvious: WHITE RACISM AND BLACK MISTRUST (SAAC 1987:2).

Rather than looking at the operation of racism in various manifestations in the Social Work Department, the Report merely commented that racism exists.

The SAAC summarised that the report, in effect, proposed to leave the 'complex matters such as policy making and monitoring to the whites' and to open doors to allow black people to join the system as object participants' (SAAC 1987:4). It had been hoped that the Report would have offered fundamental changes in existing policy which dealt with black people, but it was disappointing in this respect. SAAC and other critics saw the report as a clever public relations exercise on the part of Strathclyde Regional Council.

The Ethnic Minorities Project

As a direct result of the report, the Ethnic Minorities Project was set up, a joint Education and Social Work initiative. Along with the recruitment and deployment of ethnic minority workers in social work offices in areas with a substantial ethnic minority population, there were also workers placed within certain community education centres and home-link workers based at a number of schools. Within the office where I carried out my research, there were two Information/Advice workers from the Ethnic Minorities Project. The Project staff were to assist the Department in implementing a programme on service provision. It was pointed out that involvement of Project staff was not intended to result in the disengagement of other staff from contact with ethnic minority communities.

The project report aimed firstly to improve the uptake of existing social work services by increasing available information and publicity, developing outreach work (particularly cooperation with community-based groups and places of worship), adapting present provision, staff training and increased recruitment of black staff. To adapt present provision, the report stated that all aspects of local services should be examined to identify where immediate adaptations would make them more relevant to the specific needs of members of ethnic minority communities, for example, translation of welfare rights material, and the development of specialist provision of meals for the elderly with the Home Help Service. Staff training would involve the development and implementation of an anti-racist training strategy at all levels within the organisation involving, along with an anti-racist training package, the review and monitoring of all existing service training courses and matters. Secondly, the project aimed to improve future planning and delivery of services by introducing ethnic monitoring and developing opportunities for consultation in local service planning.

While there has been a response from Strathclyde Regional Council to attempt to improve services for ethnic minorities, it is quite telling that this response has involved the setting up of a separate 'special' project, marginal to existing provision.

The interviews

The sample of social workers I interviewed were in a number of different posts. There were six basic grade social workers, two senior social workers, one group worker, one community worker and two social work assistants. The qualified workers' experience ranged from one year to nine years, with average qualified time at six years. The length of time workers had been at the local office ranged from eight days to ten years, with the average length of time at the office three and a half years. All of the workers had had recent contact with ethnic minority clients. This contact was maximised on intake duty, with few workers carrying ethnic minority clients on their caseload. The main areas that workers were involved in with ethnic minority clients were Financial and the areas of Child and Family and Child Concern.

All the clients I interviewed were women. This perhaps reflects the wider trend within social work, where the preponderance of clients are female. Two of the clients were Chinese, seven Pakistani and two Indian. The length of time in the area ranged from four to seventeen years, with the average being nine years. Thus the sample of clients appeared to be fairly settled in the area. While the majority of families had, within their household, children under five, and three had youths, there were no elderly in any of the sample's households. This seems to reflect the generally youthful nature of the local ethnic minority population, with most of them at the stage of building families.

Most of the clients had approached the Department themselves for help, with their contact being fairly regular, ranging from weekly to monthly.

Before contacting the social work office for help, the main sources of help were identified as family and friends, with a few clients mentioning a community agency. Three of the clients did not initially approach the department for help. For two of these, social work involvement concerned suspicion of child abuse, and one client was contacted by the office in connection with a DSS problem. The most common reasons cited by the sample for seeing a social worker were Financial, Housing and Harassment.

Social workers' perception of ethnic minorities' needs, uptake of services and access

The majority of the workers believed that ethnic minorities had some different needs. Nevertheless, the tendency was to stress that, overall, their needs were not too dissimilar from white clients. Only one worker stressed that ethnic minorities' needs were different and that these were not being met by present provision and consequently required different services.

The majority of workers also thought that the uptake of social work services by ethnic minority people in the area was low. The main reasons for this were lack of clarity about social work's role, lack of knowledge about the Department's existence, and the belief that ethnic minorities prefer to seek help from their own communities. While the workers saw that the low uptake of services was partly social work's responsibility, there nevertheless still existed the notion that ethnic minorities 'look after their own' and thus do not require social work input.

To gain some further information on the access to the office by ethnic minorities, I decided to carry out a manual check on the intake record book. The month of July 1987 was picked as it was the most recent month for which information was available. This book gave details (name and address) of the person making the appointment to see a duty social worker, reasons for referral and the outcome. By means of identifying ethnic minority surnames, I drew up figures. While I am aware this method is not totally reliable, hopefully it will provide an indication of the numbers of ethnic minorities approaching the office.

From the total of 101 people who approached the office through the intake system, 27 (26.7 per cent) were identified as belonging to an ethnic minority group.

Table 1 lists the reasons for referral (categorised by the office), along with the numbers of people from ethnic minority groups seeking help.

Table 1: Ethnic minority clients and reasons for referral at the social work office (July 1987)

Reasons for referral	Number	Reason for referral	Number
Court	1	General welfare/family welfare	6
Multiple problems	1	DHSS	5
Homeless	2	Rent arrears	1
Child benefit	1	Gas Board	2
Nursery provision	1	Accomodation/housing	1
Children unattended	1	Concern re. children	2
Failed to attend appointment	2	Information sent to office on person leaving prison on probation	1

(Total = 27)

Out of the 24 who actually kept appointments (two did not attend and one referral was a letter from prison), no further action was taken on eighteen, two involved filling in forms and then no further action, one went on the waiting list (Family Welfare) and three were allocated to social workers. The three who were allocated came into similar categories: two General Welfare and one General Welfare/Respite.

While it could be argued that this is an encouraging number, as it reflects the proportion of ethnic minority people in the area, this should not be taken at face value. As discussed earlier, due to the disproportionate disadvantage and discrimination faced by ethnic minorities in this country, in general we would expect them to have more need for social worker services, but this is not reflected in the figures. The intake numbers do not reveal whether there is an on-going contact with the office, nor do they reveal those who drop out and do not return after they have initially approached the Department. Horn (1982) found that when Asian clients approached social services departments, they were quickly discouraged by language and communication difficulties, they found the services offered were culturally inappropriate and they would use the department only with extreme reluctance in an emergency.

Jackson (1979) carried out a survey in Bristol, examining the use made of the social services department of ethnic minority clients. He found a very small number of referrals of Asian clients but warned against assuming that this meant that the Asian communities were providing an effective informal welfare support system for themselves:.

> The low rate of Asian referrals may reflect a process whereby Asian welfare problems are not so much being organised into an internal welfare system, but merely being organised out of external welfare systems, such as the social services department (Jackson 1979:21).

He identified that the social workers were concerned with providing relevant services to ethnic minority clients, but were hampered by a lack of clear-cut guidelines, formulated at management level, for meeting these clients' needs. He also commented that the key to maximising accessibility lay in increasing the relevance of the service. Jackson concluded,

> At the very least, the survey demonstrates that a procedure needs to be established in social services departments whereby ethnic client needs can be systematically determined and fed into the organisation, at management level (Jackson 1979:23).

Service Provision

a) Pre-school provision

Seven out of the twelve social workers thought that existing pre-school provision was inappropriate for ethnic minority children. The clients echoed this view with ten out of the eleven saying that it was not suitable. The two most common reasons given for this were lack of ethnic minority staff and that the provision did not meet the needs of the children. Comments echoed a common feeling that these services were for white people and that they themselves were not made to feel welcome when they used the provision.

The four main changes that the social workers identified as required to improve services for ethnic minority children were the employment of more ethnic minority staff, extensive in-service staff training, changes in admission criteria to increase ethnic minority access, and the provision of resources to encourage self-help initiatives.

The changes which the client sample wanted to see for pre-school provision were the adaptation of existing provision to meet the needs of ethnic minority children, services run by ethnic minority workers for ethnic minority children, more staff training and for the ethnic minority community to set up their own provision.

McFarland et al's study based in Glasgow (1986) identified rather similar needs and recommendations in relation to under-fives services for ethnic minorities. Firstly, they found that the need for nursery and playgroup facilities was great despite some existing provision. They recommended that there be an increased recognition of the vital role of pre-school provision for women and children. Secondly, they identified little enthusiasm for child minding. Consequently they recommended that playgroup/nursery provision must continue to expand. Thirdly, they found a need for staff in under-fives services to be fully familiar with different cultural backgrounds. They recommended that facilities should be staffed by mainstream workers from all ethnic groups.

My sample expressed a need for pre-school provision and this need is present throughout the whole of the ethnic minority population. It is a need which is not being met. According to Osborn et al (1984), three-quarters of West Indian and nearly one-third of Asian mothers are employed outside the home at some period during their children's pre-school years, compared with 45 per cent of mothers in the general population. A higher proportion of ethnic minority mothers say they work from economic necessity. Also, nearly one-third of West Indian households with children under 16 are headed by a single parent, compared with one-tenth of similar white households. Contrary to assumptions, five per cent of Asian households are also in this position. Francis (1985) highlights the need for day care for Chinese under-fives; this provision -it is hoped would 'not only improve the care of children and reduce the isolation of their mothers but might discourage the sending of young children to be looked after in Hong Kong' (Francis 1985:23). This provision could also help give Chinese children a familiarity with English and education. Ethnic minority families thus have a disproportionate need for day care, much of which is at present being met by poorest quality, lowest paid and often unregistered child minders (Mayall and Petrie 1983).

Most day care is not the best that could be provided, partly because of the strain on resources and staff and because of disagreements about its role. According to Ahmed (1986) it is rare to find day care establishments which reflect the multi-racial character of their environment and clientele. Misunderstandings and ill-feelings between staff and parents are common and racism flourishes. Nursery care, in particular, often takes little account of black children's needs and backgrounds. 'Colourblind' approaches are particularly common in work with children because many white people find it distasteful to make racial and ethnic distinctions between children, lest that should imply that some groups are treated unequally on racial grounds. Many black children are disadvantaged precisely because no account is taken of their culture or appearance and it is assumed that the most natural and proper way of conducting affairs is according to the norms of the majority white culture. It is necessary to employ more ethnic minority staff in the day care setting and to train existing staff with an emphasis on an anti-racist approach. Ahmed (1986:51) stresses the need to practise 'non-racist work with all children':

> A positive policy and practice on the issue of racism is as relevant in all-white groups of under-fives as it is in racially mixed groups. It is essential that the development of multi-racial and anti-racist practices should not be confined to nurseries with a black presence. When working with young children, whatever their ethnic background, and when the nursery is all white, it is important that nursery staff counter in all children the development of negative and racist attitudes.

b) Children in care

Five of the twelve workers had experience of receiving an ethnic minority child into care. Four of these workers placed the children in local authority homes, although these placements were regarded as unsatisfactory. The other worker placed the child with white foster parents and this was regarded by the worker as being appropriate. She commented that it was very good in terms of the child's welfare, but not in terms of cultural needs. It was felt by the workers that there was no residential provision appropriate for black children. One worker cited the case of three children taken into care, where the staff of the home were at a total loss. It was recommended that the children return home as the residential placement was assessed as being more damaging to the children than the home context from where they were removed.

Black children in care have special needs that stem from their 'race', colour, culture and position in British society. These needs are on two levels, physical and emotional, and are additional to the needs all children in care have. Ethnic minority children in care need to sustain a strong identity and, if placed in an environment where black people are held in low esteem or rarely encountered at all, the outcome could be marginal identity with the white community. If a child has feelings of resentment towards and rejection by his/her own community because of being in care, he/she needs to be able to express these and get them into proportion, with someone from the same background. While in care, ethnic minority chidren need the opportunity for continuity of ethnic identity:

> Some homes may need to develop a "multi-racial ethos", with links to the appropriate communities, and appropriate staffing, while elsewhere certain homes may appropriately meet local needs by having both staff and children from one ethnic minority group.
> (Ely and Denney 1987:139).

It is imperative that authorities have a clear policy about the placement of black children. There is the need, too, to record the ethnic origin of children in care, to provide the authorities with data as well as enabling a proportionate matching of ethnic minority staff to children. The number of ethnic minority staff in children's homes is small, and more should be recruited.

Ethnic minority staff could assist in enabling ethnic minority children to cope with racism and to maintain their cultural identity. They are also in a position to increase the knowledge and understanding of the cultural and social backgrounds of the children among the rest of the staff. Existing white staff need to recognize and be sensitive to the special needs of black children. According to Coombe (1986) anti-racist training is necessary for staff, including information about the minority communities. In order to provide a multi-racial home, establishments need to build up links with the black community.

c) Fostering and adoption

Confusion existed amongst the social workers with regard to the availability of ethnic minority families for fostering and adoption resources. Six didn't know, four thought there were none and two said there were. Eleven of the workers thought that more effort should be made to recruit ethnic minority foster/adoptive parents. However one worker believed that due to their 'tight-knit' family system, Asians would not accept their child being placed with another family. 'Forward in Understanding' (SRC 1986) identified the need for recruitment of substitute parents from the ethnic minority communities. The clients I interviewed had no knowledge about fostering and adoption services.

There are a number of factors that make for the under-representation of black families as adoption or fostering resources for black children in care. The application by adoption agencies of arbitrary criteria, relating to age, marital status, religion, health, infertility, housing, education and income, can tend to eliminate black applicants. Offices are seldom based in black areas and are staffed by white workers. According to Ely and Denney (1986:165)

> Research suggests that there is a lack of information about adoption within the black community, and suspicion and anger directed at social work agencies, who represent the power to remove children rather than to restore them.
> General disadvantage also places economic constraints on the ability of black families to adopt or foster.

The recruitment of black foster or adoptive families requires a policy decision to do so, as a precondition for the allocation of appropriate resources. Thus authorities who have made no such policy decision have, in effect, made a deliberate policy decision to place black children with white foster and adoptive parents.

The placement of black children with white families is a contentious issue, arousing a lot of debate. According to Small (1986:86)

> If Britain was not a racist society, transracial adoption would not be an issue; but as long as race relations continue their current path, transracial adoption must be an area of concern. Since the aim of adoption must always be to provide a child without parents with an environment which will foster normal development the commitment must be to the child, not to the parents or to the agency.

Gill and Jackson's study (1983) found that the black children placed with white families they encountered gave every indication of living happily with their family and friends. But these children lacked a sense of who they were in terms of racial identity; they had been 'made white in all but skin colour', had no contact with the black community, and their coping mechanisms were based on denying their racial background. The Association of Black Social Workers and Allied Professions expressed their opposition to transracial placements in the following terms:

> The practice of transracial placements - whether it be for fostering or adoption - as alternative forms of family care for black children is perpetuating racist ideologies and therefore poses in ABSWAP's view, one of the most serious threats to the survival of the black community in particular and to the reality of the multi-cultural society in general. (Coombe and Little, 1986:172)

d) Youth provision

Seven of the social workers thought that existing youth provision was unsuitable for ethnic minority youth, with four of the workers not knowing. Comments included, 'There is no awareness of their culturally specific needs'; 'Black youth do not want mixed clubs - initially they need separate clubs staffed by black workers'. The needs of black youth in the area, identified by workers, were for clubs or groups and a place to meet. Additionally, workers believed there was a need for housing and employment, publicity to encourage take up of existing provision, youth work in their own culture, black workers, more mixed provision, and positive discrimination to encourage engagement and cooperation. Special provision for ethnic minority youth identified as desirable by the workers included the employment of ethnic minority workers, a self-run centre and an Asian girls group. A few of the workers were dubious about separate provision, arguing that mixed provision enables greater understanding.

None of the clients knew of any provision for youth in the area. As one woman put it, 'There is nothing for youth or younger children. Things exist for youth, but our youngsters cannot go because of the harassment they face'. There was a strong belief that what did exist was for white people and would not be suitable for ethnic minority youth. One client said, 'We are not told about the provision as it is for whites only and they do not want us to know about it'. The provision the clients saw as necessary to meet the needs of ethnic minority youth included sport/recreation clubs and a place for them to meet together.

According to Manning (1979) large numbers of black youth doubt the ability of white workers and institutions to respond to their needs. He comments that there 'will be black young people who are largely alienated by society because of a number of negative experiences they have already had at the hand of white racism'. Black adolescents, in conflict with their parents may be poorly served by social workers who often feel inadequate to tackle the number of problems which may be associated with dissatisfaction with the education system (CRE 1985, Swann 1985), with high rates of unemployment, and all manner of discrimination and harassment by the police (Smith 1981, Small 1981)

In general, low priority is given to youth by local authorities, compared to other responsibilities, and ethnic minority youth's needs in particular are neglected. In relation to social work with youth, there is a need for black workers. The Black Youth and Community Association (1982) and Manning (1979) strongly put the case for black workers to work with ethnic youth. There is discontent about the present youth provision and its inadequacies:

> In most areas the local services seem to have neither the organisation nor the potential for providing, either for the broad range of needs of adolescents in the inner cities, or for the special needs of black youth'. (CRE 1982:206)

e) Elderly services

The social workers believed that changes were necessary to existing elderly provision in order to make it suitable for ethnic minority clients.

It was seen as desirable to employ ethnic minority staff, to provide publicity for the services in different languages, to provide for religious and dietary requirements, to train existing staff, and to encourage development of self-help initiatives by the ethnic minority community. The issue of separate provision aroused a lot of debate with some of the workers totally against separate provision, believing that this increases segregation. Others identified that many ethnic minority elderly will want to go to their own establishments and that they should have separate provision if they want it. The clients perceived existing provision for the elderly as unsuitable for ethnic minority elderly. Responses included the comments 'There is nothing for Asians', 'I do not want to use white services', 'These are only for white people'.

These replies were similar to those mentioned under the Youth section (above) and are reproduced in SEMRU's (1987) Lothian study. SEMRU (1987) found from the interviews with their ethnic minority sample that clear feelings were expressed about the Social Work Department being only for white people, and that it stereotyped black people to their detriment. SEMRU state (1987:68)

> The social work services are considered to be meant for the white population, not for black people. Social workers are totally ignorant of ethnic minority people's cultural and religious needs.

The provisions that the client sample wanted for ethnic minority elderly were 'existing services adapted to meet the needs of ethnic minority elderly' and 'specialist services for ethnic minority elderly'. Additional comments included the desire for the home help service to be expanded, the provision for white elderly to be similarly provided for blacks and the need for provision for elderly to meet together.

It was clear that, for the client sample, there was a need for separate provision for ethnic elderly from the same background, with the same language and similar experiences.

McFarland et al's study (1987) also looked at the needs of ethnic minority elderly. While they found evidence for the persistence of the joint family system among their Asian sample, they argued it was important that the assumption of 'family support' must not rule out consideration of possible unmet need, especially since there is no guarantee that the present situation will continue with the increasing economic and social constraints on a joint family system. McFarland et al identified the need to prepare ethnic minority elderly for retirement, and recommended that domiciliary arrangements be modified to meet their requirements. Also, a need existed to improve the quality and quantity of information about available services. The final major need identified was the opportunity to meet other elderly people. To ensure maximum participation and benefit, SEMRU (1987) also highlighted that clubs or centres need a substantial, if not exclusive, Asian clientele.

The report by Age Concern and Help the Aged (1984) found that ethnic minority elderly are isolated and unhappy, and live in inappropriate accommodation. It also highlighted the need for authorities to work together and plan for the needs of black elderly, and for ethnic minorities themselves to be involved. It is usual to find a very low take-up by black people of officially 'integrated' services. Pursuing a 'colour-blind' policy may appear to be non-discriminatory but effectively excludes black people from its provisions.

> The argument for total integration seems ludicrous for this age group. Integration can more often mean assimilation into a dominant cultural way of life......Integration only becomes an issue when it is forced on people. There are many ethnic elders who would in old age wish to be housed with people from their own culture. The provision of housing and welfare facilites to bring about integration has the effect of limiting choice and imposing, for example certain types of food, leisure and other facilities totally unsuited to the needs of ethnic elders, while also limiting their opportunities to relate to others of their own culture.
> (Age Concern/Help the Aged 1984:26).

Take up is low whether or not services are known about. There is an unmet need for information and advice in people's own languages about services and benefits.

The political implications of setting up separate residential facilities for the ethnic minority elderly is something policy-makers find difficult to rationalise. The argument against such provision is that it is divisive and that black elderly should use existing facilities. For ethnic minority elderly, however, placement in a white-dominated residential home or day centre, geared to white culture, is likely to reinforce their feelings of alienation.

Ethnic minority elderly can benefit greatly from day care, which includes day centre facilities, meals-on-wheels, lunch clubs and home helps. Presently these services are geared to meet the needs of the indigenous elderly, with little or no account of the specific and different needs of black elderly.

It is within the voluntary sector and the ethnic minority communities themselves that initiatives to meet the needs of black elderly are emerging, as a result of a desperate need. Hopkins (1987) cites a number of alternative services for ethnic minority elderly. He examines a residential home for black residents and a day centre for elderly Asian people, concluding

> It is clear that black elderly people have special needs which are more appropriately met outside the mainstream, white dominated, services. Continuity and consistency are the mainspring of identity and for many of them the affirmation of their own identity can only come from engagement with their

peers and members of their own community in a familiar way of life. Their relationship to their community is as important as their relationship to their own family, and estrangement between the generations can make it more so. (Hopkins 1987:11).

It is clear that day care and residential services need to be reviewed and adapted. Social workers can learn much from community provision and should be prepared to work with community groups and organisations in an effort to make their work with black elderly more sensitive and effective.

General issues

In the study, questions were also asked about more general issues

a) Positive discrimination

Asking the workers about whether they agreed with positive discrimination on behalf of ethnic minority clients presented them with their biggest dilemma and more time was spent by the workers thinking through their position on this issue than on any other. The difficulty that few of the workers could not resolve was the fear of ending up discriminating too much the other way against whites. Arguments were put forward by some that everyone should be treated the same and be provided with an equal service. Seven of the workers finally agreed with the principle, with four against and one 'don't know'.

Section 35 of the Race Relations Act 1976, provides a challenge to social work delivery systems in that it allows for any act done in affording persons of particular racial groups access to facilities or services to meet the special needs of persons in that group in regard to education, training or welfare, or any ancillary benefits.

Although positive discrimination (or positive action, as it now tends to be called) is a well established general principle in social service provision (Parker 1975), there is confusion about its various manifestations. Positive discrimination in favour of ethnic minorities can involve simple recognition that individual minority members may have disproportionate problems demanding appropriate attention. More strongly, it can entail policies which give priority to a group, because of the nature and extent of the group's disadvantage. While the first definition is not particularly contentious, its significance is lost in anxious debates about the consequences of the latter version. There is fear of stigmatising those identified for special treatment and the potential for stirring up envy and hostility among whites. There seems now to be a prevailing untested assumption that all but the most subtle forms of positive discrimination will exacerbate racial hostility. Thus, social work responds by doing nothing, as this appears the safer course, but, in effect, it means accepting in perpetuity the disadvantage of ethnic minorities.

Even if the principle of positive discrimination is accepted there is no consensus as to what form it should take: 'more of the same' or the establishment of specialist or separate provision for the minorities. The latter is often dismissed as only leading to further hostility. However, such specialist or separate treatment may be necessary and positive. There are problems with the assertion of 'separate but equal': different should not be synonymous with inferiority, nor must separate become an euphemism for segregated. Cheetham (1982b) identifies that for a significant minority among ethnic minority groups, separate arrangements are the means of matching the pressing reality of needs with services that are relevant and attuned to the traditional strengths and problems of their clients' ethnicity.

b) Monitoring

Eleven of the workers agreed with the proposal to record the ethnic origin of the user of social work services. However, this was on condition that the clients should agree and the reasons for monitoring be explained.

To ensure relevance of services and provisions it is necessary to establish the needs of ethnic minorities. This can best be done by ethnic monitoring and recording, and consulting with the ethnic minority community.

> It is of major importance that the needs of the community be accurately assessed and a check made of the workings of local authority provision to ensure that there is a correspondence between need and service. If race were not an important factor in society, if people's life chances and oppportunities were not restricted on racial and ethnic grounds, it would not be important to record race. Since racial equality is a goal for our society not yet achieved, it is crucial that progress towards an equal society should be monitored.
> (CRE 1978:81)

Collecting data does not solve arguments about what ought to be done; it simply means that there is some factual foundation on which to build. There has been some reluctance to institute record keeping and monitoring services due to fears of adverse use and distaste for identifying ethnicity. Record keeping and monitoring are not, however, designed to diminish individual assessment but to sharpen thinking about pressures on people from different backgrounds and to identify the achievements and shortcomings of the service. Experience shows that recording ethnic origin can prompt further, more sophisticated examination of needs (Cheetham and Roper 1978).

c) Education and training

None of the qualified workers thought their training course adequately prepared them for working with ethnic minority clients. Eleven of the workers believed more should be included on social work courses about working with ethnic minority clients. Items the workers identified as 'needing to be included' ranged from input on culture, religion and custom, Racism Awareness Training, practical involvement through placement, and they felt that such material should be intrinsic to the course with ongoing training in the area.

None of the workers had received any in-service training on working with ethnic minority clients since they qualified. While in-service training, in general, was identified as being required, that with a specific focus on ethnic minorities was held as very necessary.

Social work courses have a crucial role to play in ensuring that practitioners are

E

adequately trained and prepared to work in a multiracial context. As Baker and Husband (1979:26) put it,

> There is a need to specifically prepare social workers for practice with ethnic minority clients, and this preparation must be founded on an acceptance of the necessity of identifying and responding to the particular needs of ethnic minorities.

Social work education must reassess the content and curriculum of its courses and examine the appropriateness of traditional social work skills in multi-racial practice. Dominelli (1979:27) states that the academic content of the social work curriculum needs to examine,

> .... [black people's] cultural background, their current postion in terms of their own aspirations and achievements and those permitted them by the opportunities British society provides; the institutionalised racism permeating the social fabric, but with particular emphasis on educational and social work practice; individual feelings and beliefs.

Cannan (1983) believes that in teaching about social work in a multi-cultural society, the focus should not be solely on the ethnic minority clients and their culture, but has to include an examination of the culture of social work and social workers. The principles and theories of social work need to be discussed as ideologies, and to be grounded in history and geography. She encourages students to stand back from social work and examine its history and philosophies with a critical eye.

Case work material should reflect a multiracial society and client expectations and perceptions should be considered more seriously, taking both class and cultural factors into account. The basic social work skills of communication and making relationships, and of interviewing, need to be taught bearing in mind that interpreters are now often used, that communication across languages is not just a matter of translation, and translation of concepts may be complicated. The intrusions of gender and status into the relationship need to be understood if the relationship is not to mean different things to each party. Students need opportunities to examine their own attitudes to racial and social differences, and for more placements in a multiracial setting.

Educational institutions should not only be employing teachers and supervisors from ethnic minority groups but should also provide educational opportunities for students from ethnic minorities currently being excluded by middle-class-biased selection processes and recruitment policies favouring the majority group.

Social work departments themselves should be pursuing in-service training initiatives for working with ethnic minorities.

Training has an important part to play within an overall programme of change in the departments, for example, through providing opportunities to discuss change and its implementation and by encouraging the development of skills which will help achieve particular employment or service delivery objectives. On a general level, training can help increase the capacity of individuals within departments to recognise the issues and deal with them effectively. However, training in itself can achieve little and departments need to work to ensure the change that begins in training is followed through in the workplace.

d) The Ethnic Minorities Project

Only one out of the twelve workers at the local office had not made use of the workers from the Ethnic Minority Project. They used the workers for information, interpreting and as co-worker on cases. The situations that had given rise to the workers making use of the Project workers were consulting on a case, duty problem and general interest. Other situations included joint visits and linking up to specific Asian resources.

On asking whether the client sample knew of the Ethnic Minorities Project, only two clients (Chinese) said they did. It was quite surprising that nine of the clients claimed not to have heard of the Project considering the extent of publicity. As well as translated leaflets and posters, a mini-launch of the Project had taken place within the area in May 1987. However, this had attracted mainly professionals, rather than the people who could directly benefit from the service.

On discussing the Project further, with all the clients, it was apparent that they knew about the Project workers and had contact with them. However all nine assumed that these workers were social workers. Thus there was lack of clarity about the roles of the various workers at the local office and it was clear that the publicity about the Ethnic Minorities Project had not even reached those using the department on a regular basis.

When asked if they had used the Project, all eleven said that they had. The major reason for contacting the workers was for advice, although three stated that they had contact with the Project workers along with a social worker. For the Chinese clients, their only contact was with the Chinese Project worker, and they had never been in contact with any of the social workers at the office.

All the clients felt that they did not know enough about what social workers do, that they needed more information on what they do, as well as more information on the services that the Social Work Department provides. It was noted by most of the client sample that all the information should be translated and readily available.

e) Identification of needs

When asked to identify the main needs of their ethnic group, clients gave the following responses most frequently. They referred to difficulties in communication and language and the need for interpreters and ethnic minority social workers; they asked for information on services in different languages; they wanted more facilities for Asian/ Chinese people and in particular, provision for learning English; they said services needed adapting to meet the needs of ethnic minorities; they wanted greater understanding from workers; and finally they spoke of the need to combat the racism and discrimination they faced in their daily lives.

f) Evaluation

In relation to social work service provision for ethnic minorites, the social workers believed that a review of all services and their appropriateness was necessary, and expressed qualified support for the adaptation of services to meet the needs of ethnic minorities.

The majority of social workers thought that ethnic minorities held a negative perception of social work. This was linked to the predominantly statutory nature of ethnic minorities' involvement with social work. Ferns (1987) shows that black people distrust statutory authorities, a view based on their personal contact with authorities such as health services, DSS, social services and police. He believes that social work has not attempted to bridge this credibility gap and that distance is maintained by 'prejudiced and stereotypical thinking' (1987:19).

When asked to evaluate the helpfulness of their social work involvement, the majority of clients felt it was unhelpful, with two of them finding it helpful. The two Chinese clients found the Ethnic Minorities Project worker helpful but could not comment on the other workers. Four of the clients commented that their problems were never completely solved, and that social workers did not keep them informed of what was going on. They talked about being left with unresolved problems and of feeling neglected by social workers. While all agreed that the Project workers were helpful, the majority had found the social workers hostile. One client stated that the social workers were not prepared to listen and did not understand.

These replies were echoed in SEMRU's Lothian study (1987), where they found that social workers were seen by ethnic minorities as unreliable, aggressive and impatient, unable to communicate effectively, ignorant of specific cultures and religions, ignorant of the specific problems they faced, in particular, of the effect of racism on the black client, and in some cases were seen to be discriminatory in their approach to black people.

Comments offered by clients at the end of my questionnaire, included the following:

Social workers are always saying that they will do something for you tomorrow, but they never seem to get it done.

Social work needs to do something about the harassment we face.

I was suspected of hitting my little girl, but the social worker never explained anything and I did not understand what was happening. There was no attempt by the worker to understand or to talk to me.

They [the Social Work Department] should employ more Asian workers.

I've had so many social workers come and go, I'm now on to my fourth one.

The Asian worker has explained more what social work is about. The social workers do not listen or try to understand my problems.

Social workers have shown me little consideration.

It is difficult for white social workers to fully understand our problems. There are difficulties with language and they know little of our background and culture, nor of the harassment and problems we face.

Discussion

I found from my interviews with the workers based at the local office, that while there were individual variations, the majority of the workers perceived social work services as inappropriate and inadequate for ethnic minorities. Some workers employed stereotypes and revealed a lack of knowledge of the background, culture and experiences of ethnic minorities. The most salient stereotype mentioned by the workers was the belief that Asian families care for 'their own' and do not want or need social work help. There was a tendency for some workers to 'blame cultures' and many were unable to identify any strengths of the various ethnic minority cultures. However, the majority of workers were aware of the shortcomings of social work and its services in relation to ethnic minorities. Just as Husband (1980) and Young and Connelly (1981) found, most of the workers in my study were making every effort to increase their understanding and improve their practice in their work with ethnic minority clients. There existed misgivings about their ability to work effectively with ethnic minorities. There was a sense that most of the workers were muddling through, picking things up as they went along and adapting their practice accordingly. An awareness existed that this was not the best way to proceed and that it was unfair to ethnic minority clients. Baker and Husband (1979) and Cheetham (1981) found evidence that professionally qualified staff felt unable to work competently with minority clients and either failed to offer adequate support or prematurely closed cases. Workers had difficulty judging the needs and problems and also assessing the strengths of ethnic minorities.

While the workers were aware of the need for change, some argued that this was not feasible due to lack of resources. Cheetham (1981:122) claims,

> It is easy now to argue that nothing can be done because of lack of resources. This is not true: in services for ethnic minority people the first essential step is for every fieldworker and administrator to consider how practice could change simply through his or her own approach to problems and how far other resources are essential.

A few of the workers I interviewed highlighted the lack of support and guidance from management, as well as the dearth of policy decisions. SEMRU's study in Lothian (1987) criticised social work for its 'ad-hoc' measures, which exist as realities, potentials or promises unsupported by a coherent plan or programme. One of SEMRU's recommendations is that Social Work Departments, besides consulting with ethnic minority organisations, should comprehensively review their organisation, policies, procedures, methods and practices in light of the wide variety of data available on institutional racism and on specialist ethnic services. The workers I interviewed felt hindered by the lack of policy decision and direction from management and the existence of unsuitable and inappropriate services. Change was seen as necessary by all workers, involving not only the adaptation of existing provision but also a full-scale review of all services and their appropriateness to ethnic minorities which was seen as a priority.

There is evidence that the ethnic minority population, in general, have a low awareness of what services are on offer. McFarland et al's (1987) study in Glasgow found that this was the case amongst the sample they interviewed, and they were struck by the extent of the lack of knowledge. The sample I interviewed knew of the existence of the Social Work Department, and had access to it. As such, it could be expected that these clients would have more awareness and, perhaps, more experience of existing provision than the ethnic minority population in general. While there was some awareness and limited experience, there still existed a lack of definite knowledge about existing provision. Nevertheless, the clients had their own impressions about the available services. Their overwhelming perception of provision for children, youth and elderly was that these services were unsuitable and inappropriate for ethnic minorities. Problems of language and communication were highlighted, along with the lack of information on social work and its services. There was an overwhelming belief that the existing services were only for white people and would not suit their needs. There also existed the perception of white social work staff as unhelpful, hostile, unaware of the cultures and customs of ethnic minorities, and ignorant of their needs and problems.

Five areas of importance in promoting a better social work service for ethnic minorities were identified by the sample in SEMRU's Lothian study (1987). These areas concurred with the recommendations made by my sample and are as follows: firstly information, that is, the need for more wide-ranging and more effectively distributed information and publicity material on social work services; secondly, the need to improve communication between the Social Work Department, social workers and ethnic minority clients; thirdly, the employment of ethnic minority social workers; fourthly, training for social workers in the cultural background of ethnic minorities, as well as greater understanding of ethnic minorities' experience in British society, particularly of racism and discrimination; and fifthly, separate provision of services, seen by my sample as necessary, particularly for ethnic minority elderly.

While the Ethnic Minorities Project workers were all regarded positively by the clients, there did exist a lack of clarity about their role and function. A precedent was emerging which has serious implications, that of ethnic minority clients having contact only with ethnic minority workers. This was particularly true in the case of the Chinese clients, who had never met with a social worker. Not only did this lead to large demands and stress on the Project workers, but also meant that the white workers' contact with ethnic minorities was further reduced. They were not being encouraged or given the opportunity to adapt their practice to meet the needs of black clients. Ferns (1987) identifies that within social work departments there has been a proliferation of posts concerned with ethnic minorities and equal opportunities:

> Creating new posts gives the impression that something is being done about racism, and this can be further enhanced if the posts are filled by black people (Ferns 1987:20).

> He goes on to warn that if the posts are merely cosmetic, then the effect would be ...to disguise the unacceptable face of racism without really taking steps to get rid of it. Many of these so-called ethnic minority posts are reduced to

advisory roles and monitoring functions, without any power to implement change. (Ferns 1987:20)

By establishing the Ethnic Minorities Project, the Social Work Department may be attempting to make its services more sensitive to ethnic minorities, but there is also the possibility that such a project is serving to divert attention away from where real changes are necessary. Within the remit of my study, I was unable to evaluate the Ethnic Minorities Project fully, apart from the observation that it has increased the numbers of ethnic minority clients approaching the Social Work Department, but, at the same time, my study suggested that the white workers' contact with ethnic minorities has not necessarily increased. More work needs to be done in evaluating such Projects, to see if they are resulting in necessary changes and improvements, or else are merely cosmetic.

Cannan (1983) sees the major problem in working with ethnic minorities not in the existence of cultural differences but in social work itself. Mayer and Timms (1976) reveal social work as a rather unusual approach to human problems with its emphasis on a professional detachment, insight giving, the importance of past, all contrasting with expectations of active, directive partisan intervention held by white working class clients. Rees's research (1978) highlights the lack of a clear public image of social work and the confusion of such elements as charity, officialdom and inspecting, income maintenance and stigmatising services in the public mind.

It is in work with ethnic minorities that traditional middle class orientated social work is being challenged as totally inappropriate and ineffectual, with no relevance to the majority of people, especially ethnic minorities. According to Cheetham (1982b:36),

... work with ethnic minorities provides an outstanding opportunity for clarity of thought and imaginative practice in matching services to needs. Seizing this opportunity will benefit the whole community and move social work towards a more expansive vision and a more flexible practice.

Social work departments and courses should reflect the multiracial character of our society with ethnic minorities present throughout the organisational structure and on courses as tutors and students. According to Dominelli (1979:29)

A non-racist practice must observe the following principles: the acceptance of a multi-racial Britain; the affirmation of the cultural specificity of different ethnic minority groups; the examination of traditional social work skills and their appropriateness in working with ethnic minorities; the development of a client-centred, community based strategy for change.

What is required for social work to progress in its work with ethnic minorities is first, actually to spend time listening to what ethnic minority consumers want and need, and then to set up the mechanisms to allow full, effective consultation to take place:

Sensitivity to people's culture and ethnic needs are 'integral to ensuring that race equality is built into provision of the personal social services' (Ahmed 1987:29).

Also necessary is a clearer perception and understanding of ethnic minorities' position in Britain:

> It is the individual's unique response to the context of their life in Britain from within the perspective of their culture which forms the dynamic which social work must grasp in working with clients from ethnic minorities. (Husband 1980:84)

It is crucial to acknowledge the pervasiveness of racism throughout our society and its presence within the Social Work Department and individual worker's practice. Recognising its influence on the experiences of ethnic minorities, we can begin to understand the special and specific needs of this group, as distinct from the indigenous white population:

> Defensiveness about the existence of racism breeds subterfuge, rhetoric, accusation and counter-accusation. Accepting racism's endemic nature makes open discussion and challenge possible and encourages realistic means of tackling it. (Ahmed et al 1986:11)

Work with ethnic minorities provides a major challenge to social work, to break out of the laissez-faire indifference that exists and to acknowledge our multiracial society and to build foundations for its subsequent development. It is in this area more than any other that the problems and shortcomings of social work, in general, are highlighted. As it stands at present, according to the available literature and in the findings of my own study, ethnic minority clients are dissatisfied with and alienated from social work and the services it provides and social workers are frustrated and feel inadequate in their attempts to judge need and problems in unfamiliar culture settings. This unsatisfactory situation cannot, and should not, be allowed to continue. Social work has to change and adapt itself so that it can operate effectively and appropriately within a multi-cultural society.

Ending on a negative, although not pessimistic note, I concur with the conclusion of SEMRU's (1987:1) Lothian study, that:

> The concerns and dissatisfaction expressed with service delivery and staffing seem to be sufficiently worrying to justify substantial changes in policy and practice in this area, coupled where necessary to relevant research and information gathering.

References

Age Concern and Help the Aged 1984 *Housing for Ethnic Elders* Mitcham: Age Concern England

Ahmed S. Cheetham J and Small J (eds) 1986 *Social Work with Black Children and their Families* London: Batsford

Ahmed S. 1987 'Sensitive to People's Needs' *Community Care* 5 November

Association of Black Social Workers and Allied Professions (ABSWAP) 1983a *Black Children in Care* Evidence to House of Commons Social Services Committee

ABSWAP 1983b Programme for the first Natural Conference on Black Children in Care

Association of Directors of Social Services and Commission for Racial Equality (ADSS/CRE) 1978 *Multi-Racial Britian: The Social Services Response* London: Commission for Racial Equality

Baker L and Husband C 1979 'How has social work education 1979 responded?' *Social Work Today* 10 (25):24-26

Cannan C 1983 'Social Work, race relations and the social work curriculum' *New Community* 11(1/2):167-178

Cheetham J and Roper S 1978 'The Roots of Change' *Community Care* 29 November : 20-23

Cheetham J 1981 *Social Work Services for Ethnic Minorities in Britain and USA* London: DHSS Report

Cheetham J (ed) 1982a *Social Work and Ethnicity* 1982 London: Allen and Unwin

Cheetham J 1982b Positive Discrimination in social work: negotiating the oppostion' *New Community* 10(1):27-37

Commission for Racial Equality 1978 *Urban Deprivation, Racial Inequality and Social Policy: A Report,* London: HMSO

Commission for Racial Equality 1982 'The Youth Service, in J Cheetham et al (ed) 1982a *op. cit*

Commission for Racial Equality 1985 *Report of the Suspension of Black Pupils in Birmingham* London: CRE

Coombe V 1986 'Black Children in Residential Care' in Coombe V and Little A, *Race and Social Work* London: Tavistock

Coombe V and Little A 1986 *Race and Social Work* London: Tavistock

Dominelli L 1979 'The Challenge for Social Work Education" *Social Work Today,* 10 {25}:27-29

Dominelll L 1989 'White Racism, poor practice' *Social Work Today* 20 (18):12-13

Ely P and Denney D 1987 *Social Work in a Multi-Racial Society* London: Gower

Ferns P 1987'The Dangerous Delusion' *Community Care* 8th Jan:19-21

Francis W 1985 'Do not let their quietness deceive' *Community Care,* 23rd May:22-4

Gill O and Jackson B 1983 *Adoption and Race: Black, Asian and Mixed Race Children in White Families,* London: Batsford

Hopkins J 1987 'Alternative services which aim to affirm an ethnic identity' *Social Work Today,* 23 Nov: 10-11

Horn E 1982 'A survey of referrals from Asian families to four Social Services Area Offices in Bradford' in Cheetham J (ed) *op cit* : 50-71

Husband C 1980 'Culture, context and practice: racism in social work' in Brake M and Bailey R
eds *Radical Social Work and Practice* London: Edward Arnold

Jackson A 1979 'Just how relevant and accessible are social services departments'; *Social Work
Today* 10 (25):21-23

Manning B 1979 'The black social workers role', *Social Work Today*, 20 Feb: 30-31

Mayer J and Timms N 1970 *The Client Speaks* London: Routledge and Kegan Paul

Mayall B and Petrie B 1983 *Childminding and Day Nurseries* London: Heinemann

McFarland E, Dalton M and Watson D 1986 *Personal Welfare Services and Ethnic Services and
Ethnic Minorities - A Study of East Pollokshields,* Glasgow: Scottish Ethnic Minorities Rsearch
Unit, Glasgow College of Technology

Osborn A F, Butler N R and Morris A C 1984 *The Social Life of Britain's Five Year Olds,*
London: Routledge and Kegan Paul

Parker J 1975 *Social Policy And Citizenship* London: Macmillan

Race Equality Unit 1988 quoted in *Social Work Today*, 7th January: 12-13

Rees S 1978 *Social Work Face to Face* London: Edward Arnold

Scottish Asian Action Committee *Comments on the Report 'Forward in Understanding',*
Glasgow: SAAC

Scottish Ethnic Minorities Research Unit (SEMRU) 1987 *Ethnic Minorities Profile - A Study of
Needs and Services of Lothian Region and Edinburgh District* Edinburgh: College of Art/Heriot
Watt University, Dept. of Town and Country Planning

Small S 1981 *Police and People in London 2* London: Policy Studies Institute

Small J 1986 'Transracial placements: conflicts and contradictions'. in Ahmed S et al (ed) 1986,
op cit

Smith D 1981 *Unemployment and Racial Minorities,* London: Policy Studies Institute

Strathclyde Regional Council (SRC) 1982 *Area, Profile and Assessment* Glasgow: SRC

Strathclyde Regional Council 1986 *Forward in Understanding* Community Development
Committee Sub-Group on Ethnic Minorities, Glasgow: SRC

Swann Report 1985 *Education for All* London: HMSO

Watson M 1984 *A Report of the Findings of a Survey of the South Asian Community Residing in
the Govanhill area of Glasgow between 19th July and 29th August 1984,* Glasgow

Young K and Connelly N 1981 *Policy and practice in the multi-racial city,* London: Policy
Studies Institute

Chapter 8

Ethnic minorities and community work: the experience of Crossroads Youth and Community Association

Clare Murray

Introduction

There is much evidence to illustrate that ethnic minorities throughout Britain still fail to gain access to services provided by both the voluntary sector and the statutory sector of social services. In 1988, the Scottish Council of Voluntary Organisations produced research clearly showing that the white voluntary sector in Scotland was not aware of the needs of ethnic minority communities and was, consequently, not responding to their needs (MacLeod 1988). The findings of the project illustrated 'just how little black people appear to be involved in the management, staffing and user groups of Scottish voluntary organisations', (conference report, May 1988, Glasgow). In 1989, a Home office research study also concluded (p.iii) that 'Asian households were found to use many less services than whites, although there is no reason to believe that they have fewer needs'.

During 1979, Crossroads Youth and Community Association had identified the same situation in its own organisation. In particular, one member of the Association's experience working as a health visitor highlighted the isolation of many Asian women living in Glasgow, and the lack of early reading material for ethnic minority children.

Having identified this lack of access to both statutory and voluntary services by ethnic minorities, including Crossroads itself, the organisation began a debate which led to the decision being taken that agency resources should be used to work towards establishing the needs of the Asian community.

This chapter will examine Crossroads' experience as a white organisation working in a multi-cultural area, in its attempts to make contact with the ethnic minority community, to assist community members to identify their needs and to provide agency resources in an appropriate way. The decision to direct Association resources in this way led Crossroads along a journey which brought it into contact with individuals and organisations, both black and white, examining the best way to ensure equal access to services. Our experience as a white organisation addresses wider questions of whether this work can or should be done by white organisations. The chapter will illustrate how far Crossroads has come and still has to go to achieve equality.

The Agency

Crossroads Youth and Community Association is a voluntary organisation working primarily in two inner city areas of Glasgow. The services of the Association, which employs twelve members of staff, include youth work provision in the Gorbals, community work support to local and city wide groups and campaigns, information and advice work in both Gorbals and Govanhill and student training, providing practice placements in community work for students on CQSW/DipSW training courses.

From the start the staff sought to combine and integrate student training with providing a local community work resource and this link was symbolized, in the early days by the fact that 'The Gorbals View' newspaper used the student unit premises as its new administrative base
(Bryant and Bryant, 1982:31).

Crossroads' roots originate from the Gorbals Group which was founded in December 1957. The Group believed in developing practical work in four areas; the personal neighbourhood relationships with families and individuals; the provision of specific services to children and young people; the involvement in community work and the sharing of common concerns with other groups and organisations throughout the city. Those involved in the Gorbals Group provided themselves, direct, personal services to vulnerable and alienated people living in that part of the city. This style has been associated with the worker priests of South America where a direct informal and committed approach was adopted. The Gorbals Group in the early days provided support in a non-judgemental way.

The philosophy however did not only seek to support individuals as victims and the group developed practice based on a model that linked the individual experience or 'private troubles' to 'public issues'. The philosophy which informs Crossroads' work was firmly established during the development from the Gorbals Group to Crossroads as we know it today. As Bryant and Bryant (1982:29) point out

The group was never static. Like all organisations, it altered in response to outside pressure and change in membership.

However the organisation may have changed in the past twenty years, many of the beliefs formed during that period remain alive today. Crossroads believes that our society is structurally unequal and that to change inequalities requires the collective organisation of people around expressed needs. Crossroads has traditionally organised amongst the unorganised in attempts to redistribute resources more fairly. Further, Crossroads in its belief that services should be locally run and accountable has encouraged the development of such services, for example the local housing association and a community technical services agency, which are run on a model of user control. Crossroads is run by a management committee made up of local residents and users of its service. These individuals have to cope daily with the rigours of survival on state benefits, in damp and inadequate housing conditions and subjected to racism and harassment. Crossroads has therefore been committed to supporting and tackling controversial and uncomfortable issues in a direct way. Crossroads' staff are expected to operate this philosophy with a partisan identification with local people and their needs and to work together with them in a relationship of mutual respect and benefit.

Commitment to race work

Records show that in 1978, Crossroads as a whole became aware that it was not providing services to members of the Asian community and further that Crossroads was not aware of that community's needs. The management committee then discussed the situation which had been highlighted to them by one of the members of the Association in her experience as a health visitor, in contact with many Asian families. She had experience of being confronted by isolated Asian women but finding herself unaware of support and contact with the outside world which would break this isolation. This situation led to much internal discussion in Crossroads. The internal debate, conducted within Crossroads involved members and staff in becoming aware of the issues involved in eradicating racism. Not all members at that time accepted that racism exists, or that it was an issue which deserved the Association's proposing redirection of resources. Activists from existing community groups complained about resources being taken away for new work to begin with the Asian community and particularly Asian women.

The outcome of the debate however for Crossroads, was to mean that a white organisation would attempt to make contact with and develop a response from those in the Asian community whose needs were not being met.

This, in reality, meant that some individuals within Crossroads had accepted the existence of racism, and had acknowledged that its effects were present in Govanhill at that time and that therefore it was the responsibility of Crossroads to investigate those unmet needs and not leave it to black people and black organisations alone to address the problem. The only valid way for Crossroads to conduct this work was by adopting existing principles, but the Association further recognised that it was not necessarily the case that existing practice would actually address and respond to expressed needs, and that methods of community work might have to be adapted in the light of growing knowledge of work in this field.

The first practical outcome of Crossroads' decision to direct its resources in this way was the production of a booklet - *Born in Glasgow*. The purpose of the booklet, for small children of ethnic minority origin, was to illustrate as normal life, black and white families in familiar situations, for example travelling on the subway, black and white children being born in Glasgow all living up the same close, eating dinner such as dhal and chappattis and washing up. The booklet was distributed widely in nursery schools and primary schools and for the first time successfully brought Crossroads into limited contact with Asian women.

This limited contact was not in itself enough to develop a response to unmet needs. Problems faced by Asian women in England had been documented by sociologists and anthropologists and provided evidence of at least two kinds of discrimination, racism and sexism. However, as far as eradicating this kind of discrimination in Scotland was concerned, there were problems to overcome. At that time, very little was known about Asians living in Scotland. The limited research that had been done focussed on housing, education, employment, health and ethnic identity, demonstrating general disadvantage clearly related to recognised inner city deprivation, but none of the work had dealt explicitly with women or confronting racism. Attempts to analyse and remedy the problems for ethnic minorities had been attacked for being ineffective, based on cosy myths that Scotland had a reputation for harmonious relations.

Action Research

Crossroads and researchers from Stirling University began a dialogue in January 1981 about the possibility of developing informed intervention in an inner city area of Glasgow where many ethnic minority people lived. The result of these discussions was an action research programme entailing community work intervention, informed and monitored by research and under the direction of the local community, in this case Asian women. There have been two action research projects both funded by the Economic and Social Research Council under their collaborative awards in social sciences scheme (now defunct). The first project began in 1984 and examined closely the lives of Asian women in Glasgow. The second project began in 1987 and examined services for and responses to Asian women suffering domestic violence. This remit was a direct response to issues raised by local women involved in the review of the first research project.

The relationship between Crossroads and Stirling University initially highlighted a large gap between research and action and involved much heart searching and debate to eventually reach a position where a joint project could be run. Alison Bowes wrote (1987)

Crossroads was primarily committed to action, and felt research was needed to fill gaps in their knowledge before community action could proceed. We (Stirling University researchers) were still trying to work out exactly what the role of research would be.

Crossroads was particularly attracted to the action research method because of its potential for community control and community involvement. This was central to Crossroads, given its commitment to local control and local people making decisions, in this case about the direction of the research. Indeed the first funding application stated clearly that both project workers and researchers would be accountable to the community and therefore the project would be locally based. Those involved from Crossroads and the University were anxious to avoid the separation of research from action, and to maintain action workers', and community members' engagement with the research process. This was achieved by establishing a management structure which operated on three levels.

As the project was locally based, regular meetings between researchers, action workers, and representatives of community groups took place. Further, a management committee for the project was made up of local Asian women, the researcher, Crossroads' management and staff and representatives of Stirling University. This committee was formally recognised as a sub-committee of Crossroads Youth and Community Association.

Finally, to ensure further accountability, review days were held regularly, and involved more local women, mostly members of the local Asian Womens Action Group. The discussions at these review days were essential for monitoring the development and assessing the usefulness of the research. The review days threw up new issues for research and action, including the topic for the second project.

Crossroads' support for action research was also based on the emphasis on qualitative research and its ability to identify issues of special concern to Asian women. We hoped that the results of the qualitative research would become the instruments of the community to use in whatever way best suited their needs, to improve their situation.

Crossroads' commitment to race work and in particular action research was reinforced by contributing funding in kind, office space and administrative support, to help ensure the success of the work

Community work at Crossroads

Earlier I attempted to outline the predominant values which guide and inform Crossroads. Community work within Crossroads developed these values during the 1970s when the community work activities were promoted by the student unit located in Gorbals and Govanhill. Both units operated a similar style and philosophy, albeit in very different geographical surroundings. Funding for these units has been forthcoming since the 1970s from three main sources: the Central Council for Education and Training in Social Work, since 1987, (Social Work Services Group before that), Strathclyde Regional Council and Glasgow District Council. Crossroads' management has usually been left to determine its own priorities for community work practice. In recent years, funders have become more rigorous in their assessment of Crossroads' work and both Strathclyde Regional Council and Glasgow District Council have decided to take up their right, under the Crossroads' constitution, to send representatives to executive meetings.

There have been conflicts with funders, one of which resulted in the Association being deprived of a grant for two years to carry out youth and community work in the Gorbals. A further threat to funding which did not result in funding being withdrawn occurred in the Gorbals over our work in the local anti-dampness campaign. Funding was never withdrawn, but Crossroads did accept conditions attached to future funding imposed by Social Work Services Group.

Since the 1970s, the values and assumptions which informed Crossroads' work have not altered drastically. As mentioned earlier, staff's community work practice is underpinned by a structural explanation of poverty and inequality as the following quote by Holman illustrates,

> deprivation is not a consequence of the malfunctioning of a few inadequates, not the grit in an otherwise satisfactory machine, but inherent in the very nature of society. The poor, or deprived, live in conditions of deprivation because they lack the power to change their situation. It is also assumed that changes of the necessary magnitude will never be altruistically conceded, but will only come as the poor themselves can influence the system through collective power (Holman 1972:9)

The focus for Crossroads' community work has traditionally been organising within neighbourhoods, such as Gorbals, Govanhill, usually around single issue campaigns, for example tenement rehabilitation and repair, anti-dampness campaigns and campaigns to maintain local services. Community work with Asian women has developed around the principles of self help organisation successfully taking up those issues identified by the women themselves (see Wardhaugh and Harvie, this volume).

Working with those in the community who traditionally have been unorganised distinguishes Crossroads practice from that which emphasises working with established organisations and leaders from existing social, political religious or trade union bodies to press for change. Traditionally our work has meant organising around single issues and encouraging self-help activity and organisations. Crossroads did not set out to change the world but to demonstrate and encourage collective action as a necessity for challenging and resolving society's problems. Crossroads believes in the active involvement of those individuals affected by poverty, racism, and unemployment in challenging and changing these circumstances which affect their lives. The process of challenging existing structures provides individuals with skills and knowledge that develop confidence in their own abilities.

Developing ethnically sensitive practice

Further examination of Crossroads developmental race work, illustrated by a number of initiatives, will explore the continuing debates about what constitutes ethnically sensitive practice.

a) Anti-racist training

Between 1984 and 1987 members of management and staff underwent anti-racist training. The management committee of Crossroads recognised the importance of this training, as membership of staff and management changed and the attitude and commitment of the Association to this work required frequent reappraisal.

The training involved frequent examination of Crossroads' attitudes towards positive action, work with black only groups, institutionalising the challenge to racist remarks and examining what sanctions were open to the Association to apply to individuals or groups who openly promoted racist ideas.

b) Staff in-service training

Crossroads also ensured that staff received training in issues which directly and specifically affected the Asian community. For example, early on, the Asian Womens Action Group produced a video to encourage the uptake of social security payments by Asian women in an attempt to maximise income. During the promotion of this video it became apparent that Asian women, particularly those most recently arrived in the UK, were reluctant to claim benefit. Many had limited knowledge of social security provision, but still refused to make claims for benefits. Their reluctance was explained to Crossroads staff as a concern by the women about their right to claim given their immigration status. Crossroads urgently required training to ensure that advice was accurate given the minefield of immigration and social security law. Therefore two members of staff attended training on this topic and resources were made available to purchase relevant publications. (See also Wardhaugh in this volume).

c) Student training

Crossroads' limited resources are frequently enhanced and supported by the presence of Social Work students placed within the Agency, as part of their professional training. Crossroads has used these placements to further develop knowledge about the needs of the Asian community, which has led to direct improvements in the quality of life of Asian users of Crossroads services. Student placements have included a welfare rights take-up campaign, a house conditions survey of Asian families in Govanhill, an examination of the needs of Asian elderly, a survey of Asian peoples experience of housing services and several community work and information work placements with black only groups in Govanhill. Student placements reflected and were defined by the actual experience and needs of the Asian community who had approached Crossroads for help and advice.

d) Location

As mentioned earlier, Crossroads has been in Govanhill for more than 15 years. Recent statistical evidence shows that 28 per cent of Govanhill residents ethnic origins lie in the Indian sub-continent. The area has mosques, saree shops, Asian jewellery shops, halal shops and its housing comprises a large amount of cheaper tenemental properties: all are contributing factors to the Asian community sinking roots in the Govanhill area.

Crossroads has always preferred shop front premises as a base, and in 1984, moved to a new central location. At that time the premises were called 'The View' which was also the name of the local community newspaper. The name was subsequently changed to the 'Govanhill Information Centre' by the management committee of Crossroads, heavily influenced by members of the Asian Womens Action Group who strongly felt that this name more adequately explained the function of the Crossroads Govanhill Unit.

This move also coincided with Crossroads successfully receiving an Urban Aid grant, supported by Glasgow District Council for an Information Work Post based in the Govanhill Unit. The award included a substantial amount for interpreting and translating facilities which could be provided locally and quickly and led to a reduction in demand on the already overworked interpreting services. Local women, under the guidance of the Asian Women's Action Group, received proper payment for this service.

It was therefore a combination of being suitably placed geographically, new staff resources and the ongoing commitment to developing work with ethnic minorities, that ensured a quick take-up of resources. Within months, 50 people per day used the Govanhill Information Centre: between 25 and 30 per cent of these were of ethnic minority origins. To make the Association more welcoming to Asian people, the management committee decided to take action over racist remarks made within the Govanhill Information Centre. It decided that racist remarks should be challenged and if necessary, the person making the remarks would be asked to leave if they were not prepared to withdraw them. This indeed happened occasionally.

e) Equal opportunities

Crossroads management are currently reviewing employment practice and service delivery to ensure a more systematic move towards Crossroads becoming an equal opportunities organisation. In reality, some of Crossroads existing practice illustrates the Association's attempts to address the issues. In employment practice for example, apart from Practice Teaching, all other posts, including community and youth work, do not require formal academic qualifications. Black workers have been employed in the organisation, but none is employed at the time of writing (November 1990).

f) Disunity over harassment

There has not always been agreement within Crossroads about our practice and direction of work. Local management committee members have reported to the Association that in the opinion of some Govanhill residents, Crossroads only provides help to the Asian community. There has been considerable debate within the organisation about our work with black only tenants groups and this can be illustrated by an examination of our support of tenants on a council estate experiencing racial harassment (see also Wardhaugh in this volume).

It is necessary to begin by explaining our historical contact with tenants from a particular area of Govanhill, which until recently had been starved of proper investment and improvements to housing and the environment. Local tenants had, with great difficulty, attempted to highlight their problems and gain improvements for their area for several years. The housing stock built under the 1919 and 1923 Housing Acts required both internal and external renovation and because this had not been done, parts of the area became 'hard to let'. There were many empty houses, and the area had a run down atmosphere.

During the period between 1984 and 1987 when, throughout other parts of the area, private sector tenemental properties were being renovated, some Asian families were being rehoused in N————. Asian people living in that area, known to Crossroads through having sought welfare rights and housing advice previously, began reporting serious incidents of racial harassment. At that time, there were probably only 15 Asian households in an area of approximately 500 houses. Crossroads began monitoring and reporting cases of racial harassment to the Police and other agencies but even with our intervention there was no evidence that action was being taken. Interviews conducted by Crossroads with all the black families indicated that harassment affected them all to a greater or lesser degree and Crossroads then proposed that a group representing those families be set up to push for action on racial harassment.

This strategy led to considerable debate internally, and to conflict between Crossroads and the existing all-white tenants association. Staff tried to set out the details of our race work in an overall framework of existing demands in the Govanhill unit. Our data showed that over a six day period there were 91 callers to the Govanhill Unit. 73 per cent of all callers were white and 27 per cent were black, Asian origin.

The current community work of the Govanhill Unit consisted of work with the Asian Womens Action Group and other single issue group work concerned with the improvement of the poorer tenemental property of the area. The membership of these single issue groups was entirely white, in spite of the fact that the groups represented residents in blocks of housing where we knew Asian families were living. Most of the groups had not been translating their publicity material into any ethnic minority languages, had not examined the ways in which they could have made black residents welcome and did not take account of the need to use translating or interpreting facilities for those Asian residents whose first language was not English. Occasionally committees would take up or refer to Crossroads individual problems of Asian people but the virtual all white image, apart from Annual General Meetings or Public Meetings, tended to go unchallenged.

This insensitivity, sometimes open hostility, led Crossroads, in traditional community work terms organising the unorganised, to support the establishment of black only groups and in particular the N—— Asian Group. The overall balance of our information work and community work reflected the proportion of Asian people in Govanhill: however, due to the reluctance of most community groups to respond to the particular problems faced by Asian residents, the only appropriate course of action that staff felt comfortable with was to support new groups organised around specific expressed needs.

The situation in N——, came to a head after the establishment of the N ——Asian Group. The Group was formed out of an increasing problem of racial harassment in the area. All Asian/black families in the area were contacted by Crossroads about their experience of racial harassment and most were able to highlight recent incidents. On calling a meeting of these tenants it was agreed that the Group should be formed and set itself the objectives of making agencies aware of the problem, to accept its existence and to use the Group to push for the rehousing of those tenants that wished it to areas not so badly affected by racial harassment. The existing Tenants Association discouraged the use of a local community flat for a meeting of the black only tenants group. The N—— Action Group, adopting a colour blind approach, stated that it represented all sections of the community and its needs, and that there was no need for Asian tenants to meet and organise separately.

Within Crossroads, a strong argument was put that a separate organisation representing black only tenants weakened all tenants in that area and that all tenants should be united behind one banner of a united tenants association. The counter argument to this was that the white tenants association had shown no sign of tackling the one single issue uniting the black tenants, which for them was the most important issue, racial harassment.

Following traditional community work practice, meetings took place with Crossroads staff and the black families where a strategy was evolved to pursue certain objectives which the black families felt would resolve their growing fear of further racial harassment. The meetings were conducted in Urdu with translation into English. The community work support to this group involved helping the group to identify objectives, offering practical support such as typing and photocopying and advising the group on the various methods of raising issues with other agencies to ensure that these agencies included the issue of racial harassment on their agendas. For most of the families at that time, although not all, their favoured solution to their problems entailed vigorously pursuing rehousing applications, some of which were ultimately successful. The group encountered several different responses to their statements and evidence of racial harassment by housing officials, ranging from outright denial that it occurred, to blaming black and white tenants equally for creating the situation, to laying the blame on poverty and unemployment without giving any credence to the specific effects of racism on black people facing harassment.

Crossroads staff saw part of their function to be assisting the black tenants to prepare a case which evidenced their actual experience. In this process of gathering information and evidence, the tenants showed their trust for Crossroads as an agency prepared to listen and respond to their problems as they defined them. Crossroads supported them in their attempts to bring about change, by making available resources that allowed meetings to be conducted in Urdu with a paid translator. Staff, recognising the dangers in becoming a spokesperson for the group in meetings with the Police and other officials, made strenuous attempts to involve members of the group in the presentation of their case, seeing this as part of our attempts to develop ethnically sensitive practice.

The strategy of the N—— Asian Group concentrated on resolving individual problems created by racial harassment through pursuing rehousing. Whether eventually this Group would have adopted a strategy which placed emphasis upon targeting the white tenants association to fight racial harassment involving the black tenants is unclear, as the Group eventually became less active following successful rehousing and less frequent attacks of racial harassment on its members.

g) Asian Womens Action Group and community work

Contact with local Asian women was steadily built up during the early days of our move to new shop front premises. In ones and twos, Asian women would come into the shop to explore what kind of organisation we were and what kind of services we had to offer. Crossroads staff were able to spend time cultivating these contacts, who sought advice and help on a range of issues from tenemental repairs to dealing with difficult children. As the number of individual callers grew and demands for the service increased by word of mouth advertising, community work staff in Crossroads began discussions with the women about setting up a self help group and in particular exploring with the women measures that would break down the isolation that they recognised many Asian women experienced and suffered.

This early work, examined in detail by Wardhaugh (this volume) formed the embryonic beginning of an organisation which still exists today. The success of the group was due in part to the following factors. The group was quick to gel and get off the ground. They successfully tapped into resources for Asian women, e.g. by raising funds for informal adult education activities. The strong personalities of the first office bearers ensured an atmosphere which was non-judgemental towards women whose circumstances were different from accepted norms. The group organised successful events which attracted a much wider support than only their existing members. The group members stretched themselves by setting up relevant training opportunities, e.g. office organisation classes, welfare rights training. Individual members of the group provided emotional and practical help to local women in trouble.

The group of women who set up the Asian Womens Action Group in December 1984 chose the name and the issues around which they felt Asian women would get organised. Their objectives were to break down the isolation of Asian women by educating and socialising with each other in an environment in which different circumstances would be tolerated. Since December 1984, the membership has altered, with old members leaving and new members coming, with many of the most committed members now in full-time paid employment or on various training courses. The attempts of the group to help Asian women expand their horizons and in so doing change their social circumstances has had some success. The Asian Womens Action Group has not eradicated racial inequality or racial harassment, but in the process of pursuing their own objectives the involvement of women in the Asian Womens Action Group has managed to increase the confidence and participation of some.

The most recent initiative of the group was to support an Assertiveness Training course for local women who were interested in training which would develop their confidence in a variety of settings. This shows the continuing role of the group in encouraging new women to stretch themselves. Twelve women successfully completed the course, which included relaxation training, a discussion on racism, interviewing techniques, confidence building and the management of stress. We insisted that there be a black tutor to accompany the white tutor who had more experience and this greatly enhanced the discussion which was often conducted in Urdu. From this training several other ideas to be developed have been suggested by the women including setting up a community business in the area, run by the women, to provide halal food to schools and day centres in the area.

Since 1984, the bulk of community work practice with Asian women has been carried out by a white English only speaking community worker. Crossroads management committee funded this worker through a language course but the benefits of this in reality have been limited linguistically. The benefits of this initiative however were significant in that the local Asian women were impressed by it and took a great deal of interest in the course and in encouraging the worker to use some Urdu vocabulary. Communication between staff and activists has been helped by the resources of the information and translating budget which forms part of the funding of the Association. However, there are limitations in a community group setting in picking up suggestions and points which are made in the course of a lively and often heated discussion. Staff rely heavily on bi-lingual activists feeding information back in order to ensure that implementation of ideas and suggestions can be carried out by staff.

Staff have built up strong relationships with local Asian women activists and the strength of these relationships depends upon the continuing relevance of the support offered to the women. We attempted to create an atmosphere that would minimise the feeling of superiority and in reality the strong relationships that were established were the backbone of the development of the community work with the various community groups in Govanhill. Trust can only be earned between activists and community workers and does not depend upon ignoring differences or disagreements. For example, strong reservations were expressed by the Asian Womens Action Group members when they were addressed by a speaker from a young persons hostel who was seeking their ideas about setting up a young Asian womens refuge. Crossroads staff supported the view that a small refuge was necessary and differed with the general view of the group which was against such a resource. The strength of the relationships ensured that the group knew that the workers were there to help the group develop resources and strengths to meet its needs, although the starting point for staff and activists and indeed between activists themselves, would often be very different. Honesty about different values did not prevent the development of good working relationships. The activists however depended not only on good relationships but also on the quality of information and advice that accompanied them. Furthermore, an openness to learn about different cultural interests and a willingness to challenge racism cemented the trust.

h) Govanhill Asian Self Help Housing Group.

The recent development of the Govanhill Asian Self Help Housing group illustrates some of the particular skills and background knowledge needed to provide good community work practice with a black only group by white workers.

This group emanated from contact made with 22 Asian families with housing problems in the Southside of Glasgow. Having interviewed the families, Crossroads established their aspirations and current housing conditions. Our findings bore out many of the findings of the Home Office Research Study (1989) which offers a detailed explanation for the low take up of statutory and voluntary sector services by the Asian community. The survey suggests (p 43) that 'many local services are unsuitable or unavailable to the Asian community, or are seen by that community as being so.' At the first meeting of the Asian Self Help Housing Group, at which all dialogue was translated into English or Urdu as necessary, one of the members told another member that it was only possible to apply to one Housing agency at any one time and that therefore, for example, it was not possible to have an application with the local community based housing Association and the District Council at the same time. This mistaken view was expressed by an experienced community activist and could easily have been picked up and passed around to other members of the community. Given the prevalent dependence upon word of mouth information about services within the Asian community, systems must be devised which overcome inaccurate information being circulated. This places responsibilities on statutory and voluntary organisations which have major responsibility for ensuing equal opportunity and access to services.

The first meeting of the Govanhill Asian Self Help Housing Group also illustrated that in fact people did have some knowledge of the various forms of housing tenure available in the area including local authority, although there was much less knowledge about the community based Housing Association. It was not necessarily lack of knowledge therefore that was preventing housing problems being resolved: other factors came into play. As mentioned already, local knowledge, if inaccurate, could prevent problems being solved. Also the belief that public sector housing was for 'white people only', another view expressed at the meeting, suggests that services must be seen to be appropriate and eligible for the Asian community and this will also mean that agencies have to be more pro-active in their attempts to provide equal access to services. Workers attending these meetings had to familiarise themselves with the kind of barriers, both real and felt, that prevented Asian people overcoming their housing difficulties. Workers also required to have basic knowledge about local housing policy and allocations systems which in a practical way offered solutions to some of the problems presented.

This group is still working out its objectives and aims but is clear that the individuals making up the group will educate themselves to help others overcome individual housing problems. There will still be long queues for better housing in better areas, tenants will still have to wait to get repairs done or to be rehoused, but the role of this group will ensure that Asian families will not be disadvantaged due to lack of information. The group will push for bi-lingual staff to be available for appointments and the translation of signs and information to be available in different ethnic minority languages, at the local Housing Department and Housing Association. They will ensure that tenants do not have to bring their own interpreters and that repairs will not go unattended because Housing Department staff fail to pick up problems. Perhaps most importantly, the group will in the future feel confident about tackling the policy vacuum that currently exists around the issue of racial harassment in the area. The better informed the individuals of the group feel, then the more confident they will become as activists and collectively challenge the poor quality of service in Govanhill. The link between private ills and public issues will continue to develop the work of this group to deal appropriately with the unmet needs of the Asian community and hopefully to generalise this experience city wide.

Conclusion

Crossroads is not yet satisfied that it has achieved racial equality in its work. We have learnt that the process is a continuous one, changing and developing as our knowledge improves. Community work with ethnic minorities has differences from other forms of community work practice, primarily in the field of content of the work itself, which for example requires an appreciation of black perspectives on many issues. The form of community work practice is essentially the same, as good community work practice should be informed by a perspective that accepts and understands the influence and impact on black peoples' lives of racism. Working with ethnic minorities around issues that specifically affect them, such as racial harassment, or in working with white only groups in a non-discriminatory and anti-racist way, will demand that community workers are confident in the issues and the methods required to challenge them.

Racism, which leads to discrimination and disadvantage, forms part of a society in which inequality, poverty and suffering are further evidence of the need for people to organise to challenge those structures which make the decisions that influence all our lives. Community work has a role to play in providing a method of challenging these structures in which individuals themselves play a role in overcoming their problems.

References

Bowes A.M. (ed) 1987 *Asian Women in Glasgow: an Action Research Project*   Glasgow: Crossroads Youth and Community Association

Bryant B. and Bryant R. 1982 *Change and Conflict: a Study of Community Work in Glasgow* Aberdeen: Aberdeen University Press.

Dominelli L. 1988 *Anti-racist Social Work*   London: MacMillan

Home Office 1989 *Race, Community Groups and Service Delivery*   (Research Study 113) London: HMSO.

MacLeod L. 1988 *Irrespective of Race, Colour or Creed?*   Edinburgh: SCVO.

Chapter 9

Asian women: campaigning for self-help

Julia Wardhaugh

Introduction

This paper is based on research carried out as part of a joint action-research project sponsored by Stirling University and Crossroads Youth and Community Association. Crossroads is a community agency serving Govanhill, an inner-city area in the South side of Glasgow, which is the centre of one of Glasgow's main Asian communities. Being an action-research project, there was close involvement with local community organisations, the aim being not only to observe and document their activities, but to feedback research results which might contribute to their development (Lees and Smith 1975, Leonard 1975, Bryant and Bryant 1982).

The first part of the paper considers the processes involved in the development of self-help groups - their formation, their values, their growth and expansion and their relationship to the wider community - and the second part outlines some of the issues addressed by two of these groups - welfare benefits, housing, racial harassment, and domestic violence. The first of the groups is the Asian Women's Action Group (AWAG), a broadly-based women's group aiming to meet a range of material, social, cultural and community needs. The second group, the Asian Housing Group (AHG), was a mixed group formed on the basis of tackling racial harassment on the North Govanhill housing scheme. The account of these two groups is based on participant observation and in-depth interviews carried out in Govanhill between 1984 and 1986. All names used have been changed.

Group formation

Of the large number of people who share membership of a particular category - in this case Asian women in Govanhill -only a minority will take direct action on this basis by joining a community or self-help group. It is worth looking, then, at some of the factors which favour Asian women joining a group, and those which militate against this.

As a minimum, there must be some discontent with the status quo, a belief in the possibility of change, and a willingness to take action to effect this change. In addition, in the case of the women's group, founder-members had certain resources facilitating their activism, including some or all of: middle-class origins, urban rather than rural origins in the subcontinent, and a level of further education (Saifullah Khan 1987, Wilson 1978).

This was less the case with the housing group whose members had few of these resources: membership of this group was determined largely by residence and by the intervention of Crossroads, who provided the motivating force for group formation. For members of the women's group, positive factors for group membership had to be weighed against negative factors especially male opposition to the formation of a women's group. For many women, the (temporary or permanent) absence of husbands or fathers from the household was a central factor in their being able to become active in the women's group. Others, with husbands present, were acutely aware of the restrictions thus imposed:

> *He thinks I'm at the shops now, you know (laughs)....I'm not really supposed to be here....I can't stay too long, though, as I can't explain being out for more than a couple of hours. (Woman at AWAG meeting)*

A large part of the strength of the group derived from the ability of such women to negotiate the restrictions imposed on their lives.

Group norms

While AWAG was not necessarily familiar with the theoretical or ideological background of the feminist and community action movements, it did share many of their principles, in particular, a commitment to egalitarian, accountable groups, with all members sharing in decision-making processes (Curno 1978, Lowe 1986, Mayo 1977, Morgan 1970). Importantly, however, AWAG drew not only on Western feminist and socialist traditions, but also on well-established procedures within the women's own community, drawing on traditions of organising from within the Indian sub-continent. It was commonplace for group members to consult widely with women outside the group on important issues, using a range of informal contacts, to ensure participation by both English and Urdu/Punjabi speakers, and to base all action on consensus opinion (Bryan, Dadzie and Scafe 1985, Davies 1983, Foster-Carter 1987).

This contrasts with AHG, where male group members often took a leadership role in terms of dominating both discussions and decision-making processes: further, discussion was almost exclusively in English, thus excluding Urdu/Punjabi speakers, as while almost all men spoke English, many women did not (Brown 1984).

While AWAG became increasingly independent of Crossroads, formulating for themselves their own values, norms and procedures, AHG remained heavily dependent on Crossroads during its short existence. This does not reflect on the group or on Crossroads, but is simply a measure of the enormous task facing the group, their relative powerlessness, and the many obstacles in the way of effective group development (Cheetham 1981, Henderson and Thomas 1981).

Group expansion

Central to the question of group expansion is whether a particular group is single-issue, or whether it is more broadly-based. Single issue groups, by definition, are likely to have a limited constituency, for example there were only around a dozen Asian households on the North Govanhill scheme thus ruling out the potential for the expansion of the housing group. AHG was of course aware of shared interests with Asian households in the rest of Govanhill, many of whom suffered some form of racial harassment. However, factors militating against making such links included, firstly, the geographical isolation of those in North Govanhill; secondly, the main target of campaign for AHG was the District Council Housing Department, while the majority of Asian households in Govanhill belonged to the private sector; and thirdly, members of AHG experienced the most severe racial violence while many others experienced mostly verbal abuse which, while serious, did not provide such a strong basis for action.

AWAG, in being a more broadly based group, was successful in attracting new members. This is not to say there were no periods when the group was static, failing to expand: however, precisely because it was flexible and varied in its aims and approach, it could always adapt in order to respond to the needs and priorities of Asian women in the community. Thus, by means as varied as the making and showing of a video, lectures and talks, the provision of sewing classes and the sharing of cultural and social events, many new members were attracted and incorporated into the group.

Wider context

Groups need not be narrowly defined in terms of their regular members, but the concept can be expanded to include a 'floating' membership, that is, those with only occasional contact with the group. Such members were not of peripheral importance for AWAG - rather, they represented an important 'natural constituency', the women whose needs the group aimed to serve, and to whom they held themselves accountable. Thus, AWAG frequently consulted a wide range of women, using their own informal network of contacts and this allowed grassroots organising to take place on a solid basis (Jeffery 1976).

As should be clear by now, AHG had no such 'natural constituency' as they were both socially and geographically isolated from the mainstream Asian community. Women in AHG did not also become members of AWAG due partly to isolation within their own homes and the enormity of problems they faced, including poverty, racism, and poor housing. Furthermore a significant level of male domination - both domestically and within AHG - reduced the possibility of their taking independent action within a women's group (Bhatti 1976, Dahya 1965).

Welfare benefits

Action on welfare benefits was the first major project undertaken by AWAG and this served not only to improve the material circumstances of many women (in particular, several women received substantial payments from the Department of Social Security as a result of benefits checks) but to further the development of the group itself. In particular it crystallized questions of group identity, and the nature of its liaison with Crossroads. Closely connected with group identity were fluctuations in group membership, especially the fact that some founder-members left, to be replaced by new women. Slowly the group expanded to encompass women of all backgrounds and interests. The important thing was to establish a coherent group identity and sense of purpose which could transcend fluctuations in group membership and variable attendance at meetings. This was in fact achieved, largely because the group remained at all times grounded in the wider community. The question of liaison with Crossroads remained an ongoing one for many months: at first the group relied heavily on Crossroads for material, emotional and political support. Gradually, however, and in line with Crossroads policy, the group became increasingly self-reliant, and took more of the initiative for new and ongoing projects and activities.

However, and certainly in the first year of its existence, liaison with Crossroads was very important, as was the development of what was to become a triangular relationship between AWAG, Crossroads and researchers. The nature of this relationship, and the development of the group, can perhaps best be illustrated by an outline of one of the group's projects.

The first major project undertaken by the group, in Summer 1984, was the making of a video about the processes involved in making a claim for welfare benefits. The idea was to raise a subject relevant to many Asian women's lives, and by making a video in Urdu with English subtitles, for it to be as accessible as possible. The video could be shown at various venues, with a threefold aim: to pass on useful information on the benefits system; to encourage women to seek further advice on a range of problems; and to attract new members to the group. In making the video, technical aid came from Queen's College, Glasgow, advice and help from community workers and students, while the Asian women themselves wrote the script and acted the roles. The result was a half-hour long video, well-made and well-presented, telling the fictional but fairly representative story of a young Asian woman's life. Briefly, her husband leaves her to return to Pakistan, leaving her with little money and with children to care for. She has little knowledge of the English language, so a friend goes with her to the Department of Social Security to help translate, and to explain how the system operates. The same friend helps her through the subsequent processes: home visits by the Department of Social Security officer, filling in application forms and supplying the necessary documentation, awaiting payment, and finally visiting the supermarket.

The video, then, dramatised the range of obstacles faced by Asian women in dealing with the benefits system, the complexities of a bureaucratic system being compounded by lack of familiarity with the English language. A major aim of the video was to address the material conditions of Asian women's lives, and to this end the video proved to be of considerable practical value. However, it was also of importance in the development of the group: firstly, in increasing group members' confidence in their own skills and abilities; secondly, in giving a clear focus to the group through their joint work on a shared project; thirdly, in defining a target group towards which their activities should be directed; and fourthly, as the subsequent showing of the video attracted new members, it allowed the group to broaden its base, and to connect with a wider reference group.

Once the video was completed, in the Autumn of 1984, AWAG members, community workers and researchers all engaged in several weeks of discussion concerning the appropriate venue for the showing of the video, and what was hoped to be gained from the exercise. The consensus was that choice of venue was very important, as this had implications for the type of audience it would reach. for example, the saree shops were used primarily by Muslim rather than Sikh women, while Sikh as well as Muslim women could be contacted through the local nursery school; furthermore, certain groups of Muslim women were more likely to use one rather than another of the five saree shops in Govanhill. Other possible venues considered were the private houses used by the more religiously-observant Muslim women for prayer-meetings on Friday evenings.

In the end, the 'Parents Room' at Annette Street primary school was chosen, for several reasons: firstly, it was a venue familiar to most Asian women in the neighbourhood; secondly, it was equally used by all sections of the Asian community so no-one was likely to feel excluded on religious, kinship or any other grounds; and thirdly, the meeting could be arranged to fit in with the school timetable, thus allowing women to attend unhindered by responsibility for children, or their husbands' negative attitudes to their leaving the house without 'good reason'.

The showing of the video in December 1984 was deliberately planned as a joint action-research event, with Crossroads providing video facilities and welfare advice, AWAG advising and translating, and the researcher observing and documenting the proceedings. It was felt to be important to record the whole event as it was a new kind of activity for AWAG, in that they were undertaking outreach, rather than contacting women already known to them.

Around 10-12 women attended each day, first watching the video, then seeking detailed advice on welfare, housing and immigration issues. The set-up was very informal with women forming and re-forming small groups to suit their needs. There was also discussion amongst the women, not necessarily with group members, on personal and family problems. As usual, discussion was in both Urdu and English, much of it being translated so that everyone could understand most of what was said.

It is important to note that, along with a range of practical aims, these days were also a social occasion. This was an important end in itself, given the extent to which many women were confined to their home, and had few other meeting-places. It was also important in that socialising helps to break down isolation, and is often the first step towards the recognition of shared interests. Later, if women became involved in community action, their personal and social contacts made for a stronger and more cohesive group.

The showing of the video did, in fact, attract some new members. It is interesting to note the process involved in becoming included in the group. One women's experience can serve as an illustration: arriving early in the day, there were few others there, and she sat alone, obviously feeling awkward. She exchanged a few words with one or two members of the group, then watched the video. Before the video was over she had visibly relaxed, and began to enter into more animated conversation, in Urdu, on both practical and personal matters. She met with a warm response and so began her gradual acceptance into the group.

It is interesting to note the transformation of the event from a tense, slightly formal beginning, with community workers taking a lot of the initiative, to stay more relaxed, informal atmosphere later in the day, when community workers had moved slightly into the background, and Asian women were communicating freely amongst themselves. Conversation ranged from immediate welfare problems, to the question of arranged marriages:

> I had an arranged marriage myself, but I don't think I would do the same for my children...mind you, I don't blame my parents, they were just doing what they thought was best for me.

This reply, after some slight hesitation, to the community worker's question on the subject, indicates a level of trust in the white people present not to judge as 'strange' Asian culture and customs. This pattern of slight hesitation to discuss certain subjects with white people, followed by the decision to trust, was also evident on several other occasions, most notably in relation to the question of arranged marriages, and immigration and nationality issues, all of which are the object of much misunderstanding and prejudice (Wilson 1978).

After the meeting, group members discussed the success of the event, and debated the future direction and development of AWAG. They noted that women were much more interested in attending what they perceived as social events, rather than occasions more formally presented as 'community action' meetings. In reality, the distinction between the two, for AWAG at least, is artificial: 'social' occasions were often the setting for self-help and community organising, while 'action' group meetings were also important in terms of social interaction. Nevertheless, in order to attract new members to the group, AWAG were beginning to realise that presentation was important, and that they should perhaps organise more overtly 'social' occasions, in order to attract new members, and by this means introduce them to community activism.

Housing

The second major project for AWAG was involvement in conducting a series of housing interviews, carried out by the researcher, and designed to document the housing conditions and the housing needs of Asian households in Govanhill. These interviews provided the opportunity for close collaboration between the researcher and AWAG, in that AWAG's network of contacts provided a number of people willing to be interviewed, group members provided translation where necessary, and researchers, group members and Crossroads workers all benefitted from discussions arising out of these interviews.

The two major issues to emerge from the interviews were the appalling housing conditions many households had to endure, and the strong desire of many households for entry into the public housing sector (Henderson and Karn 1984, Robinson 1980, Runnymede Trust and Radical statistics Race Group 1980). The group and action-research workers then discussed the potential for organising community action around these two issues. After several meetings it was agreed that as Crossroads was already deeply involved in the issue of housing conditions it was better to encourage Asian households to join existing groups, rather than to form new ones, because as both tenants and homeowners, Asian households shared many needs and interests in common with their white neighbours.

In terms of housing access, however, the group were concerned that Asian households did not simply share a position similar to that of others in Govanhill, but were in fact subjected to systematic racial discrimination in gaining access to the city's public housing stock. In meetings, group members referred to their own experiences:

You go down to Argyle Street (housing allocations department for City Centre and South, which includes Govanhill) and they just don't want to know, no-one shows you how to fill in the forms, or helps you to decide which choices to make.

and:

They're all right on the 'phone, then when you go down and they see a black face, that's it, you know you've got no chance.

However, despite their concern the group was not at that point ready to take action: they realised the extreme difficulty of tackling the whole question of the operation of the allocations system, although in the longer term they did aspire to having some influence on housing policy and on the decision-making processes of the Housing Department (see Dunleavy 1980, on the importance of documenting non-action over housing issues).

In the shorter term, then, the group decided to focus only on those housing issues which were likely to meet with some fairly tangible success. In particular, they became concerned with the question of hostel provision for battered women, as this was the issue which was increasingly preoccupying the group, both in personal and in wider community terms. Throughout 1985, then, and into 1986, the group became very concerned with the question of refuge provision for Asian women. The group's concern with violence against women in general, and refuge provision in particular, is discussed in more detail in a following section (and related issues by Pahl 1985, Rose 1978).

While housing conditions and access to housing did not become central to AWAG's community activism, the importance of these issues to the group's social and political development should not be underestimated. The case-study of Sheraz Begum illustrates the extent to which one woman's housing experiences were pivotal not only to her own involvement in the group but also to the group's own development.

A woman in her late twenties, Sheraz Begum lived until 1985 in an owner-occupied three-apartment house in the heart of Govanhill's Asian community. She came to this house from Pakistan, nine years earlier, in order to join her husband, Mushtaq Ali, a man then in his late fifties. Speaking very little English, and therefore unable to deal directly with public institutions and services, Sheraz was very dependent on her husband.

As there were four children, the main problem for the household was overcrowding. Other conditions were fairly typical, especially of the older housing in Govanhill - cold and dampness, inadequate heating facilities, poor wiring, but, unlike many others, there were at least bathroom amenities and running hot water. At the time of the interview, May 1985, major improvements were being carried out on the house.

Before deciding to invest money in these improvements, they had considered other alternatives. They had thought of moving house, but in terms of private renting, they felt it was impossible to find a reasonable place without any major defects. They also thought of renting from the council, but had been deterred from applying, for two reasons. First, they wanted to stay in Govanhill but realised that there were long waiting-lists for the area (that is, the decent council housing, not North Govanhill), and secondly, that, if they lived in council accommodation they felt they were far more likely to face severe levels of racial harassment. At present they had few problems with their neighbours. When asked, they said they knew nothing of the existence of the local Govanhill Housing Association.

This, then, was the situation in May 1985. Later that summer, however, it became clear that Sheraz was being repeatedly and severely beaten by Mushtaq. The situation was intolerable, but for a woman with four children, speaking little English, and with little or no money, the prospects of survival on her own were not good. However, with the practical help and advice of Crossroads, and the emotional support of the Asian Women's Group, Sheraz did leave the marital home for the Asian women's refuge outside the city.

Once settled into the temporary accommodation of the refuge, Sheraz had to begin thinking about permanent rehousing for herself and her children. The few weeks she stayed there were spent in various consultations with the Housing Department, social workers and her solicitor, as, apart from possible rehousing by the council she also had to clarify her legal position with regard to rights of residence in the marital home. While in law Sheraz did have some rights in this respect, she decided not to pursue them, deterred mainly by her husband's hostility and aggression. Deciding that her main priority was safety, she reluctantly left Mushtaq in possession of the marital home. Financially, she had to make a claim for Supplementary Benefits, both the usual weekly allowance, and single payments for furnishings for her new accommodation (single payments have now been abolished). During and after this period she received continued support from Crossroads, and from the Asian Women's Action Group, in the form of advice on her legal, housing, and welfare rights, and translation of discussions with the relevant agencies.

In September 1985, Sheraz Begum was offered temporary accommodation in Toryglen, an area adjoining Govanhill. As the house was in reasonable condition, was near to the Asian community in Govanhill, and was in any case only a temporary measure, she decided to accept the offer. The council policy on those in temporary accommodation is that they should be offered permanent housing very quickly, but it was in fact February 1986 before any further action was taken.

On 12 February, Sheraz was offered a house in the Hillpark/Mansewood area of the city (a district lying a mile or two to the south of Govanhill), with the stipulation that she should accept or refuse the offer within twenty-four hours. Sheraz wanted to be rehoused in either Govanhill or Pollokshields, as she felt she needed to live within an Asian community. Otherwise, speaking little English she would find it very difficult to shop, or seek help from neighbours in dealing with everyday matters such as electricity bills, and especially, there would be no-one to help with the children if she was ill, or was faced with some other crisis.

In discussion with a community worker from Crossroads, officers from the Homeless

Persons Unit insisted that there was no possibility of Mrs Begum being offered accommodation in either Govanhill or Pollokshields. They regretted this, as they realised that the proposed new move would make it difficult for Mrs Begum to send her children to the mosque, some 3-4 miles away in the Gorbals. While this remark was supposed to show some sensitivity to the importance of area of residence to Asian families, for Sheraz Begum, nearness to the mosque was not one of her priorities: rather, she needed the practical and moral support she was used to receiving within an established Asian community.

On inspection, the house itself proved to be damp, lacking a sink, and badly in need of decoration. The housing officers stated, however, that if these problems could be overcome, then Mrs Begum would have to accept the house, as she would receive only one offer. This was standard council policy on rehousing the homeless. While, clearly, a sink could be installed, and the house decorated, it was difficult to see, as the community worker involved commented, how the problem of dampness could be 'overcome'. Sheraz was eventually satisfactorily rehoused, but without the extensive support of both Crossroads and the Asian Women's Action Group it is difficult to believe that this would have been possible.

While this advocacy role was an important aspect of AWAG's community activism, it should not be confused with the system of patronage that exists both within the local political system and within the Asian business community. AWAG deliberately avoided such methods, and consciously adopted a more egalitarian approach. Thus, while they certainly did much to help individual women, the relationship was reciprocal in that, firstly, these women frequently became active members of the group, and secondly, even if this was not the case, they were very much a part of group development in that they helped in defining priorities, in developing organising methods, and in consolidating group identity. Individual experiences such as that of Sheraz Begum were central to these processes.

Racial violence

The Asian Housing Group (AHG) was established to tackle the problem of racial violence on the North Govanhill council scheme. The group was initiated by Crossroads who contacted all the Asian households they could trace in North Govanhill (around 12-13 households) and invited them to join an action group: about half of those contacted responded positively to this invitation. AHG was a mixed rather than women-only group and it is worth considering the position of women in this group. Mr Sharma expresses the position of the men clearly:

I would prefer to be in a group with men, I don't know what to say to Asian women... in our culture women are second-class citizens, they don't know how to relate to men. I can talk to you, though, that's different.

His comment also reveals the 'token male' status accorded to the white woman academic (cf. Bhachu 1985, Papanek 1964, Pettigrew 1981).

In meetings, men took leadership roles, and women did little of the talking: united by

F

their experiences of white racism, the group was nevertheless divided by gender. This division was one barrier to the effectiveness of the group and another was the sheer enormity of the problems they faced, along with their extreme vulnerability and relative powerlessness. Some comments by group members will serve to illustrate the extent of the problem:

> *Mrs Ahmed: All the time, it happens nearly every day, they call us 'black bastard' and 'Paki'....but what can you do, there's so many of them and so few of us.*

> *Mr Mohammed: It's just happening nearly every day now, over the past two weeks the children have had bricks thrown at them - one had to go to hospital for stitches - my wife is shouted at in the streets, they're writing on our doors and keeping us awake at night. I don't know how much longer we can take it.*

These and many other similar comments alerted both the group and Crossroads to the need to document the extent of racial violence, as a first stage in the process of tackling the problem. Thus the action-research task was formulated, namely that the researcher should interview households in North Govanhill, and document their experiences. These accounts would then form the basis of the group's community activism.

As well as providing a campaigning tool, consideration of individual life-histories served as a focus for the group as a whole, as they engaged in the process of assessing the meaning and the implications of their individual and collective experiences. Over the course of several weeks, during the Winter of 1984, the following accounts were constructed.

The Ahmed household were living temporarily in council accommodation in North Govanhill, while they waited for improvements to their own house to be carried out. Furnishings consisted mainly of the most basic seating and bedding, floors remained uncovered, and several windows were broken, the result of repeated racist attacks. Mrs Ahmed told her story thus:

> *Well, as you can see I have six children, that's the oldest there, he's twelve. My husband isn't here at the moment, he went back to Pakistan on a visit, three months ago - I'm not sure when he will be back. What is it you want to know? There is just so much to tell. It happens all the time, the children will tell you. They attack them in the playground, or when they are on their way to school, or when they are coming home. See his face, that's how he got that cut. You call the police but they don't do anything, and anyway when it's children there's nothing they can do, it's mostly young boys who do it, you know. But I do blame the headmaster, he could be something about it, at least he could make sure it doesn't happen in the playground.*

> *Then when they come home it's just the same, if they go out the children throw stones at them, they shout names at them, call them 'Paki'. They call me names as well, every time I go out, sometimes they throw things as well. One time a group of them came up and they pulled the dupatta off my head, I was very frightened. You know, I can't even get to the telephone to call the police because that's where they stand, I can tell you they will always be up there by the shops, and in the park, that's the other place. I have to send the children to the shops for me, but often they will come back crying, saying they have stolen the money from them or something. I just don't*

know what to do, can you do anything to help?

This story was told slowly and with difficulty, with some of the older children providing help with translation. Mrs Ahmed shifted from despair to anger in the telling of her story, and on one occasion turned inwards in her depression and was unable to speak of her experience at all. Elements of her story, and her response, were to be repeated again and again in the documentation of racial violence in North Govanhill. While the impact of such experiences cannot of course be quantified, the experience of the Mohammed household was perhaps the most severe in North Govanhill. As Mrs Mohammed speaks virtually no English, Mr Mohammed tells their story:

Come in, this is my wife, she is having another baby soon. She has to lie here in the living-room as the bedroom is too damp, but it is not good for her with all the children running around, it is too noisy. The house is far too small for nine of us, and the children are young, they need to run around and play outside, but we can't let them because the neighbours complain all the time. Anyway, we're scared to let them out now, in case they're attacked again. Just the other day I did let her play outside, she was only there, just in front of the window where I could see her, but after only a few minutes the bigger boys were throwing stones and calling her names, so I had to bring her in. I wish I knew what to do. I have got family in the Midlands, I've thought of going down there, and perhaps there would be more chance of a job. But I don't really think it would be any better, probably it would be worse, there might be more attacks.

Later -

The past few weeks have been the worst, I suppose you've heard a bit about them? I didn't believe people could do such things. First they put a bottle through the letterbox, it was full of bees, they were still alive, another time it was a bottle filled with urine. Than late at night they started putting fireworks through the door, setting light to them first, they really scared my wife and the children. The worst, though, was when they set light to the door, they fastened a sack or something to the door, poured petrol on it and set it alight. Luckily we were all still awake, well, I hardly dare go to sleep at night, I'm always waiting for something to happen. So no-one was hurt but we've had enough now, they'll have to move us, we just can't stay here.

In the next stage of the group's community activism, their intention was to use these accounts to publicise the nature and extent of this problems, in an attempt to influence the relevant agencies, and thus to bring about some improvement in their situation. In terms of eradicating the problem of racial violence, group effectiveness was inevitably limited (see Kraushaar 1981, on the difficulties of organising for change in Britain). However, they did achieve certain objectives, firstly the issue of harassment was raised with the Housing Department, police and local councillors: while meeting with no immediate positive response, the issue was at least placed on the political agenda. These moves were consolidated by Bowes, McCluskey and Sim's research, which further raised the question of racial harassment with the District Council (see their chapter in this volume).

Secondly, the main research role was to document experience of racial harassment. During this process, however, other related issues began to emerge, for example, the links between racial harassment and health problems. Mrs Shah, for example, suffered severe panic attacks due to the harassment she experienced:

My own health is poor anyway, and it's getting worse with all the stress...the children become frightened too, and it's them I worry about most, they're so small and can't understand what's happening.

Thirdly, while harassment in general was not eradicated, at least the position of some of the most vulnerable households was improved, either by rehousing or by support from group members and Crossroads.

Domestic violence

By the Autumn of 1985 significant changes had become apparent in the Asian Women's Action Group. The numbers of women involved in the group was steadily increasing, much of the new membership coming from women attending the sewing-classes established by AWAG in association with the Community Education Department. Funding for these classes came from the European Community Social Fund, AWAG, Crossroads and the Community Education Department having worked hard together to secure funding from this source. This was a considerable achievement within an economic climate where funding for 'social' causes was increasingly difficult to obtain. There was a greater demand for these classes than could be accommodated, and one session soon grew into two per week. While women clearly did want to learn to sew, for many it was equally important as a social event, and the provision of a free creche meant that at least for a couple of hours each week they were free to pursue their own interests.

On the surface, sewing classes may not seem a radical step, rather a means of reinforcing women's roles. However, for many Asian women, simply leaving the house and meeting with other women is a radical step (Hobson 1978). In addition, several group members noted that going to a sewing class, on the surface a 'respectable' activity, enabled them to engage in a range of social and political organising. Consciousness-raising, shared childcare, advocacy, problem-solving, adult education and planning community action tactics all took place at the sewing classes. During this period of expansion the group began to consolidate its identity as a group, and to consider addressing new areas of concern. Levels of confidence and optimism were high, and the group now felt able to address controversial issues such as racial harassment and domestic violence. In the course of several discussions, they outlined the scope and nature of racial harassment in Govanhill, noting that it was widespread and took many forms, from verbal abuse, to racist graffiti, to physical attacks. Domestic violence was not a new phenomenon, but this was perhaps the first time it had been publicly discussed. Some of the group had experienced it themselves, and were coming into contact with increasing numbers of other women who had been subjected to violence.

While some women were initially a little reluctant to discuss domestic violence, the strength of feeling on the subject soon overcame their hesitation: discussion of the issue was often intense and prolonged, reflecting the extent to which it had long been a hidden problem, shrouded in shame and secrecy. Some of the most vocal women were, understandably, those who had experienced violence themselves; discussion of their experiences was clearly an important step, as this was the first time that they had been communicated to outsiders.

The consensus of the group was that Asian women in Glasgow needed far more service provision, as well as practical and emotional support to enable them to leave violent husbands, and they were of the opinion that sympathy should lie with the woman, not with the man. As one woman expressed it:

People say you shouldn't leave him, you should give the man a chance. Well, I gave my husband a twenty-year 'chance', and it didn't get me anywhere.

At this time, group members were beginning to take action in support of battered women, and were also very concerned about the quality of help available to them. In addition to the frequent inadequacy of police, legal, and social work services, they were also concerned about the Asian women's refuge some distance outside the city. Based on the experience of one member of the group, and their visits to the refuge, they felt that it was inappropriate in several ways: it did not encourage visits from a women's friends, important as the refuge was twenty miles from the city, and thus women, especially those speaking little English were very isolated (one woman travelled the twenty miles by bus every day, with four children, simply for the help and support she received from AWAG). It also seemed that refuge workers were not always supportive of a woman's decision to leave her husband, and sometimes encouraged her to return. Workers were educated, middle-class Indian women and many of the AWAG women, often semi-literate, working-class Pakistani women, felt they could have little in common with them (see Ubero: 1965 on the divisions between educated and non-educated Asian women).

However, despite these disadvantages, the group still believed that it was essential that there should be refuge provision specifically for Asian women. They believed that only such a refuge could provide Asian women with an understanding of, and support for, their experiences of racial as well as domestic violence; protect them from white racism within their place of refuge; and provide the necessary language facilities, as well as a sensitivity to dress, dietary and cultural norms.

Discussion around these issues took place at several group meetings over the period Autumn 1985 - Spring 1986, and the group clarified its position on many issues relating to domestic violence. However, group members were of course at different levels of awareness, and/or had different priorities. It was one of the many strengths of AWAG that they were able to encompass these many different levels of need and experience.

In the Summer of 1986 the third major review of the action-research project provided a forum for extended discussion of domestic violence to take place. The following transcript of part of that discussion reveals in particular the extent to which the group were comparing themselves firstly with other, non-activist Asian women, and secondly with the experiences of white women. Both of these comparisons were essential to the process of defining group identity, and focusing on appropriate courses of action.

Nasira:	*Most battered women won't go to the authorities, they're scared to go to the police, they might suffer badly with their relatives if they did. Asian women won't speak out or complain about their problems, they'll only discuss them amongst themselves.*
Carol:	*Yes, the problem does seem to be hidden.*
Julia:	*Would women speak to a researcher, if they could be sure it was confidential?*
Nasira:	*Some would, some wouldn't.*
Carol:	*What about involving the women from the refuge?*
Nasira:	*But women won't go to a refuge, people will talk, say she's a bad woman.*
Ellen:	*But your group doesn't condemn these women.*
Nasira:	*No, but we have a bad reputation ourselves...but we will defend ourselves against these accusations...I still believe women should leave violent husbands.*
Carol:	*But they often don't, as there's nowhere for them to go.*
Nasira:	*Men just think women are their property.*
Amarjit:	*This is all nonsense, I could knock a man down, I'd just hit him back if he hit me.*
Rehana:	*But not all women are as strong as you.*
Ellen:	*What you need then is a class in self-defence...you know, you should remember that it's not always easy for white women either, we've had much the same problems.*
Nasreen:	*But it is easier for white women, they can just leave their husbands.*
Ellen:	*No, not always, they face the same problems of money and housing, and are often still condemned as bad women. We haven't had refuges that long, it's been a struggle. I remember the first women's hostel in Glasgow, people set the door alight, they did everything to get them out. I thought it was a terrible place myself, very poor conditions, but for the women there it was a safe place, it was what they needed.*
Carol:	*Yes, those refuges were only set up fifteen years ago, they faced lots of difficulties...it's the same for you now, but you have to start somewhere, start in small ways and build slowly on that.*
Sheraz:	*I know one woman, her husband used to tie her hands and leave her in the house all day, he'd come back to untie her to she could cook his meal, then tie her up again. She's in a refuge now.*
Nasira:	*Perhaps you do have lots of the same problems, but it's still different for us, we have no choice, we have to marry just anyone.*

This discussion was central to the development of the group's perception of, and attitudes towards, marital violence. This particular day, the third Project Review, marked an important point in the group's history. One focus of the day was the transition between the first and the second action-research projects, and in particular a shift in focus away from housing issues and towards domestic violence.

There are several major features of the Asian Women's Action Group at this period. Firstly, a strong, cohesive group had emerged, one that worked constantly to respond to emerging needs, and was continually adapting to integrate new members. Secondly, the balance of power, which had been slowly shifting over the two-year period, had now been clearly resolved, in that group members no longer relied so heavily on Crossroads, but were much more confident in articulating their needs, and in defining the focus for their community activism. Thirdly, this shift contributed to the development of a strong action-research relationship, with group members increasingly clear about what they wanted from researchers. Clearly, the second project would be beginning from a much stronger base than the first. However, the two years of the first project had proved to be an invaluable learning experience for all those involved: group members, community workers, and researchers.

Conclusion

The development of AWAG contrasts sharply with that of AHG, which met with far less success, in terms of both its own development, and the achievement of its stated aims. There are several reasons for this, including of course the severity of the problem, racial violence, which they were attempting to tackle. Furthermore, as a single-issue group they were unable to diversify when faced with organisation problems on this issue. Thirdly, they were very isolated as a group, having little substantial contact with the wider Asian community in Govanhill, and of course facing considerable hostility from their white neighbours. Finally, there were also significant internal divisions, in particular between men and women, with the men frequently taking leadership roles, thus preventing the emergence of a cohesive group based on full and equal participation by all members.

It is worth considering the extent to which the experiences of Asian women organising in Govanhill can be generalised. In some respects, the accounts presented here are very particular to the local situation, in that they represent a fairly detailed history of the two groups. Both belong to Glasgow's tradition of community action, AWAG especially continuing the long history of women organising for change at grassroots level (Madigan 1984, Melling 1983). Further, the group's histories are located in Govanhill, and are inevitably influenced by this context: here, the influence of Crossroads is central, as Asian community groups elsewhere in the city developed along very different lines, due partly to their own needs and priorities, but also partly due to the influence of the community organisations with which they were associated (Wardhaugh 1989).

There are, however, important ways in which the experiences of these two groups in Govanhill can be generalised, and the implications for Asian women's community activism can be considered. Firstly, the history of AWAG challenges the myth of the passive Asian woman, and demonstrates that action groups can and will emerge, especially, perhaps, where needs are strongest. Secondly, at least in the early days, a group is likely to rely heavily on certain key members who have the necessary personal resources to steer a group through its difficult early stages of development. Note, however, that this does not necessarily mean 'leaders' in the conventional sense, that in fact Asian women are as likely to draw on strong community traditions of consultation and shared decision-making, as they are to emulate patterns of leadership and control.

Despite their considerable resources, it must also be remembered that groups are likely to need support, whether material, personal or organisational. Most commonly this support will derive from various community organisations, but may also include research, technical or financial support. In all cases, needs and priorities are ideally established by groups themselves rather than by the supporting bodies. While groups may often be fortunate in receiving such support, at other times they may have to face opposition. In particular, it is worth remembering that any 'community' is not a single entity but is often divided against itself. AWAG, for example, were frequently opposed by men within the community who perceived them as undermining the family unit. While they were prepared to risk this hostility, and were successful in negotiating a place for the group within the community, gender divisions within the mixed AHG proved to be too much for an already vulnerable group.

Any community action or self-help group is likely to experience some combination of positive and negative factors during the course of its existence: given sufficient positive conditions a group can bring about considerable personal and social change. AHG may have failed to eradicate racial violence on one of Glasgow's council schemes, but they did achieve the rehousing of some group members, they did begin to take seriously the experiences of some of the most vulnerable and abused members of the community, and they did begin the process of demanding that the District Council recognise and take seriously the problem of racial violence.

The Asian Women's Action Group achieved a wide range of things, from improving the material conditions of women's lives, to organising a range of social, community and political activities, to bringing about a change in consciousness within themselves and a validation of their own lives. At the time of writing they are now in the seventh year of their existence and can well serve as example and inspiration to Asian women's groups elsewhere.

References

Bhachu P. 1986 *Twice Migrants: East African Sikh Settlers in Britain*   London: Tavistock

Bhatti F.M. 1976 'Language difficulties and social isolation' *New Community* 5(1-2):115-117

Brown C. 1984 *Black and White Britain: The Third P.S.I. Survey* London: Heinemann

Bryan B, Dadzie S and Scafe S. 1985 *The Heart of the Race: Black Women's Lives in Britain* London: Virago

Bryant B and Bryant R. 1982 *Change and Conflict: a Study of Community Work in Glasgow* Aberdeen University Press

Cheetham J. 1981 *Social and Community Work in a Multi-Racial Society* London: Harper and Row

Curno P. (ed) 1978 *Political Issues in Community Work* London: Routledge and Kegan Paul

Dahya Z. 1965 'Pakistani wives in Britain' *Race* 6(4):311-21

Davies M. (ed) 1983 *Third World, Second Sex: Women's Struggles and National Liberation* London: Zed Books

Dunleavy P. 1980 *Urban Political Analysis* London: Macmillan

Foster-Carter O. 1987 'Ethnicity: the fourth burden of black women-political action' *Critical Social Policy* Autumn.20:46-56

Henderson J and Karn V. 1984 'Race, class and the allocation of public housing in Britain' *Urban Studies* 21:2 115-27

Henderson P and Thomas D N. (eds) 1981 *Readings in Community Work London:* Allen and Unwin

Hobson D. 1978 'Housewives: isolation as oppression' in Centre for Contemporary Cultural Studies *Women Take Issue* London: Hutchinson

Jeffery P. 1976 *Migrants and Refugees* Cambridge University Press

Kraushaar R. 1981 'Policy without protest: the dilemma of organising for change in Britain' in Harloe M. (ed) *New Perspectives in Urban Change and Conflict* London: Heinemann

Lees R. and Smith G. 1975 *Action-Research in Community Development* London: Routledge and Kegan Paul

Leonard P. (ed) 1975 *The Sociology of Community Action* University of Keele

Lowe S. 1986 *Urban Social Movements* London: Macmillan

Madigan R. 1984 'Women and housing' in Glasgow Women's Studies Group *Uncharted Lives: Extracts from Scottish Women's Experiences. 1950-1982* Glasgow University Press

Mayo M. (ed) 1977 *Women in the Community* London: Routledge and Kegan Paul

Melling J. 1983 *Rent Strikes: People's Struggle for Housing in West Scotland. 1890-1916* Edinburgh: Anchor Press

Morgan R. 1970 *Sisterhood is Powerful* New York: Vintage

Pahl J. (ed) 1985 *Private Violence and Public Policy: The Needs of Battered Women and the Response of the Public Services* London: Routledge and Kegan Paul

Papanek H. 1964 'The woman fieldworker in a purdah society' *Human Organisation* 23: 160-63

Pettigrew J. 1981 'Reminiscences of fieldwork among the Sikhs' in Roberts H. (ed) *Doing Feminist Research* London: Routledge and Kegan Paul

Robinson V. 1980 'Asians and council housing' *Urban Studies* 17:323-31

Rose H. 1978 'In practice supported, in theory denied: an account of an invisible urban movement' *International Journal of Urban and Regional Research* Vol.2 No.3:521-37. October

Runnymede Trust and Radical Statistics Race Group 1980 *Britain's Black Population* London: Heinemann

Saifullah Khan V. 1976 'Pakistani women in Britain' *New Community* 5(1-2): 99-108

Uberoi N. 1965 'Sikh women in Southall' *Race* 6(1):34-40

Wardhaugh J 1989 *Asian Women and Housing: The Potential for Community Action* Unpublished PhD thesis University of Stirling

Wilson A. 1978 *Finding a Voice: Asian Women in Britain* London: Virago

G

Chapter 10
Sexual violence and the voluntary sector:
Asian women and wife abuse
Lynne Harvie

Background

This chapter documents and discusses the results of a UK wide survey of provision for Asian women in women's refuges. The survey was carried out as part of the action-research programme at Crossroads Youth and Community Association (see Murray and Wardhaugh, above), at the instigation of the local Asian Women's Action group.

The first refuge for women experiencing abuse in relationships emerged in 1971. Originally established as a Women's Advice Centre, the Chiswick group was over-whelmed by the numbers of women experiencing violence from their partners. 'Their need was so obvious and so great that the group broke the terms of their lease....' (Sutton 1978:576) and began providing women with safe refuge, 24 hours a day. Sutton (1978:577) adds that due to changes in rules regarding homeless accommodation which allowed men access to emergency housing, 'Between 1966 and 1971 the only major safe places for battered women were with friends or relatives, or in a prison, a hospital, or a mortuary.' Erin Pizzey, the founder of the Chiswick refuge, succeeded in forcing the issue of abuse of women by partners onto the public agenda through her clever use of the media (Marsden 1978, Sutton 1978, Dobash and Dobash 1980, 1987). In the following years support groups were set up by women across the country, with a national co-ordinating group being established in 1975. In the same year the Chiswick group split from the National Women's Aid Federation as differing perspectives and principles conflicted (see also Martin 1978, Sutton 1978, Dobash and Dobash 1980, 1988). The aims of NWAF were (Sutton 1978:580):

i)   to provide temporary refuge on request, for women and their children who have suffered mental or physical harassment;

ii)   to encourage women to determine their own futures and to help them achieve them, whether this involves returning home or starting a new life elsewhere;

iii)   to recognise and care for the emotional and educational needs of the children involved;

iv)   to offer support and advice and help to any woman who asks for it, whether or not she is a resident, and also to offer support and aftercare to any woman and child who has left the refuge;

v)   to educate and inform the public, the media, the police, the courts, social services, and other authorities with respect to battered women mindful of the fact that this is a result of the general position of women in our society.

Although previously all under the one body, there are now four national organisations: Scottish Women's Aid (SWA), Northern Irish Women's Aid (NIWA), Welsh Women's Aid (WWA), and Women's Aid Federation (England) (WAFE), the latter only re-opening in 1988 after having to close for some years due to lack of funding. Most refuges in the country are affiliated with their relevant national body, however there are a fairly large number of unaffiliated refuges operating in England. There are now approximately 200 groups in Britain, although accurate numbers are hard to obtain as new groups are setting up all the time and others are closing continually due to funding problems. What is clear is that present provision is still well below the recommendation made by the 1975 Select Committee on Violence in Marriage (HCP, 553, Vol XXXV) that there should be one refuge place per 10,000 population (see Binney et al 1981).

The 1980s saw a new development in the refuge movement. Despite adopting the feminist principles of self-help, power sharing and mutual support (Pahl 1978:47) and maintaining a non-hierarchical user-controlled structure, for many women in Britain existing refuge provision was not offering a real alternative to sexual violence. In the last decade a number of refuges have been established by women from ethnic minority groups in response to the issues and problems which denied them access to refuges, or made life in predominantly 'white' refuges difficult.

In the context of the action-research project the study of refuge provision for Asian women developed from a number of sources. Originally there had been discussion in the AWAG about the Asian women's refuge locally. During a previous action-research project (Wardhaugh 1989 and above) concern had been expressed about both the location of the house and the practical workings of the refuge, indeed it was the experiences of some women who had used the refuge which raised the issue of sexual violence in the group in the first place. Some investigation into refuge provision available to abused Asian women was clearly necessary. Initial work focussed on the existing Asian women's refuge in Scotland and a new refuge, then in the early planning stages. I examined the history, structure, principles and support offered by both groups. As a result of this and some more intensive discussion and observation with the local refuge, it was decided that similar information should be collected from other groups across the country, since provision in Scotland was low and one of the groups was only just getting off the ground. Meetings were arranged with four other refuges for Asian women, and written information received from other groups. Subsequently, all Asian women only groups known to WAFE, SWA, WWA, and NIWA were contacted by post to gain a complete picture of the specific provision available for Asian women in the UK. The results of this part of the project are presented and discussed elsewhere (Harvie 1990).

Members of AWAG also asked what kind of service and support Asian women could expect in areas where there was no Asian women's refuge or where a woman chose not to use an Asian women's refuge. Some of the difficulties facing Asian women in existing refuges had been raised in the material received from Asian only groups. Those were, that separate refuges emerged because of racism, language difficulties, religious and dietary needs, immigration fears and difficulties, and the greater social isolation of Asian women.

AWAG wanted to know whether it was possible to overcome any of these problems in refuges and if it was possible that any groups, where no Asian women's refuge existed, had managed to find ways round these difficulties and to provide a service which was accessible for all women regardless of ethnic origin. A postal survey of all known refuge groups in Britain was carried out to assess the level of provision for Asian women in predominantly 'white' refuges, to ascertain whether Asian women used such refuges, if at all, and to attempt to identify the extent to which groups were sensitive to and receptive to the specific pressures faced by Asian women in this country. Postal questionnaires were distributed via the four national Federations, and the response rate was 54 per cent (110 refuges).

The data from this survey is presented here to highlight some issues raised in service provision for ethnic minority groups, and to identify some of the practical manifestations of both personal and institutional forms of racism. It is not intended as a direct critique of the women's refuge movement as the issues discussed are similarly raised in other women's organisations (from personal experience), voluntary organistions as a whole (see MacLeod 1988), and within statutory forms of provision as is discussed elsewhere in this book.

Survey results

a) Use of refuges by Asian women

The survey aimed to discover the extent to which refuges not specifically geared towards Asian women were in fact being used by Asian women. 27 per cent of all groups had never been approached by any Asian women, 53 per cent had only ever been used occasionally by Asian women (from once, ever, to once or twice in the past year), and only six per cent of groups were used regularly by Asian women. 70 per cent of groups nevertheless described themselves as being 'mixed' refuges, or 'open to all women'. 15 per cent of groups did recognise their failure to translate the idea of equality of provision into actual practice, describing themselves as 'white refuges', qualified with statements such as 'not a policy decision', or 'not intentionally' or 'in practice', adding that they were 'attempting to meet Asian women's needs'.

Some groups therefore recognised that although they would like to think they were open to all women, in practice they operated as a refuge for white women only.

Not all the groups recognised the fact that Asian women did not, in practice, use their refuge. 75 per cent of those groups which had ever been used by Asian women nevertheless regarded themselves as providing a service for all women. One group stated;

We don't find these descriptions helpful. Our refuge is open to any woman who needs us, regardless of colour.

It is clear from these figures that Asian women are not on the whole using refuges which are not specifically structured for Asian women. Only six per cent of refuges were used frequently by Asian women, yet 70 per cent of groups saw their refuge provision as being open to all women regardless of race or creed. Where groups think they are providing a service which is equally accessible for all women, questions may therefore need to be raised regarding their actual use by Asian women, and by women from other minority groups, to assess whether the principle is in fact a reality, and whether the service is in fact as open as refuges perceive it to be.

b) Equal opportunities policies

To gain an idea of the extent to which groups had taken on board the issue of racism and discrimination in their service, the questionnaire asked whether groups had adopted any written statement regarding equal opportunities.

37 per cent of groups had a written equal opportunities policy; two percent mentioned that the Women's Aid Constitution encompassed this but had no separate policy; 46 per cent had no policy, though five of these groups were in the process of writing one. All the refuges used frequently by Asian women had a policy, whereas 80 per cent of those which had never been used by Asian women had no written equal opportunities policy.

Clearly having a written policy on equal opportunities in an organisation will not, in itself, make a difference to service provision and subsequent use by Asian women. However it appears that *without* such a policy the likelihood of achieving any real and lasting accessibility for women from any ethnic minority group is greatly reduced because of the lack of a firm commitment to challenge racism. A written policy statement may be crucial firstly in defining a commitment to anti-racism, then in placing a formal and constitutional obligation upon the organisation to examine and combat any directly or indirectly discriminatory practices and policies. In combatting racism, choices regarding priorities will inevitably have to be made. For example, a group must decide whether to invest time in challenging racism, or contacting Asian organisations, or to continue as they are supporting the women already contacting them. Resources may alternatively be needed for translating information material, or repainting the refuge. Written policy is essential to inform and support any decisions taken. Without such a policy, or without adhering to a commitment to support all women, 'white' organisations can exclude Asian women through inaction as much as through action (see also MacLeod 1988).

c) Provision for Asian women

The survey also examined the level of provision for Asian women in the refuges. Sixty per cent of all refuges had no special provision for Asian women. This was especially the case amongst the 83 per cent of groups which had never been used by Asian women. Only seven per cent of the groups which had never been used by Asian women mentioned any form of provision for Asian women, such as access to translators, and referring women on to an Asian women's refuge. 17 per cent of all of the groups without provision for Asian women felt that there was no need for special provision to be made. Of the groups who believed there was no need to give any special consideration to the needs of Asian women, some adopted a 'colour-bind' approach, that is, they believed equality of service provision to be best achieved through treating all women the same. They commented:

All women are treated equally, regardless of race or creed.

We treat all women, whatever colour, race, creed, the same.

We do not feel any special provision is necessary, we treat all women the same. To us, colour, race or religion is not an issue, we are all sisters.

Some groups said that because workers were responsive to the individual needs of every woman who approached them, then the workers would be responsive to the needs of any Asian woman approaching them in the same way:

When a woman comes to our refuge they are all treated with the same sympathy and they all receive the same amount of help. As Women's Aid workers we are sensitive to women's needs and respond to them in the manner we feel most appropriate.

Q. What special provision does your group have to meet the needs of Asian women?

A. None, apart from that we are supportive of all women.

Others took a similar stance and stated individual needs would be dealt with if and when the situation arose.

If the situation arises we will do our best for the woman.

Any special need or request would be catered for if it were possible.

We would give them as much help as they needed if the situation arose.

They would be welcome to use us if the need arose.

Clearly sympathy and understanding are crucial in supporting battered women. However these factors alone may not be sufficient to provide support to all battered women, for example, if these qualities are not accompanied by any understanding of the specific pressures faced by Asian women in their day to day lives. To a white woman, 'colour, race, or religion' may not be an issue, but for an Asian woman who is all too aware of the facts of discrimination, or daily racial harassment, who is treated like a second class citizen, or who faces strong cultural pressures if she leaves her husband, 'colour, race, creed' are, through necessity, very much an issue (see Wilson 1978, Allen 1980 1987, Davis 1982, Carby 1982, Hooks 1982, Parmar 1982, *Feminist Review* 1984, King 1988). The support and advice deemed 'most appropriate' by a white worker may not feel appropriate for an Asian woman, given the added pressure she may face. There are likely to be problems for Asian women who approach a refuge which assumes the typically middle class, white woman's view of the world is necessarily a neutral one. For groups to therefore improve the provision available within refuges, a starting point may be to acknowledge the bias which is inherent in a 'colour-blind' attitude to service provision. Some groups acknowledged that their approach was very much an ethnocentric one, and that although they might provide the same service to all women, it did not necessarily follow that the service was equally accessible to all women:

[Our service is the] ... same as for any woman, but probably inaccessible for many Asian women.

Because we are a mainly white organisation most Asian women do not feel comfortable here.

The 'colour-blind' approach to service provision does not result in the provision of a neutral service as is often assumed (see MacLeod 1988). Rather it allows an organisation to ignore the fact that its services and structures have been shaped around a particular 'class' of women. This problem was highlighted by the comments of some groups, who although having had no Asian women in their refuge had had experiences of other minority groups using the refuge. Some such groups stated that they had realised the ethnocentrism of their support when approached by traveller or Irish women in the past. Only when women from these groups approached them did they become aware of, for example, the problems prejudice and disadvantage could cause for some women. Treating all women as equals (equals, that is, to white women) will not result in a service which is open equally to all women. To ignore that some women face particular difficulties, such as racism, racial harassment, language difficulties and cultural pressures in escaping abuse, will not result in equality of access to that service. Groups can in fact promote inequality by doing nothing to counteract or challenge the various forms of disadvantage and discrimination faced by women from ethnic minority backgrounds. We do not live in an equal world, and to act as if we do, does nothing other than promote inequality.

Despite 60 per cent having no special provision for Asian women, some groups did state that they had considered the needs of Asian women in structuring their service. One quarter of all groups did have some form of provision for Asian women. Of these, one-fifth were used frequently by Asian women, three quarters were used occasionally by Asian women and the remainder were never used by Asian women.

The provision which these 28 groups provided was as follows: 15 groups had access to interpreters, 11 had information in minority languages, seven had an Asian worker, eight referred to Asian organisations for advice and support, six kept details of local Asian shops, classes and support groups, six maintained links with Asian women who had used the refuge, four had non-meat cooking facilities as standard, three had contact with individual Asian workers elsewhere and one group had a purpose built hostel which was 'designed and equipped with Asian women very much in mind , with interconnecting rooms for larger families, a non-meat cooking area, a quiet lounge and a bidet'.

Thus some groups had taken positive steps to try to make their refuge more accessible for Asian women. The vast majority of these groups were used by Asian women. It might be helpful for groups to follow their example and seek positive steps to open up their services to all women.

d) Other forms of support

All groups were also asked about any other forms of support they might have for Asian women outwith the actual refuge, to see whether Asian women were receiving support in other ways from women's refuge groups. 67 per cent provided no form of support for Asian women other than in the refuge. 34 per cent did provide some other form of support for Asian women not living in the refuge.

The provision mentioned included; access to interpreters for counselling, aftercare work with women who had left the refuge, contact with Asian women who had used the refuge in the past for advice, counselling, and translation as necessary, contact with local

Asian women's support group, outreach work with Asian women, the running of support groups for Asian women, and a phone line with an Asian language speaker available.

Some groups then had managed to find ways of attempting to make their service more accessible to Asian women, through support work outwith the actual provision of a refuge for abused women. Nevertheless, 47 per cent of all groups had neither special provision for Asian women in the refuge, nor had they any other form of support for Asian women. Thus, out of the total of 60 per cent of groups with no special provision for women in the refuge, only 13 per cent of all groups had attempted to fill this gap in service through some other type of support for Asian women. Nearly half (47 per cent) of refuge groups had no provision in the refuge, or in terms of wider counselling and support. The gaps in service provision outlined in the previous section are not being filled by alternative forms of support as almost two thirds of those groups with alternative support also had special provision for Asian women within the refuge. It is clear then that many groups had made no special effort to provide services for Asian women.

e) Problems Asian women faced in refuges

An examination of some of the problems groups felt Asian women who had used their refuges had faced in the past might provide an indication of the reasons for Asian women's infrequent use of the refuges. According to the groups who had provided support to Asian women at some time, many of the difficulties these women had faced were consistent with the general problems which had led to Asian women only refuges being established. Thus, 37 per cent of groups mentioned racism as a difficulty, stating that women were 'subjected to racial abuse from whites' and to 'blatant racist comments eg food stinks' and to generalised 'racism from other women'.

Another reason for separate refuges is, as one Asian women's refuge stated, that refuge is 'a safe place, not only in relation to violence, but it is an environment they can identify with. Language creates a bond'. 32 per cent of groups mentioned language as being a problem, referring to 'language barriers with other women staying in the refuge', and stating 'women who do not speak English have felt very isolated.' 28 per cent mentioned the practical difficulties Asian women can face because the refuge did not cater for dietary or religious needs, referring to 'practical problems over cooking facilities'. Other problems mentioned were that Asian women experienced more isolation (nine per cent), difficulties due to women having different lifestyles and expectations (eight per cent), problems due to religion (eight per cent), differences in child rearing practices (five per cent), cultural misunderstandings (five per cent) and greater cultural pressures faced by Asian women to return home (three per cent).

As has been already stated, these are precisely the types of problems which became the driving force behind the setting up of separate refuges by and for Asian women. All abused women need a safe and secure environment from which to decide upon their futures. For Asian, and other ethnic minority women in Britain, this may mean an environment which is free from racist abuse, free from feelings that one is 'different' or a 'problem', free from practical difficulties and where women can feel comfortable in getting support from other women in the refuge. In light of the many problems raised above and which have been facing Asian women for many years, Asian women only refuges are essential in providing this.

However, the existence of such refuges should not lead to complacency on the part of existing refuges as to their provision for Asian women. There may be, as will be discussed later, circumstances in which an Asian woman cannot use an Asian only house, because there is none in the area, because of lack of space, or because she chooses not to use one. Asian women undoubtedly need separate refuges, but Women's Aid groups should try to confront as many of the problems faced by Asian women as they can. The existence of separate provision is not an excuse for inaction on the ethnocentric provision of support.

The survey has shown that provision for Asian women in 'mixed' refuges is minimal, and I take that as an indication of why these refuges are underused by Asian women. Many of the problems Asian women are known to have faced in such houses have not been overcome.

f) Why refuges are underused by Asian women

All of the groups were asked if they had any ideas why their refuge was not used more by Asian women. Five per cent said that their refuge was used frequently by Asian women, 17 per cent did not respond and 10 per cent said they had no idea why Asian women did not use the refuge. Responses range from the direct 'no idea' or 'don't know' to the more ambiguous 'We've never come across the situation [of an Asian woman using the refuge] so we cannot comment.'

Others had clearly never considered why this was the case, one group responding, 'No idea. You would have to ask an Asian woman in the area to find out why'.

A total of 28 per cent of groups in the survey therefore did not appear ever to have considered or confronted the fact that very few Asian women ever used their refuge. Some of these felt that Asian women used Asian women's refuges, or wanted to deal with violence in their own communities, stating for example 'They probably use the one in the —— area' or 'they prefer to go to —— where workers speak the language,' 'Asian women prefer to be in a refuge with other Asian women,' 'They would prefer to go to someone within their own community', or 'Because of the town's relatively small Asian community, we have found that most local Asian women prefer to discuss their problems with the local Asian women's group.'

Despite having very little contact with Asian women, Asian women's groups or refuges, some groups assumed that Asian women would not want to use a mixed refuges. As will be discussed in more detail later and as mentioned above, this assumption may not always be justified, as some Asian women may prefer to use white/mixed refuges in some circumstances.

Some groups gave other reasons for Asian women not using their refuge. One quarter said their refuge was not used because of the size of Asian community in the area, and noted 'a very small percentage of Asians in the area,' '...Few in the area,' 'There aren't any in the area', or 'The Asian population in —— is extremely small, the actual need is probably almost negligible.'

More than half the groups giving these reasons were in areas with an Asian population of between 0.2 per cent and 0.5 per cent. But one quarter were situated in areas where the Asian population made up one per cent or more of the total (these figures are derived from 1981 census figures, and are probably underestimates).

Some groups again, had made assumptions about the Asian community in the area without accurate knowledge of the communities they were basing their assumptions upon. A one per cent Asian population is a fairly significant number of people in a city or district. The number of Asians living in an area, however, is not a significant factor on which to make assumptions about the relative need for service provision for Asian women. There are a number of points which need to be raised here.

Firstly, it was mentioned by some groups that Asian women who had used their refuge in the past had usually come from outwith the local area, some women moving to refuges some distance from their home towns. Pahl (1978:20), in her study of a refuge in Canterbury, similarly found that many women who were using the refuge came from outwith the Canterbury area (53 per cent). One group in the present study, stated

> Most of the Asian women coming to our refuge are from out of the area and moved mostly for reasons of safety.

Thus Asian women, like many other women, may need to use refuges outwith the locality of their homes. In assuming that there is no need to provide a service which is responsive to the needs of abused Asian women, 'because there aren't any in the area', refuges may be effectively closing this avenue of support for some Asian women. If groups aim to provide for all women then it is necessary for them to be committed to providing such support regardless of the size of the Asian community locally.

Secondly, it should be stressed that the size of the Asian community is irrelevant to the need to provide support for Asian women who experience sexual violence. Assuming that most groups accept that the number of abused women in any town is immeasurable, but is likely to be far higher than is commonly acknowledged, then there will be women experiencing sexual violence in any community regardless of its size. Even if there are only a few hundred Asians in the area, there will still be abused women. This is one of the fundamental principles of the women's refuge movement, that 'Women need refuges'.

A third point which is worth highlighting here is that refuges which are in predominantly 'white' areas should perhaps have more of an obligation to ensure that their services are open to all women. In such areas there is much less likelihood of there being a refuge specifically for Asian or other ethnic minority women. Given the point made above, it could be argued that existing refuges should therefore be more equipped and prepared to offer support to Asian women who have experienced sexual violence.

Aside then from the groups who felt that Asian women did not use their refuge because of the small Asian population in their area, 23 per cent of all groups felt that cultural constraints and pressures discouraged Asian women from approaching their refuge. They mentioned 'pressure exerted on them from within their own communities to stay at home', and 'cultural barriers'. Some groups did not locate the reasons for their lack of contact with Asian women in purely external causes, that is lack of demand from Asian women, as did the groups above. Some groups saw flaws in their own service provision which might prevent Asian women from using their refuge. 19 per cent of groups felt that Asian women didn't know about their service. They commented:

Many Asian women are not aware of Women's Aid.

Asian women in —— probably don't know our service is here.

Women don't know about our service. Lack of knowledge that there is somewhere for them to go.

13 per cent saw the lack of Asian speakers in the group as a problem which might discourage Asian women from using the refuge. Five per cent of groups felt racism could be a factor which influenced a woman's decision not to use their refuge, referring to 'fear of racism within the refuge'. Four per cent mentioned the fact that Asian women might not contact them because they did not feel the refuge was for them. One group stated ...because we are a mainly white organisation...most Asian women do not feel comfortable here'. A further four per cent felt that a major factor was that they received most of their referrals through statutory agencies which themselves were not accessible to Asian women:

We are part of a range of services that Asian women do not connect with (or that do not connect with Asian women). White women come to us via Social Services, CAB, Housing, etc., which are all agencies which fail to provide a service to Asian women.

This 'filter' most certainly does play a part in reducing the number of Asian women being referred to any refuge, especially if that group has little direct contact with Asian women. An important point to note here however, is that four out of five Asian women's refuges contacted separately stated that their referrals came mostly through these same organisations. This in itself then, is not preventing Asian women from using refuges. It might be the case, nevertheless, that statutory and voluntary agencies are less likely to refer Asian women to refuges which do not directly publicise their support as being open to all women, and may also assume that Asian women do not use, or do not want to use certain refuges.

It is important therefore that refuges begin to look at possible reason why their service is not used more by Asian women, or women from other minority backgrounds, and that in doing so groups look at both the internal and external reasons why this might be the case. Refuges will only succeed in offering the best support possible if they are aware of and try to counteract all of the factors which prevent Asian women from contacting them.

g) Improvements in services

To investigate awareness of possible ways of improving their service, groups were asked if they thought there was anything that might make it easier for Asian women to use their refuge. Over half of the refuge groups (52 per cent) could suggest no changes that they could make to their service which might make it easier for Asian women to use the refuges.

The 53 groups (48 per cent) which suggested positive changes raised several points .

About half felt they needed to produce more information in ethnic minority languages, or more publicity specifically directed at Asian women, suggesting perhaps more advertising:

> 'We should be better advertised, and may also advertise specifically for Asian women': 'We should ....have multi-lingual literature.'

One third felt that they needed an Asian worker:

> It's important to have an Asian worker employed in the refuge.
> Having an Asian language speaker/volunteer.

One quarter saw a need to make more links with and to have more contact with Asian women, referring to

> More contact with Asian women and outreach work.
> A better form of communication between our organisation and the Asian population in ——.

or stating

> we feel we must ask Asian women what support it would be effective to give them.

One quarter stated that their service would be improved if they had better access to translators. One-fifth believed racism awareness training of some kind was essential for both workers and women in the refuge. They suggested

> Consciousness raising for the white workers within the organisation, and racist [sic] awareness courses, but it would have to be constant and ongoing as we have a large turnover of women.

Other proposed improvements mentioned were having Asian women involved on their management/support groups, better cooking facilities, a larger refuge (because the group believed Asian women did not like sharing or cramped conditions), more workers (not necessarily Asian women), the support of the local council to improve their service and an Asian women's support group.

On the whole, most groups thought that positive steps they could take were to have more contact with Asian women, to aim more publicity specifically at women from ethnic minorities, to provide for languages other than English, to involve Asian women in all aspects of the organisation and its management, and to develop a greater awareness of the specific pressures facing Asian women who experience sexual violence.

Some groups commented on the fact that services were shaped to meet the needs of white women, and not all women, and that groups should begin to acknowledge and challenge this:

> Basically start to question our service to Asian women.
> All Women's Aid groups should be made more aware of the problems women from all ethnic minorities...have in addition to domestic violence and be aware of the problems of racism etc in white refuges; racism should be continually

tackled in white refuges, regardless of if Asian/black families are in the refuge. Refuges are in effect not directly offered to many Asian women.

This last statement was made by a group who had only ever had one Asian woman through their refuge and who were situated in an area where only 0.1 per cent of the population were Asians.

The comments of all these groups have indicated the need for all groups to look closely at the practical steps that can be taken, if they are to achieve their aim of openness to all women. This needs to be underpinned by a genuine questioning of the basis of their services, and its relation to the needs of women from many ethnic minority backgrounds, for example how the service is publicised, how the service is delivered, and the practical and emotional support provided.

h) Referral to Asian Refuges

Groups were asked whether they would automatically refer Asian women to an Asian women's refuge, in order to ascertain the extent to which Asian women could choose to use a white/mixed refuge if they preferred to do so. It was possible that groups might immediately refer Asian women to an Asian only refuge because they, rather than the woman, saw that as the best form of support. The major of groups (66 per cent) said that they would not refer women automatically but would tell them that such groups existed and ask if they would prefer to go there. Some groups stated that Asian women, in their experience, preferred to go to an Asian only house, or that Asian women moved there (to the Asian refuge) for reasons of safety. They commented

The refuge is situated in the middle of the Asian community and is not seen as a safe or secret place..

...because we are very near to the mosque...Asian women who come here often do not feel safe.

It is difficult for Asian women to use local refuge groups because they are so easily identified the minute they go out shopping etc.

Many groups however said that often Asian women who came to them, did not want to be referred to or move to an Asian women's refuge:

In the main...[Asian women]... do not want to be referred to an Asian women's refuge.

No...women have stated that they don't want to go there.

We inform Asian women of the existence of Asian only refuges but no-one has ever wanted to be referred on.

The crucial point which has been raised here, is not that Asian only refuges are not needed, but that Asian women need a choice of services. The fact that some Asian women may not wish to stay in an Asian only refuge should be acknowledged. As has been highlighted earlier, some groups may assume Asian women will use Asian only refuges, and thus not confront their own directly or indirectly racist practices and policies. Given the added pressures faced by abused Asian women, it is important that they are able to choose freely which form of support best meets their needs, and situation. In general, Asian only refuges may be more equipped to support Asian women, but in some circumstances, white refuges may be able to offer the best support for a particular woman. Asian women may feel that 'they will be less easily found' or that the address 'will be less known to the Asian community.' Clearly this underscores the fact that all groups need to ensure that their refuge is truly open to all women, and should not shirk responsibilities for meeting the needs of Asian women simply because there is an Asian refuge nearby.

i) Contact with other organisations

The level of contact groups had either with refuges for Asian women, or with other Asian organisations was noticeably low. Only 14 groups had an Asian refuge nearby, and of these, five said they rarely contacted them, four said that their only contact was if referring women on to the refuge, four had regular contact and meetings with the group and one did not specify what contact they had with the group.

Contact with any other Asian organisation was also low. Two thirds of all groups had had no contact with any Asian organisations, one quarter had had some contact, and the remainder did not respond. The contact which groups mentioned varied from regular meetings and discussions, to occasional meetings, or written correspondence. Such groups included formal community organisations like Community Relations Councils, Community Associations, and the Commission for Racial Equality, and more informal groups such as Asian women's support groups and advice centres. Given many of the issues raised here and elsewhere regarding the direct and indirect effects of racism (see for example Brown 1984, Gordon and Newnham 1985, MacLeod 1988, Bowes, McCluskey and Sim 1989), and the issues raised by refuge groups themselves, increased contact and liaison with Asian organisations and groups might be a first step in the development of a service which is sensitive to the needs and demands of Asian women.

j) Children

Years of experience supporting women who are coping with sexual violence in their lives have shown that the welfare of children involved is of major concern to women when deciding about their future (Pahl 1978, Binney et al 1981, Scottish Women's Aid Children's Office, n.d.). How children adjust to and cope with life in a refuge or other temporary accommodation can be a crucial factor in a woman's decision about whether to return to her husband or to set up a new life on her own. Binney et al (1981:63) discuss at length how children experienced life in refuges. In the present study groups were asked about the provision they had for the children of Asian women, since the effects of racism on children can clearly be far-reaching.

Two thirds of all groups had no special provision for the children of Asian women. Many of these groups added that they had no provision for any children due to lack of funding or lack of space in the refuge. Only 19 per cent of all groups had any form of provision for the children of Asian women. Of these groups, 42 per cent said that they had a Play Worker for all children, one quarter had games and books in ethnic minority languages, and others had anti-racist toys and games, contact with a local Asian mothers and toddlers group, links with a school with a good record for anti-racist policy and practice, or contact with Asian support groups.

The generally low level of provision for children in refuges indicates that there has been little change in groups' abilities to fund children's projects since the Binney et al (1981:64) study which found that 56 per cent of refuges had no playroom, and 44 per cent had no arranged play for children under five years old (Binney et al 1981:67). If anything, the situation seems to have worsened for children in refuges although a more detailed study of provision for children would be needed to assess this more comprehensively. For the children of Asian women, the situation is worse still, with less than 20 per cent of groups having any form of provision for these children. Clearly this is in part related to the lack of provision for children generally (due to lack of funding for workers, lack of space, and lack of resources). However, if groups have taken no steps to accommodate the children of Asian women in refuges by providing games and toys in minority languages, or stocking only anti-racist books and materials, the problems faced by children adapting to life in a refuge are likely to be compounded for these children. Feelings of being 'different' or less valued are likely to have a lasting effect on young children, a factor which may lead some Asian women to decide not to stay in a refuge.

k) Experiences of abuse

Groups were asked whether they believed the experience of abuse was any different for Asian women than it was for white women, in order to gain some indication of groups perceptions of Asian women, and to gain any further information on the extent to which groups had considered the pressures faced by abused Asian women. There were 28 per cent 'don't knows' or no responses, and seven per cent unelaborated 'yes' replies. 17 per cent said no, there was no difference:

> No. All women feel pain.

> No. Violence is violence.

47 per cent felt that although the experience of abuse itself was the same for all women, the effects of that abuse and the aftermath might be different:

> We think Asian women find it harder to seek help.

> It's more difficult to get away. Especially somewhere like —— where the Asian community is so small - there's more hassle once she's away.

> We feel unqualified to comment, except where traditional domestic roles are strictly demarcated, the scope for abuse of power has to be greater, and the escape routes may well be more limited.

Many of these groups felt that Asian women's experiences differed only in so far as

> Language, cultural and social factors...make escaping the violence more difficulty.

Refuges felt that Asian women faced additional pressures from families to remain with abusive husbands:

Increased family pressure to stay in a relationship may bring particular problems for Asian women.

It is more difficult, because of family ties, for Asian women to leave a violent partner. When the break is made, the woman often has to break with the whole family.

We have had Asian women in the refuge who have had good support from their families. However in two cases the families rejected the woman and this also led to a sense of isolation in the wider community.

There was also seen to be much greater cultural pressure upon Asian women to remain with their husbands:

Perhaps [the experience of abuse is different] because their culture teaches them that a woman should stay with her husband regardless.

Not emotionally [different for Asian women] but culturally they have greater difficulty possibly in leaving home and beginning a new life alone.

Asian women are inclined to feel more trapped in relationships as the future for them if they leave is bleak...being classed as a 'loose woman', and outcast from the Asian community and even possibly their own family, the future marriage potential for their children being detrimentally affected.

The ostracism and resulting isolation for Asian women from their community after leaving a violent relationship is something which fewer white women experience.

Similarly groups recognised the difficulties which faced Asian women, if they set up home alone, as a result of abuse from white community:

She may be more vulnerable as a single parent on larger estates.

[She may have] a great fear of trying to survive in a white society on her own.

The experience of abuse is worse because of the added problems for an Asian woman of racism outside her home, and for many women the difficulties of surviving in another culture which is hostile to their needs.

Other groups discussed how these factors all combined to isolate Asian women to a great extent:

We think the isolation suffered by white women must be compounded for abused Asian women and their position of powerlessness when faced by authority must be increased.

[The] sense of isolation and feeling of failure can be stronger for Asian women. Asian women tend to be more isolated and have more barriers, eg religion, language.

Although few groups discussed the variety of pressures faced by Asian women who experience sexual violence from husbands, or in the home, many (47 per cent) were aware of some of the difficulties they faced. Language problems, isolation, institutional and individual racism, community and family pressures all combine and interconnect to reduce Asian women's self-esteem, confidence, awareness of services, options for independent living, and likelihood of receiving benefits and services, generally making the decision to leave harder for the majority of Asian women. One Asian women's refuge (contacted separately) stated that,

> One cannot isolate women's experiences of 'domestic violence'. However one has to take account of the specificity of Asian (black) women's experiences in a racist and sexist society. It is always going to be that much harder for Asian women to deal with problems.

Thus, although the actual experience of abuse may not be different in any way for Asian women, the repercussions of that experience and the difficulties faced when trying to cope with sexual violence are necessarily influenced and shaped by the sexist and racist society in which the experience occurs. Any support network for Asian women has to be aware of, and committed to challenging, such compounding factors, if it is to be truly accessible to Asian women.

Groups were also asked about their feelings about the experience of children witnessing abuse. Seven per cent felt that it was different for the children of Asian women, stating

> In Asian families children learn that violence is permissible.
> [There is] cultural firming up of the sexist attitudes in which children are brought up.
> Perhaps being in a minority makes children of Asian women witnessing abuse feel even more insecure and isolated than their white counterparts feel.

A small number of groups did feel that witnessing abuse would have a more detrimental effect upon the children of Asian women than was the case for the children of white women. Again, further research would be needed to assess fully the effects witnessing abuse has upon all children; however, it is unlikely that Asian rather than white children are any more susceptible to becoming more violent or sexist as a result of witnessing abuse, than their white counterparts. About half the groups nevertheless felt that there were no differences between children's experiences of witnessing abuse:

> Violence is violence. The colour of a child's skin makes no difference to how it affects a child.
> In our experience the effect of domestic violence on children has the same far reaching psychological disturbances regardless of cultural differences/roots.
> We feel that the experience of abuse and it's effects are universal; that race is secondary. They are women and children first.

Groups thus felt that although the after effects of sexual violence might be different for Asian women, the experiences of children witnessing abuse were much the same for all children.

l) Statutory agencies

Though the research was not specifically focussed on statutory agency responses to Asian women experiencing sexual violence, it was of interest to gain some indication of the responses women did receive, if they approached any such agencies for support. The refuge groups were asked about their experiences of supporting Asian women who had come into contact with statutory agencies.

A total of 64 groups (58 per cent) had had experiences of Asian women contacting agencies such as Housing Departments, Police, DSS, Social Work Departments and so forth. Groups were asked about their experiences of such agencies in general. Of these 64 groups, 30 per cent felt that Asian women experienced no specific problems, and 48 per cent said Asian women did face problems and difficulties which white women, in their experience, did not encounter. The remainder either did not know or did not respond. Of the 31 (48 per cent) groups who mentioned problems with statutory agencies, 81 per cent referred to a failure to provide translation facilities, 42 per cent said that staff were racist, with a further six per cent saying that staff were rude, and another six per cent saying that staff stereotyped Asian women. 16 per cent said staff were ignorant of cultural or religious backgrounds, ten per cent said staff were generally unhelpful, and six per cent said Housing Departments lacked sensitivity in rehousing Asian women. One group said that Asian women were often suspected of benefit fraud and one that the police often colluded with violent men. These figures are clearly generalisations about a variety of different statutory services and cannot be presented as conclusive proof of failure in service provision. However, it is clear that there is great scope for many agencies to improve their accessibility to Asian women generally, and specifically to women experiencing sexual violence.

Many of the problems and difficulties raised here by women's refuge groups were similarly raised by Asian women themselves in Govanhill. Some of the difficulties may be a result of wider institutional racism, or of indirectly racist policies (such as problems in rehousing women in areas where there is known to be racial harassment). However many of the issues raised here would not require major restructuring to put right. For example, on the basic level of providing translation facilities, 81 per cent of groups mentioned that agencies had no access to translators. This figure alone gives some indication of the very limited extent to which major institutions are adapting to the needs of a multi-lingual society, and perhaps begins to indicate their willingness to adapt. Furthermore, more than half of refuge groups noting problems with agencies said that Asian women directly experienced racism from staff in statutory agencies:

The attitude is condescending when dealing with Asian women.

...They need more proof of violence, Asian women are questioned more, more likely to be disbelieved, assumption that all/most black/Asian men are violent anyway and it's not as important.

The problems raised here are furthermore not unique to this research, many others having noted similar problems in other areas. Given the many difficulties faced by all abused women (see Borkowski et al 1983, Stark and Flitcraft 1983, Radford 1984/7, Johnson (ed.) 1985a, Pahl 1985a, Stanko 1985, Davis 1988, Kurz and Stark 1988, Maguire 1988, Hanmer et al 1989) the compounding effects of racial and sexist discrimination when seeking support will be highly debilitating. Adding a class dimension to the issue, and acknowledging the many difficulties facing working class women in their contact with state agencies, further closes the avenues of support open to women.

Many refuge groups will be aware of the problems of sexism and classism when abused women have to deal with the state, many more should familiarise themselves with the workings of and effects of racist oppression if they are to adequately support Asian women who experience sexual violence.

Conclusion

Certain practical conclusions arise from the survey results which would enable refuge groups to improve their service to Asian women. First, refuge groups should examine their policies and practice regarding the provision of a service which is genuinely 'open to all women'. Second, all groups should adopt and enforce a policy of equal opportunities, which can inform and support priorities and decision which may have to be made regarding practices, policies and the allocation of resources. Third, groups should be committed to challenging any ethnocentric bias in their service provision and take positive steps to shape provision to account for the specificity of Asian women's experiences. This is necessary as some Asian women may choose to or have to use white/ mixed refuges. Such provision might include access to interpreters, the employment of Asian language speakers, producing information in minority languages, providing non-meat or halal cooking facilities as standard, maintaining information on local Asian shops, classes and support groups, and building contacts with Asian women and with workers in other organisations, or more generally, as one group put it 'basically start to question our service to Asian women.' Fourth, groups should maximise contact with Asian women and organisations so that they can challenge their own services from an informed basis. Fifth, networking or centralising of resources and developments in services, through national bodies, may assist groups who wish to confront their lack of accessibility to Asian women. Sixth, refuges need consciously to ensure that toys, books and so on for children are neither racist nor ethnocentric. Provision of material in minority languages is essential. Seventh, groups should consider the variety of pressures which face abused Asian women. Language barriers, isolation, institutional and individual racism, community and family pressures, and the reality of daily racial harassment all combine and interconnect to reinforce low self-esteem, low confidence, low awareness of services, difficulties in living independently, problems in receiving benefits and social services, and generally 'make the decision to leave harder for the majority of Asian women'.

These issues have all been highlighted by this survey, with many groups stating that they had previously given little or no thought to their support of Asian women, but that it was an issue which they should be tackling:

> We feel this survey has highlighted our inexperience and lack of expertise and knowledge in this area. Although we rarely deal with any ethnic minorities here we should be equipped to deal with them if necessary.

> Your questionnaire has highlighted the fact that we know very little about the Asian population in the —— area.

> We are glad to have had the chance to fill in your questionnaire as it has made

us aware that until now we have failed to address this issue.
We think that we are non-racist but filling in this form has made us realise
that we are not positive enough towards anti-racism. We feel that many other
refuges are like us and it would be good if WAFE initiated a serious, ongoing
campaign.

These comments indicate how any research carried out is not simply a process of
'taking' information for the researchers own purposes, but that research can and does have
an effect on the subjects of that research. In this case it is hoped that the effects will be
positive ones. The survey was carried out in order to gain a clearer picture of the support
available for Asian women who experience sexual violence from their partners. It has
outlined some of the problems which prevail if there is no refuge specifically for Asian
women in the area, or if a woman chooses not to use that refuge. Many of these problems
may not be insurmountable.

From a research point of view the survey has been invaluable in providing a detailed
picture of support across the country. On the action side, it has provided material to
support any future plans for support for abused women by local Asian women. Furthermore it is hoped that refuge groups themselves will view the survey as a positive piece
of work rather than a negative or critical one. Many of the issues raised here will not be
specific to women's refuge groups (see MacLeod 1988).

One group concludes,

Although we would like to think that our and other refuges were available to
abused Asian women and that they could benefit, as white women do, from
living with women who have shared that experience, we are aware that many
factors interfere with this... at this stage the most appropriate service for
abused Asian women is an Asian women's refuge. We would, however, hope
that with continued learning and communication, this situation will change
and that the Women's Aid network [and other refuges] will genuinely be open
to *ALL* abused women.

This data has therefore raised many issues about service provision for ethnic minorities
in general, although the focus here was on the women's refuge movement specifically.
The survey emphasises how there often exists a gap between the *idea* of equality and the
practical provision of services, and that this gap frequently is unacknowledged by service
providers. It is clear that within the voluntary sector the *scope* for change exists as
statutory limitations on services are less restricting, but change will only be achieved if
the *intent* to challenge our own racism is evident. Within the women's movement
specifically we need to ask why our practice often fails to meet up to our theoretical claim
of equality by challenging the basis of our many assumptions about support for all women.
Most crucially we must be open to constructive criticism from black women and be
willing to challenge our own racism if services are to be genuinely 'open to all women'.

References

Allen S. 19880 'Perhaps a seventh person' *Womens Studies International Quarterly* 3(4):325-338

Allen S. 1987 'Gender, race and class in the 1980s' in Husband C. (ed) *'Race' in Britain: Continuity and Change* London: Hutchinson

Binney V. Harkell G. and Nixon J. 1981 *Leaving Violent Men* England: Women's Aid Federation, England.

Borkowski M. Murch M. and Walker V. 1983 *Marital Violence: the Community Response* London: Tavistock.

Bowes A.M. McCluskey J. and Sim D. 1989 *Ethnic Minority Housing Problems in Glasgow: a Report to Glasgow District Council* Glasgow: GDC Housing Department.

Brown C. 1984 *Black and White Britain: The Third PSI Survey* London: Heinemann

Carby H.V. 1982 'White woman listen! Black feminism and the boundaries of sisterhood' in Centre for Contemporary Cultural Studies *The Empire Strikes Back* London: Hutchinson.

Davis N.J. 1988 'Battered Women: implications for social control' *Contemporary Crisis* 12(4):345-372.

David A. 1982 *Women, Race and Class* London and New York: Women's Press.

Dobash R.E. and Dobash R.P. 1980 *Violence Against Wives* Somerset: Open Books.

Dobash R.E. and Dobash R.P. 1987 'The response of the British and American women's movements to violence against women' in Hanmer J. and Maynard M. (eds) *Women, Violence and Social Control* London: Macmillan.

Feminist Review 1984 *Many Voices, One Chant: Black Feminist Perspectives* Vol. 17.

Gordon P. and Newnham A. 1985 *Passport to Benefits? Racism in Social Security* London: Child Poverty Action Group.

Hanmer J. Radford J. and Stanko E. 1989 *Women, Policing and Male Violence* London: Routledge.

Harvie L.T.S. 1990 *"Fighting the Whole World?" Action-research on Sexual Violence Against Asian Women in Glasgow* unpublished PhD thesis, University of Stirling.

Hooks B. 1982 *Ain't I a Woman? Black Women and Feminism* London: Pluto Press.

Johnson N. (ed) 1985 *Material Violence* London: Routledge and Kegan Paul.

King D. 1988 'Multiple jeopardy, multiple consciousness: the context of a black feminist ideology' *Signs* 14(1):42-73.

Kurz D. and Starke E. 1988 'Not-so-benign neglect: the medical response to battering' in Yllö K. and Bograd M. (eds) *Feminist Perspectives on Wife Abuse* California: Sage.

Maguire S. 1988 'Sorry love - violence against women in the home and the state response' *Critical Social Policy* 23(8):34-45.

Marsden D. 1978 'Sociological perspectives on family violence' in Martin J.P. (ed) *Violence and the Family* Surrey: John Wiley and Sons.

Martin J.P. (ed) Violence and the Family Surrey: John Wiley and Sons.

MacLeod L. 1988 *"Irrespective of race, colour or creed?" Voluntary Organisations and Minority Ethnic Groups in Scotland* Edinburgh: Scottish Council for Voluntary Organisations.

Pahl J. 1978 *A Refuge for Battered Women* London: HMSO.

Pahl J. 1985 *Private Violence and Public Policy* London: Routledge and Kegan Paul.

Parmar P. 1982 'Gender, race and class: Asian women in resistance' in Centre for Contemporary Cultural Studies *The Empire Strikes Back* London: Hutchinson.

Radford J. 1984 '"Woman Slaughter": a licence to kill? the killing of Jane Asher' in Scraton P. and Gordon P. (eds) *Cause for Concern: British Criminal Justice on Trial* Harmondsworth: Penguin.

Radford J. 1987 'Policing male violence - policing women' in Hanmer J. and Maynard M. (eds) *Women, Violence and Social Control* London: Macmillan.

Scottish Women's Aid 12989 *Women Talking to Women* Edinburgh: Scottish Women's Aid.

Stanko E. 1985 *Intimate Intrusions: Women's Experience of Male Violence* London: Routledge and Kegan Paul.

Stark E. and Flitcraft A. 1983 'Social knowledge, social policy and the abuse of women: the case against patriarchal benevolence' in Finkelhor D. Gelles R. Horaling G. and Strauss M. (ed) *The Dark Side of Families: Current Family Violence Research* California: Sage.

Sutton J. 1978 'The growth of the British movement for battered women' *Victimology* 2(3-4):576-584.

Wardhaugh J. 1989 *Asian Women and Housing: the Potential for Community Action* unpublished PhD thesis, University of Stirling.

Wilson A. 1978 *Finding a Voice: Asian Women in Britain* London: Virago.

Conclusion
David Alexander, Alison Bowes and Duncan Sim

Research and action

All the contributions to this book, whilst they have presented the results of research and practical experience, have also raised further questions and issues for action. In no sense have we comprehensively covered all the work that is to be done with black people in Scotland.

Bowes, McCluskey and Sim focused on Glasgow District Council's Housing Action Plan, stressing that this, if fully implemented, would begin to improve black people's prospects of getting council houses in Glasgow, and to alleviate the problem of harassment. They suggested that the implementation of the Action Plan could usefully be monitored by research, and noted that specific research questions concerning the allocations process needed to be investigated via the waiting list.

Sim's review of Scotland-wide housing association policy led him to suggest improvements in policy to adapt it more specifically to the Scottish situation, and thereby to make it more effective. Dalton demonstrated a need for radical changes at the individual housing association level, suggesting that the whole procedure, from advertising housing association services, through the application procedure to housing allocations needed radical reform. Sim and Dalton both argued that continuous critical review of policies at national and local level would be necessary to ensure effective results of change.

MacEwen dealt with issues of discrimination in legal terms, showing the need for improvements in the 1976 Race Relations Act. Whilst, as the case of Edinburgh District Council showed, public bodies can adopt seemingly effective non-discriminatory policies and practices, MacEwen urged that more effective laws are needed to ensure that they do so. The role of research here is to investigate the precise effects of policy and practice, which may not be as intended or predicted.

Brailey's work moved into an area where there is very little information: she emphasised that research remains necessary on the nature of black Scots' special housing needs, and on the provision that might meet these needs. She showed that black people's special housing needs are distinct from white people's in certain ways, and referred to precedents for meeting them in England.

Social work training was severely criticised by Chakrabarti, who noted that existing anti-racist guidelines were not being implemented. Social work management, he argued, must bear major responsibility for this failure, and for future improvements. He raised several practical issues, which improved training would help social workers tackle more effectively. These included fostering and adopting black children, the care of black elders and community care. For research, he urged the development of black perspectives, which would ensure that research findings truly reflected black people's experience, and could then be used to improve it.

McCluskey's focus on social workers in black communities revealed considerable frustration. They needed better training, information and management support to do their jobs satisfactorily. McCluskey argued that social work in general, from training to practice, from management to grassroots, needed to adopt and implement a truly anti-racist strategy. She noted a dearth of systematic research on social work with black people at the local level, and in particular argued that initiatives such as Strathclyde Region's Ethnic Minorities Project needed monitoring for effects and effectiveness.

Implementing anti-racist strategies in community work, Murray showed, involves constant effort. Crossroads Youth and Community Association has experienced both problems and successes in working with black people and has often done so in the face of white opposition. Community work needed constant monitoring, to ensure its effectiveness and the maintenance of anti-racism. Murray stressed how, in the programme of action-research, research questions directly relevant to local people were raised, and information and analysis were available to the communities which had inspired them. She urged that research must be closely in touch with black people themselves, to maintain its relevance.

Wardhaugh's study showed some of the practical results of anti-racist community work, and emphasised that these were not necessarily predictable. One of the black community groups, the Asian Housing Group, was rather weak in campaigning, though did support its members, whereas the Asian Women's Action Group became stronger and stronger, offering, Wardhaugh suggests, inspiration for other such groups and emphasising the potential of locally-based, self-help activity. Like Murray, Wardhaugh is an advocate for action-research, responsive and relevant to ordinary people.

The Women's Aid movement stresses the right of all women and children to a place of refuge from violent situations. Harvie's survey of provision for Asian women experiencing sexual violence exposed a wide gap between principle and practice. Harvie revealed that Asian women were effectively denied refuge in many areas of Britain and examined the issues that needed to be faced if provision was to be improved. Like MacEwen and McCluskey, she stressed that espousing principles was insufficient, as the practices then implemented did not necessarily produce the desired results. As part of Crossroads' action-research programme, Harvie's work was suggested by and fed back to the Asian Women's Action Group, who have been using the information in their campaign on refuge provision.

General issues

Many of the contributions to this book were discussed at a conference held at Stirling University in February 1990, attended by practitioners and researchers in housing and social work from many parts of Scotland. It was a day of lively, often heated, discussion, and developed a broader perspective on the issues arising from our work. Two parallel sessions, one on housing, the other on social and community work, were held, and everyone came together at the end for a free-for-all plenary session.

In the housing sessions, the first area of debate concerned the existence of a specifically Scottish dimension to the issue. Speakers had sought to emphasise that the experience of ethnic minorities was substantially different in Scotland from elsewhere in the United Kingdom, and that there was a danger in generalising from research undertaken south of the border. However, speakers from the floor were of the opinion that discrimination and prejudice were the same everywhere, and that specifically Scottish research offered little that was new. A compromise position could be put forward; the processes underlying racism were not unique to Scotland, but the manifestations might be, not least because of the distinctive cultural and institutional framework.

Much discussion focused on the practical steps to be taken in combatting disadvantage. One view was that it was not enough to ensure that information (on access to housing or indeed any other social service) was available to ethnic groups; it was vital also to use the most appropriate channels and to monitor the use being made of information. Barriers of access could often be explained in terms of information flows.

Neither was it enough, some argued, to seek to improve access. Without changes to employment and management structures within the social service agencies, there could be no commitment to redressing the disadvantage experienced by ethnic groups. Agencies should examine their recruitment and training policies to ensure that ethnic groups were properly represented in the provider agencies, and to counter the effect of institutional racism.

In the last analysis, however, the problems of access to housing were of a structural nature. Racism was deeply rooted in power structures, and only at this level could fundamental changes be achieved.

Much debate concerned the role of the research process. Even with the evidence of the research which formed the basis of this conference, there was a shortage of information on the nature of the disadvantage experienced. Little research had been conducted in Scotland outside Glasgow; and hardly any work had been based on the needs and wishes of the ethnic minority population. But it was universally agreed that the lack of information should not be used as an excuse for lack of action.

A final but fundamental concern was the control of the research process. It was pointed out that the research which had been presented reflected the perceptions and priorities of the dominant white population. It was felt by some participants that this inevitability shaped the outcome and limited the usefulness of the research. Other participants argued that the key to achieving change was to make the results of the research available to the ethnic minority population. Much remained to be done, but much could be done with the evidence already available.

The social and community work discussion began by focusing specifically on the statutory sector. Details were presented of recent efforts by the Ethnic Minorities Project to improve social work services to black people in Glasgow: despite these, the criticisms raised in conference presentations and discussion of statutory social work still seemed to apply. In particular, it was noted that social workers tend to come into contact with black people for 'control' purposes, such as taking children into care, and that their relationships often therefore start badly. Far-reaching reform of services was felt necessary, and this would lead to a general improvement for everyone, not just black people.

Everyone should have access to suitable services, and there should be a degree of choice for the individuals concerned between, for example, separate services for black people or multiracial provision.

The voluntary sector, some people felt, was just 'chipping away' at a vast, unyielding and ultimately racist structure, and might simply be giving statutory services an excuse for inaction. Generally though, it was felt that all change for the better, however small, was worthwhile, and that work on a broad front was needed. This feeling was echoed in the discussion of self-help groups, whose work was considered important as part of a much broader approach which would entail policy changes, a clear lead from influential individuals such as social work management, and work with white people to develop anti-racist attitudes.

The assumption that white people know best what is good for black people came through particularly clearly in the survey of women's refuges. Whilst equal opportunities policies were admirable in principle, to be effective they needed to be translated into practice: 'colourblind' assumptions that true equality of access existed had to be challenged. There was evidence that this was happening in the Womens Aid movement, as groups were becoming more aware.

In plenary discussion, the need for a black research perspective was stressed, to help ensure the relevance of such work and to increase the likelihood of subsequent action. The importance of challenging racism at all times was raised, and considered especially important for those involved in decision-making bodies.

A research agenda

Four key themes for further research and action are raised in our work, in the book and by the conference.

The first of these is that the development of a Scottish perspective on black issues is essential. Whilst the manifestations of racism may differ rather little from one place to another, its underlying causes and supports undoubtedly vary. All the chapters stress the distinctive structures of Scotland as compared with England and Wales. These structures are legal, institutional and ideological, so that the framework for anti-racist work in Scotland is distinct. Furthermore, the black population has a particular structure in Scotland, therefore experiencing some distinctive problems.

The second theme concerns the relationship between research and action. Collectively, we have echoed the Scottish Asian Action Committee's remarks that in this field, research for its own sake does little to alleviate black people's problems: in itself, a research project can only collect and interpret information. On the one hand, we have argued, it is important for research to reflect black people's real concerns, and, on the other, it is important that research findings can be practically orientated, and translated into action.

Thirdly, we have argued throughout the book that institutions and those who run them have a major responsibility for ensuring that change occurs and for giving a lead in its implementation. They include Scottish Homes, local authorities responsible for housing and social work services (District and Regional Councils), voluntary agencies, managers and senior staff in all such bodies, and housing and social work educators and educational bodies. Researchers and practitioners in turn must constantly challenge such organisations and individuals.

Fourthly, we have all stressed the fundamental issue of racism, as a major underlying cause of black disadvantage in this society. Racism certainly exists in Scotland at all levels, institutional and personal, and all the reform agendas we have set entail tackling it as an important part of their work. We see our work as an early stage in a major effort, whose success can only benefit all the people of Scotland, black and white.

INDEX

East African Asians, 24
Edinburgh
    council house allocations, 70-2, 76
    District Council, 71, 76
    patterns of black settlement, 11
elderly, services for, 84, 88, 106-7, 126-7
Ethnic Minorities Outreach Project, 43
Ethnic Minorities Project, 118-9, 131, 132, 134, 135
ethnic monitoring, 30, 43, 71, 90, 129

Fair Employment (Northern Ireland) Act (1989), 77
Family Housing Association, 39
Federation of Black Housing Organisations, 37, 41, 87
fostering and adoption, 100, 101, 124-5

Glasgow:
    City Council, 21-33, 52-3, 56-7, 83, 88, 90-1, 143
    Forum on Disability, 84
    Homeless Unit, 160-61
    housing profile of ethnic minorities 22-24
    housing renewal, 47
    patterns of black settlement, 11
Gorbals Group, 140
Govanhill Asian Self-Help Housing Group, 150-51
Govanhill Housing Association, 42, 43, 46, 51, 52, 160
Greater Glasgow Health Board, 83, 116
Griffiths Report, 82, 107

Hackney, 7, 69, 72
harassment, 26-27, 71, 146-8, 160, 161-4
Help the Aged, 127
house size, 26, 54, 159
Housing Action Areas, 40, 47, 53
housing associations, 23, 35-44, 46-58, 66, 83, 86, 87, 88, 90;
    black housing associations, 38, 65, 91-2;
    nominations to housing associations, 39, 52, 56-7
Housing Associations Act (1985), 54
housing allocations, 24-6, 30, 39, 51-2, 53-6, 66-78, 159-60
housing conditions, 49-50, 158-9
Housing Corporation, 36-8, 40-1, 47, 54
Housing (Homeless Persons) Act (1977), 66
Housing (Scotland) Act (1986), 54
Housing (Scotland) Act (1987), 66, 67
Housing (Scotland) Act (1988), 86, 87

PUBLICATIONS

This publication was produced by SCVO, which is the independent council for voluntary organisations in Scotland. SCVO provides an information service, training opportunities, publications and a wide range of other services to its members, who comprise over 400 local and national voluntary bodies active in the fields of social welfare, health, housing, education, economic development and the environment.

The following SCVO publications may also be of interest.
Copies can be obtained from SCVO Publications, 18/19 Claremont Crescent, Edinburgh EH7 4QD (prices include post and package).

IRRESPECTIVE OF RACE, COLOUR OR CREED ?
The results of an action research project into the response of the white Scottish voluntary sector to the multi-racial nature of Scottish society. **(£3.50)**

WORKING FOR RACIAL EQUALITY
A training workpack which shows how organisations can plan a programme of action which will promote racial equality in the opportunities they offer to the public. Working through the pack will provide a framework for initiative and policy changes. **(£5.50)**